**Developing Student Autonomy
in Learning**

Developing Student Autonomy in Learning

Edited by David Boud

Kogan Page, London
Nichols Publishing Company, New York

First published 1981
by Kogan Page Ltd,
120 Pentonville Road, London N1 9JN

British Library Cataloguing in Publication Data
Boud, David
    Developing student autonomy in learning
    1. Education, Higher
    2. Independent study
    I. Title
    378'.17943   LB1049
    ISBN 0-85038-416-8

First published in the USA 1981
by Nichols Publishing Company,
PO Box 96, New York, NY 10024
ISBN 0-89397-101-2
Library of Congress Catalog Card No 812726

Printed in Great Britain
by The Anchor Press, Tiptree, Essex

Contents

Preface

Let me try to put this book in the context of its appearance at this particular time in the history of our civilization. Seeing it in this context may help you to perceive its significance — and I view this as a most significant book.

Prescient observers of our civilization — H. G. Wells, Aldous and Julian Huxley, Pierre Teilhard de Chardin, Bertrand de Jouvenal, George Orwell, Edgar Faure, Donald Schon, Alvin Toffler, to mention some of the most outstanding — have been trying to prepare us during much of this century for the emergence of a drastically different kind of civilization in the next century. They have convinced me that as we approach the 21st century we are facing a major turning point in human history. The assumptions and ideologies — about the nature of man, the distribution of power and wealth, the stability of knowledge and technology, and about many other things — on which past and present civilizations have been operating have become dysfunctional in a world of accelerating change. The axioms of the last century are becoming the myths of the next century. And a society that is operating on the basis of myths is in deep trouble.

The set of assumptions, ideologies and myths to which this book is directed concerns the purpose and nature of education — or, to be more accurate, of learning. Traditional education has been based on the premiss that the central purpose of education is to produce knowledgeable persons. Often this purpose has been couched in the term 'socialization', by which is meant providing individuals with the concepts, values, and skills required to function reasonably well in the world as it is now. Accordingly, educational systems consisting of primary schools, secondary schools, technical institutes, and colleges and universities were established. Individuals were permitted to 'graduate' into life at any level prepared to function in society in roles for which that level of education had equipped them. Learning was perceived as being 'terminal' almost anywhere along the line.

This assumption about the purpose of education may have been appropriate in a world of relative stability, in which people could function reasonably well for the rest of their lives on the basis of what they had learned in their youth. But this assumption is a myth in a world in which the half-life of a fact or a technical skill or a value or an attitude is

7

shrinking year by year. People whose personal equipment became fixed at 16 or 20 or 25 will be largely obsolete within a few years — or, in some areas of life, within months. This is the great risk of continuing to operate on this myth of socialization — the impending obsolescence of man.

The new assumption about the purpose of education, to which the authors of this book subscribe, is that it is to produce autonomous *lifelong* learners. As Edgar Faure and his associates proclaim in their seminal book, *Learning To Be* (1972), if lifelong learning is to be the organizing principle for all of education, the primary mission of education for children and youth must be the development of the skills of self-directed inquiry rather than the inculcation of subject-matter content. The test of the readiness of students to leave formal schooling would be demonstration of the mastery of the skills of autonomous learning. What a different curricular structure and what a different set of teaching-learning strategies this would require. There are signs, though, that islands of primary, secondary, and higher education institutions are beginning to experiment with ways of doing this. Being an optimist, it is my hope that the generation of my grandchildren will emerge from schooling as highly skilful autonomous learners so that the tertiary educators of that era will be primarily educational brokers with responsibility mainly for linking autonomous learners with appropriate learning resources.

Meantime we are faced with the reality that most people seeking higher education have learned only the skills of learning by being taught. They do not know how to diagnose their own needs for learning, for formulating their own learning objectives, identifying a variety of learning resources and planning strategies for taking the initiative in using those resources, assessing their own learning, and having their assessments validated. The 21st century will not wait for my grandchildren to have acquired these skills; survival under its mercurial conditions will require that this generation of adults has those skills. Thus there is an urgent need for all programmes of higher education between now and the end of the century to be geared to developing the skills of autonomous learning at the front end of their sequence of learning experiences and that subsequent units of the sequence be designed as self-directed learning activities. This is to say that the new emphasis in higher education must be on the *process of learning*, with the *acquisition of content* (rather than the transmission of content) being a natural (but not pre-programmed) result.

To reorient higher education around the world in this direction is a tremendous challenge. It is a concept that is foreign to most educators. It has not been part of their training (ie socialization). It requires a redefinition of their role away from that of transmitter and controller of instruction to that of facilitator and resource person to self-directed learners. It is frightening. They do not know how to do it.

For such a drastic transition to occur, therefore, teachers in higher education throughout the world need (1) to know that there is a respectable (preferably research-based) rationale for autonomous learning, (2) to know that its benefits have been successfully demonstrated in practice, and (3) to have specific guidelines and techniques for implementing it. These are precisely the things that this book gives them.

Returning to my opening statements, I would like to emphasize that I do not view what we are talking about here as a passing fad or a cosmetic improvement in education. I am convinced that we are talking about a fundamental restructuring of our way of thinking about the purpose and nature of education. We might say that we are now beginning to perceive that the purpose of education is *learning*. And we are beginning to realize that frequently *teaching* interferes with learning. As Allen Tough has demonstrated (in his *Adult's Learning Projects* [1971]), when adults undertake to learn on their own they tend to follow a sequence of steps, move at a pace, make use of a variety of resources, exhibit a style, and assess their learning in ways that are uniquely their own. If we want to facilitate their learning, we 'teachers' will follow the flow of their natural process rather than impose our teacher-made sequence on them.

I am certain that the next two decades are going to be the most innovative, revolutionary, full of ferment, and painful but exciting in the history of education.

Malcolm S. Knowles
Professor Emeritus
North Carolina State University

Acknowledgements

I would like to thank the contributors to this book who felt that it was important and gave it their unflinching support, my colleagues John Powell and Elizabeth de Rome for their particular assistance, and my wife Susan Knights who was a continuing source of encouragement. I am also grateful to the R. D. Laing Trust and to Tavistock Publications Ltd for permission to quote from *Knots* by R. D. Laing.

Introduction

David Boud, *Tertiary Education Research Centre,*
University of New South Wales

This book is about a very important goal of education and how it can be translated into practice. It concerns ways in which teachers in higher education can enable students to become more autonomous in their learning; that is, how students can learn without the constant presence or intervention of a teacher.

Few people would dispute the central theme of this book, that the role of teachers is not just to transmit knowledge but also to help students take increasing responsibility for their own learning. This idea has received a great deal of token support but has rarely received the depth of consideration exhibited in the contributions presented here.

Many of those who agree, in principle, that one important aim of education should be to produce students who will eventually be capable of functioning independently of their teachers and their set texts, are at a loss when it comes to organizing their courses to achieve this end. 'Students don't want to be autonomous'; 'The institution isn't set up for this'; 'What about the problem of assessment?' are some of the common responses to the question: 'If you believe this to be important why aren't you doing something about it?' In this book, academics from different disciplines and from different institutional settings show how they are attempting to produce autonomous students by describing their experiences of introducing alternatives to the traditional modes of teaching and course design. They provide personal accounts of their experiences rather than exhortations about what should be done. It is not intended to be a recipe for how-to-do-it but rather a source of information, encouragement and even inspiration for others who wish to pursue the goal of increasing student autonomy but are not quite sure whether it is possible or, if it is, how they might start.

Many terms have been used to describe approaches to developing student autonomy in higher education: independent study, self-directed learning, student-initiated learning and project orientation are a few. Some of these have been used to refer to particular practices or to specific contexts and have special connotations for some people. The theme of this book, however, encompasses all these approaches and examines them with respect to their common element – the goals of developing independence, self-directedness, and responsibility for learning.

Although the focus will not be on teaching methods *per se*, but on strategies for fostering learning within the context of particular courses, various methods will be described. These include the use of learning contracts in which students prepare a formal plan for their learning and its evaluation which is validated by a staff member; one-to-one learning in which students work in pairs to facilitate each other's learning; student planned courses in which students work on their own and in groups to initiate their own projects and put them into practice; peer support systems in which newly arrived students are assisted in problems of personal and academic adjustment by students with longer experience of the institution; and collaborative assessment in which staff and students cooperate in establishing criteria for student assessment and make judgements on the basis of these. Each of these approaches is described in a particular context from the point of view of the teacher using the approach.

Why should we be concerned about creating opportunities for students to develop and exercise autonomy in learning? The reasons emphasized in this book are not primarily theoretical and philosophical but practical. Independence in learning may or may not be a desirable personal goal for an individual; it is, nevertheless, a vital requisite for someone to be able to function effectively in modern society. Anyone acting in a responsible position needs to be able to plan his or her own learning and draw upon a variety of resources to assist in putting his or her learning plan into action. He or she needs to draw upon the experience and expertise of others, but it is his or her own responsibility to ensure that the answer needed is found.

If people outside educational institutions do, by force of circumstance, act more or less as autonomous learners, and there is evidence to suggest that they do (Tough, 1979), then the activities within educational institutions should be structured in such a way that they prepare students for 'learning after school' and assist them to develop the skills that they will need to exercise responsibility for learning effectively. If students enter these institutions with a very limited capability of being independent learners, one of the important roles of colleges and universities should be to provide the circumstances in which they can develop this capability. Unfortunately, at present, the assumption of most institutions is that students can satisfactorily conduct their own learning. They are dismayed when they find evidence to the contrary, but provide little in the way of training in the skills which are needed, focusing instead on the presentation of new subjects and increasingly sophisticated problems.

The assumption of the contributors to this volume is that if a skill is as important as that of autonomy in learning, then it is the responsibility of teachers in higher education to do something about creating the conditions in which it can flourish. They believe that it is the responsibility of all teachers to ensure that they construct their courses to foster autonomy and that this goal is compatible with the discipline-centred goals which often predominate. No matter what the professional background of the teacher, and irrespective of whether he or she has had any formal educational training, it is possible to design and conduct courses on this basis.

The book is composed of three parts. The first three chapters provide the reader with a general orientation towards the issues which will be considered later in practical detail. In Chapter 1, I survey some of the key issues which have been canvassed in recent years concerning the ideal of autonomy and how it might be manifest in higher education practice. Some of the assumptions which underpin the work of many practitioners of independent learning methods are presented, and some principles which can be used for the design of learning experiences aimed at promoting the transition from dependence to autonomy are summarized. In Chapter 2, Jane Abercrombie outlines the premises underlying her belief in the need to create more opportunities for student autonomy and suggests a reformulation of the student-peer-teacher relationship using three case studies drawn from her own experience to illustrate how this can work in practice.

Assessment practices are often the major barrier to developing increasing student responsibility: if students always look to others for judgements of their competence, how can they develop their own ability to assess their own learning? John Heron, in Chapter 3, argues that the transactions between students and teachers are critically affected by the balance of power — where it rests and how it is used determines the quality of learning. Assessment is the clearest example of this power in action, and he advocates the use of collaborative forms of assessment to overcome the authority problem whilst still meeting the need for a certificate of intellectual competence.

Part 2 comprises the bulk of the book and consists of case studies in which practising teachers in universities and colleges describe the ways in which they have confronted the problems raised in Part 1. Examples have been drawn from many disciplines: history, engineering, medicine, psychology, architecture, nursing; from many parts of the world: England, Australia, Canada and Switzerland; and all describe courses which require formal accreditation of student performance.

Student reticence and resistance to taking responsibility for learning are likely to be among the first problems the teacher will meet. Many existing courses unconsciously encourage dependence and, if a teacher who wishes to foster independence finds him or herself immersed in such an environment, problems can and do arise. In Chapter 4, John Powell gives a personal account of his own struggle against these forces as he deliberately tried to reduce his own control over his course and give it to his students. In Chapter 5, Harry Stanton identifies the main problem as being one of students' lack of confidence in handling a more open-ended approach to learning. His solution to this was to incorporate training in enhancing self-confidence as an early part of his course.

Students can learn as much, or even more, from their peers as from their teachers, but the help students can give to each other is a severely under-utilized resource in higher education. It is recognized that it may occur informally, but it appears to be assumed that it is not really the concern of teachers to involve themselves in this rather unstructured activity. That there is enormous potential in peer learning is clearly demonstrated by David Potts in Chapter 6. His course is structured around the basic principle of students helping each other to learn, with the teacher providing the environment and materials needed. On a broader scale, Marcel Goldschmid in Chapter 7 considers the problem of inducting students into what is to them a strange and new institution and how staff are able to foster student support activities which then become self-sufficient.

Medicine and health care are one of the most sensitive areas in which to make changes towards autonomous learning. Graduates must possess a high level of competence when lives are at risk. This does not, however, prevent this area of higher education being one of the areas in which the greatest steps have been taken in recent years towards developing self-directed learning. The Faculty of Health Science at McMaster University in Canada has been one of the leaders of this trend and is represented in both Chapters 8 and 9. In Chapter 8 Barbara Ferrier and two of her medical students, Michael Marrin and Jeffrey Seidman, describe their experiences of participating in a self-directed course in medicine, and in Chapter 9 Mary Buzzell and Olga Roman describe one particular method which is becoming increasingly widely used throughout the world: the use of learning contracts.

The final case studies move away from developing autonomy within part of a defined course of study to student involvement in the design and conduct of an entire undergraduate programme. John Stephenson in Chapter 10 describes the most well-known example in Britain of a course of independent studies, that of North East London Polytechnic, and focuses on its successes in helping students who would not normally be served well by the higher education system. In Chapter 11, Barrie Shelton provides the most substantial programme of all in independent learning which pre-dates the British examples and is little known outside its locale. The School of Environmental Design in Tasmania has a three-year undergraduate and three-year postgraduate course which, although it has hardly any formal requirements, has been nationally recognized and accredited by the professional architectural associations.

In the concluding section Malcolm Cornwall and John Powell reflect on the issues which have been raised by the preceding contributions. Malcolm Cornwall addresses the problem in Chapter 12 of how independent learning activities might be introduced into a traditional institution and what arguments can be put forward to respond to the critical questions of colleagues who may be initially unsympathetic to the ideas of putting autonomy into practice. In conclusion John Powell analyses some of the reports presented in earlier chapters on developing student autonomy in learning and points to some of the difficulties which remain if these ideas are to have a significant impact on higher education as a whole. He ends with a brief discussion of the educational significance of independence in learning.

One of the privileges which an editor has is to indulge his own views and to present his own account of what he regards as significant in the area on which he reports. For the most part I have refrained from this in the rest of the book, and you will have only the unconscious selection of authors and material to guide you. But in closing the Introduction I would like to add a personal note in keeping with the autobiographical accounts of many of the other contributors.

When I was preparing this book for publication I began to reflect on my own experience as an autonomous learner. I tried to identify those educational events in which I acted independently from teachers and which I regarded as significant learning activities. My first discovery was that there were very few experiences of this type which I could recall while I was in formal educational institutions. Most of those of importance occurred without any intervention by teachers. Of those which remained three were crucial. The first occurred in my last two years at secondary school. I was at an inner London comprehensive school that co-existed with many local grammar schools, the latter having supposedly creamed off most of the talented students. This meant that many A level subjects were taught in very small classes; indeed in Chemistry I was the only student. Luckily funds were not as restricted then and the class was not cancelled. I had a teacher, but did not have access to him for the usual number of periods. I had therefore to fall back on my own resources. At first the teacher tried to arrange it as a normal class in which he set work for me to complete and return to him for marking. This worked satisfactorily for a while, but as the examination drew near I took a more functional approach to the subject, concentrating on the need to pass the examination. I discovered the official syllabus and examination papers and used these as a guide for study, only calling on the teacher when I needed advice on difficulties I had met in my self-defined study and when I required his experience on the importance, or otherwise, of certain topics in the examination. Although I was working towards an externally set objective, passing A level Chemistry, I had through force of circumstances been engaged in self-appropriated learning and experienced the exhilaration of taking charge of my own learning in what I have always regarded as a difficult subject.

The second memory of being an autonomous learner is one I share with many of my contemporaries at university and is one which has been documented more widely. In my final undergraduate year, the last term before graduation was devoted to a major project in physics. Each person was required to find a project and a project supervisor from amongst the staff of the department or elsewhere. Usually projects were nominated by staff in areas of their research interest. I chose a topic out of interest, which combined physics, education and the foundations of science, and out of regard for the supervisor whom I felt I could get along with. Luckily my supervisor expected me to take full responsibility for what I was doing and acted as a sounding board and interpreter of difficult concepts. I was required to define the scope of my inquiry and its orientation, and to identify the resources which I needed and generally get on and do it. I soon found myself beyond the stage where I could take my problems and difficulties to my supervisor, as I was moving into areas in which our knowledge was more equal than before. I experienced a sense of buoyancy and freedom which contrasted with my begrudging tolerance of the prescribed courses of lectures and examples classes. My experience of the final-year project encouraged me to enter research where I thought I could find more of this excitement. My experience of the subject, however, did not encourage me to enter the same field. I was able to separate the feeling of being an independent learner from the content of the subject, which was purely a vehicle for this personal experience.

My final recollection of independence in learning takes me to the time when I was beginning a research studentship shortly after graduating from the course I have just described. Rather than continue my study of physics I had decided that my interests lay elsewhere and that I was more interested in the processes of education than the physical sciences. I joined the Institute for Educational Technology at the University of Surrey as its first full-time research student. It was a new institute in a subject new to the university, headed by a physicist with a powerful commitment to education. All the staff and students were new and were entering what we then regarded as a new field of endeavour. The most striking thing was that no one had defined the scope of the field in which we were working. We often had discussions and arguments about what was and was not legitimately included within the orbit of educational technology.

This meant that I, as a new research student, had no well-trod path to follow to guide me to a choice of thesis topic. I was forced by circumstances to become a self-directed learner. I had to decide for myself what was and was not important and had to plan my own programme of study and research. Of course, I had my supervisor to talk to and other members of the institute to share ideas with, but in this they were fully my peers and, although they brought a wealth of experience and expertise to the discussions, none of them could be identified as *the* expert in educational technology and thus authoritatively able to advise me on what I should do if I wanted to make a contribution to the field.

On thinking about these varied events I began to notice some common themes. The first of these was that in none of these situations did I have a long-standing commitment to the subject; they all happened to be of interest to me at the time, but most were not of enduring interest. The opportunity to work independently generated more interest than did a prior interest in the actual subject matter. The second is that circumstances pushed me into taking the initiative. In most other aspects of my student career I had been as conformist as many of my colleagues, but on these few occasions I had had the opportunity, sometimes planned but mostly not, of having to take responsibility for what I had to learn and of being personally accountable for the results. Finally, I realized that, especially when I was in school, I would not have voluntarily entered into a situation in which I felt I would be entirely responsible for everything I had had to do. I would not have opted for A level Chemistry, for example, if I had realized in advance the circumstances under which I would have to study it. The fact that one of these experiences (the final-year project) was deliberately scheduled by staff encouraged me to think that it is possible to make plans for independent learning in formal settings. In comparing notes with fellow students about the final-year project, I realized that although the potential was there to develop autonomy it was not always manifested. Whether it was or not appeared to depend on the ways in which the staff supervisors saw their role, and the degree of constraint and direction they placed on their students.

When I found myself in a teaching role, I was determined to operate in such a way as to maximize the opportunity for student-initiated learning within the context of a specific discipline (Boud and Prosser, 1980). I felt obliged to take into account my major experiences of independence in formal education, when planning and conducting my own courses, rather than follow the path that led to acceptability rather than excitement.

These personal experiences have supported my reading of the literature on autonomous and independent learning and led me to believe that teachers can facilitate or block student autonomy depending on the ways in which they act. Teachers cannot make someone autonomous: all they can do is create situations in which autonomy in learning may develop. They can, however, easily stifle its development. By creating a rigid and unresponsive structure they can severely inhibit student self-directedness and establish an unhealthy dependency which not only turns students away from learning in its wider context, but which diminishes the teacher as a person.

For those people who have accumulated most of their experience in the formal educational system it is often difficult to see what the alternatives might be. It is for this reason, that is to see how courses might be differently constructed, that this book has been written.

Part I Issues

Part I Issues

1. Toward Student Responsibility for Learning

David Boud

Introduction

What do we mean by developing student 'autonomy'? How can this 'autonomy' be developed? When teachers aim to develop independent learning activities what do they expect of their students? The notion of autonomy in learning is not a simple one and is the subject of much debate amongst philosophers of education. However, independently of this debate and unaware of many of the subtleties of the arguments, many practitioners throughout the world are trying to establish ways in which they can assist students to become less dependent upon them as teachers and to design courses which involve students more deeply in learning and in making decisions about what they will study.

The aim of this chapter is to present some of the ideas of educational philosophers on what is an 'autonomous' person; to clarify what is a legitimate objective for teachers who wish to decrease student dependence on themselves; to examine the assumptions made by proponents of independent learning; and to introduce some principles and guidelines for planning courses which aim to pursue student autonomy. It will do so by focusing on the work of people who are not represented directly in this book and who have made major contributions to understanding in this area. In this way it will also provide access to other literature about developing student responsibility in learning. The related literature on adult learning (Knowles, 1970; 1973; 1975) and experiential learning (Keeton *et al*, 1977; Keeton and Tate, 1978; Boud and Pascoe, 1978) will not be addressed directly.

One of the difficulties in discussing the field of autonomy in learning is the relative lack of conceptual and empirical research. As Wedemeyer points out in his encyclopedia entry on independent study 'the literature describing independent study is almost uniformly parochial' (Wedemeyer, 1971, p 548). The situation has changed in the last ten years but it is still puzzling that a topic so close to the heart of the educational enterprise should have received so little attention over the years. Compared to the plethora of literature on classroom research and educational testing the area is almost completely neglected. One reason for this might be the fact that it is very hard to be clear about what is a realistic goal for autonomy in education. Is it to produce an autonomous person — a product-oriented approach — or is it to introduce activities which require students to act autonomously — a process-oriented approach? (Lewis, 1978). A programme which allowed for students to be autonomous in the process of learning would not necessarily lead to the production of an autonomous person. But before we enter too closely into the debate let us examine briefly what has been said about autonomy as a goal of education.

Autonomy as a goal of education

The original concept of autonomy can be traced back to ancient Greece and to a political context. It was concerned with the property of a state to be self-ruling or self-governing. Its educational usage, by analogy, refers to the capacity of an individual to be an independent agent, not governed by others. R. F. Dearden has devoted many articles to discussing autonomy and education and defines it thus:

> A person is autonomous to the degree, and it is very much a matter of degree, that what he thinks and does, at least in important areas of his life, are determined by himself. That is to say, it cannot be explained why these are his beliefs and actions without referring to his own activity of mind. This determination of what one is to think and do is made possible by the bringing to bear of relevant considerations in such activities of mind as those of choosing, deciding, deliberating, reflecting, planning and judging. (Dearden, 1972, p 461)

Benjamin Gibbs elaborates on this:

> an autonomous individual must have both independence from external authority and mastery of himself and his powers. He must be free from the dictates and interference of other people, and free also from disabling conflicts or lack of coordination between the elements of his own personality. He must have the freedom to act and work as he chooses, and he must be capable of formulating and following a rule, pattern or policy of acting and working. (Gibbs, 1979, p 119)

In a later paper Dearden gives a further description of the qualities which could be observed in a person who would be thought of as autonomous:

> (i) wondering and asking, with a sense of the right to ask, what the justification is for various things which it would be quite natural to take for granted; (ii) refusing agreement or compliance with what others put to him when this seems critically unacceptable; (iii) defining what he really wants, or what is really in his interests, as distinct from what may be conventionally so regarded; (iv) conceiving of goals, policies and plans of his own, and forming purposes and intentions of his own independently of any pressure to do so from others; (v) choosing amongst alternatives in ways which could exhibit that choice as the deliberate outcome of his own ideas or purposes; (vi) forming his own opinion on a variety of topics that interest him; (vii) governing his actions and attitudes in the light of the previous sort of activity. In short, the autonomous man has a mind of his own and acts according to it. (Dearden, 1975, p 7)

These definitions encompass the important distinction made by Riesman (1950) between self-direction, other-direction and inner-direction. The autonomous person must not only be free from direction by others external to himself, but also from his own inner compulsions and rigidities. Autonomy is more than acting on one's own. It implies a responsiveness to one's environment and the ability to make creative and unique responses to situations as they arise rather than patterned and stereotypical responses from one's past (Jackins, 1965).

So far we have seen ideals: the autonomous person here is an abstraction, not something which we can realistically expect to emerge from any given course. Even at this level these views have been challenged, by Phillips, who finds difficulty in distinguishing an autonomous person of the type defined by Dearden and a person lacking in autonomy (Phillips, 1975), by Crittenden (1978) and, more seriously for practice by Lewis:

> To approve 'autonomy' as an ideal for students is one thing: to commend 'autonomous' methods of learning is another — however 'autonomy' is defined. If, for the purposes of argument, we gloss it as independence, it is not quite obvious that independent methods of learning promote independence — auxiliary causal relationships must be established. (Lewis, 1978, p 152)

We should be careful in following this path too far. Although it may be in doubt that independent methods of learning in themselves promote independence it is certainly unlikely that dependent, teacher-dominated methods would so so. We must therefore look at methods which claim to foster autonomy through autonomous ways of working to see if they in fact do so.

Autonomy cannot be pursued in a vacuum: it does not necessitate isolation from the ideas and experience of others. Its exercise has a social context:

> Mature autonomy requires both emotional independence — freedom from continual and pressing needs for reassurance and approval — and instrumental independence, the ability to carry on activities and cope with problems without seeking help from others and the ability to be mobile in relation to one's needs. Simultaneously, the individual must accept interdependence, recognizing that one cannot receive benefits from a social structure without contributing to it, that personal rights have a corollary social responsibility. (Chickering, 1969)

Even with independence as the goal there is an unavoidable dependence at one level on authorities for information and guidance. *Inter*dependence is therefore an essential component of autonomy in action.

Turning to the practical implications of our definitions, Lewis' caution is echoed in a different context by Dressel and Thompson in one of the few surveys of independent study in the United States:

> At the heart of the problem of definition is the fact that independence has not been defined adequately in an academic context. It has come to mean independent of classes, independent of other students, or independent of faculty. Acceptance of any one or even all of these as essential would be missing the most important aspect of the whole process which is that the student becomes capable of self-directed study. (Dressel and Thompson, 1973, p 3)

That is, there has been a failure to discriminate between independent study as a learning experience and as a capability to be developed (Dittman, 1976). They then make their own statement on independent study which can serve as a working definition despite an element of tautology:

> Independent study is the student's self-directed pursuit of academic competence
> in as autonomous a manner as he is able to exercise at any particular time.
> (Dressel and Thompson, 1973, p1)

However, we cannot wait for unambiguous definitions at this stage of development. Undeniably, independence and autonomy are highly rated goals of teachers and it is encouraging to note that this view is shared by students. In a study of the university experience of a group of students at the University of Melbourne, Little (1970) found that, of all the aims provided, the one stating that 'the university should develop in its students habits of independent intellectual inquiry' was rated highest. It is necessary for teachers to act on what seem reasonable assumptions in the area of autonomy in learning and to reflect at a later date on the action they take in the light of the philosophers' concerns.

Some working assumptions

Although proponents of independent and self-directed learning might not agree on a common simple definition of their goals, there are many shared assumptions about the nature of students, the role of teachers and the principles which should inform their practice. These cannot be found in any one source, or even group of sources, and I have made my own selection of the assumptions which underlie my practice. Not all the contributors to this volume would subscribe to every one of these, but they do give the general flavour of the assumptions which are implicit in many of the case studies which follow in later chapters. As this is a composite list drawn from a large number of sources it is not possible to acknowledge the origins of each in detail.

The first group of assumptions refers to the nature of autonomous learning in higher education.

Autonomous learning is not an absolute standard to be met but a goal to be pursued; what is important is the direction — towards student responsibility for learning — not the magnitude of the change in any given situation.

This follows the distinction made by Lewis (1978) and others between independence in the process of learning and the production of an autonomous person. The only realistic goal for higher education is that students should be more autonomous when they leave the course than when they enter, not that they will have reached some arbitrary point along some established continuum of autonomy.

The goal of developing student autonomy needs to be as actively pursued and as clearly stated as any other; it is unlikely to be effectively pursued if it remains unarticulated in particular courses.

It is not sufficient that student autonomy only exists as a global goal of an institution. Unless it is included as an integral and explicit part of courses, no plans will be made for its pursuit and it will only be developed through spin-off from other activities designed for other purposes. It is not just one goal among many but rather a characteristic of all of the others; it is the manner in which all skills should be displayed and all beliefs held.

Autonomy in learning does not mean that students work on their own in isolation from others. Autonomy in learning does not imply that there should always be a one-to-one relationship between a student and a teacher or supervisor. It is compatible with autonomous learning for learners to opt to be 'taught' in situations in which they have decided that it is desirable for their own ends. Developing autonomy does not simply involve removing structured teaching; it may require a greater degree of structure than didactic teaching, but of a different kind.

The fact that so much independent learning at present occurs through students working on individual projects supervised by one teacher should not lead us to believe that this is the only appropriate mode for developing autonomy in learning. It is desirable that students learn to work with their peers, and it is legitimate for many students to relate as a group to one teacher, or indeed for one student to relate to many teachers on one project. Some classroom teaching in the usual sense of the word is not incompatible with autonomy. A preponderance of classroom teaching obviously is, and so also are those forms of classroom teaching which place the teacher in the centre of activity, unilaterally controlling what takes place.

The centrality of the goal of developing autonomy in learning in higher education is such that it cannot be limited to peripheral topics or extra-curricular activities and it cannot be pursued partially. The exercise of autonomy cannot be realistically limited to any one part of the learning process: for example, in course content, but not assessment or in choosing one's own pace but not one's objectives. Autonomous learning, as all learning, involves the whole person, not just the intellect; what is to be learned should not be seen separately from the motives and desires of students. Postponement of the opportunity to exercise responsibility for learning actively discourages the development of the capacity to do so.

It is tempting to argue that there are already some opportunities for students to work independently through student societies and optional activities and therefore there is no need to touch the core of the curriculum. Unfortunately, doing this gives the clear message that the goal of independent work is not important enough for it to be pursued in the main part of the programme. The same applies to providing opportunities for students to make decisions about parts of a course, such as the topics to be included, but not to crucial aspects, such as assessment. The message is the same: you are not to be trusted with important decisions, you should be content with the minor ones. It may be necessary for external reasons for this to occur at the early stages of some courses, but unless students can see a progression to wider involvement the claim to be developing autonomy is suspect. The third assumption above does pose something of a dilemma: the tension between the requirements of the student and the requirements of the subject as interpreted by the teacher. It does not necessarily follow that a student who seeks his own solutions will come close to human knowledge which is thousands of years old (Lewis, 1978). In this circumstance the teacher as an agent of the institution is obliged to decide whether the course exists for the student or the subject in that specific situation and to communicate this clearly to the student in advance. Neither the teacher who professes his subject oblivious to the response of students, nor the totally responsive teacher who gives solely what the students ask, are acceptable in educational institutions today.

It does not follow that in autonomous learning that which is to be learned must be original; what is essential is that the goals of learning should derive from the needs of the learner.

Strictly speaking it is not a necessary part of autonomy that thinking should be done correctly: a person may be thinking autonomously, but may be making errors of which he is unaware (Hare, 1975). However, this is certainly not something which is to be encouraged and it is no part of the argument in favour of autonomy that standards of excellence should not be applicable. Autonomous learning is not to be identified with discovery learning, or at least with the distortions of this idea which seem to be much in common currency in recent years. Just because a student is responsible for his own learning there is no reason why the experience of others should be hidden or withheld. The issue here is: when is it appropriate for this information to become apparent? In traditional teaching this occurs right from the start: the knowledge of others is the starting point for learning, but when autonomy is the goal this will be very rarely the starting point. This brings us to the final assumption in this section.

Moves towards developing autonomy can be blocked if extrinsic rewards and incentives do not support it.

There is no point in introducing independent learning if students are to be judged and rewarded on grounds which are incompatible with the goal. If the form of assessment emphasizes the memorizing of a set body of knowledge, when the learning which precedes it has gone well beyond this and has not focused on the memory component, then independent learning and the students themselves will be discouraged. Evaluation and assessment, if externally conducted, must reward the component skills of independent learning as well as the competence of the final product.

The second group of assumptions relate to the characteristics of students.

Students bring a great deal of prior learning and experience to any situation; this should be utilized. Students are in the best position to know what their own learning needs are: however, they are not always able to identify their own needs unaided, especially if they have been 'educated' in a system which places a low value on this activity. Individual students have individual needs which must be treated as such.

There are no situations in which students can be treated as if they were empty vessels. Even the newly arrived first-year student enrolled in a subject which is not available in school brings a vast wealth of experience about related areas, about learning and about his or her own reasons for taking that course. If this is ignored then teaching will be inefficient and the student will receive the message that his or her experience is valueless. Although students may not be able to articulate their needs in the same language as teachers, they are the only people with access to their reasons for choosing an area and what they are learning for. They may need assistance in relating this to a pre-existing body of knowledge and the needs of others, but teachers have no right to deny their needs. A vital and often neglected skill for teachers which is especially important in developing autonomy is that of facilitating the identification of students' aims and objectives, and of assisting them in learning from their own standpoint. Students who, like the majority, have been brought up in a system in which all learning was externally defined by examination syllabuses, will often be resistant to assessing their own needs and desires and will be bemused and inhibited by the prospect of doing so. If teachers wish to encourage autonomy they have a responsibility to help their students overcome these conditioned responses and take the initiative.

All students are capable of working independently, it is not the exclusive province of the most able. Autonomous learning can take place at any level or at any age; however, it will not manifest itself in the same ways in all situations. Students themselves are a significantly under-utilized resource for teaching in higher education; given suitable conditions they can facilitate and support each others' learning.

All students should be given the opportunity to work autonomously; there are no educational grounds for limiting the availability of independent study. Obviously not all students will be able to perform at the highest levels of competence, as with teacher-dominated learning approaches a range of performance is to be expected. Often the grounds for excluding some students from independent study programmes are expedient: it would demand more of the supervising teachers and make the system more complex to administer. But any institution which takes this point of view is making a poor contribution to learning if it selects only those students who are already able to work autonomously and then sets up programmes to allow them to do so whilst neglecting those students who require more help with their learning. There are no single paths to autonomous learning: they will differ depending on the backgrounds of students, their levels of knowledge and skill and on the abilities of teachers. It cannot be expected that the facilitation of autonomy in learning will be identical in all years of a course, or for all students within a year. It is possible, however, for students at similar states of readiness to work within a common framework, and there are frameworks (see the example of contract learning in Chapter 9) which are very robust and can accommodate a wide range of ability within the same approach. Many approaches to independent learning are based upon students working together, not just as co-learners, but as learners and facilitators to each other (see Goldschmid and Goldschmid, 1976 and Chapters 6 and 7). Not only does this provide a valuable learning experience in working together interdependently, but it also supplements the resources which are available from the institution and can be useful in saving costs (Black and Boud, 1977).

The third group of assumptions are specifically related to staff.

Teachers are still necessary. Teachers are usually more effectively used as facilitators of learning rather than transmitters of information.
It should not need saying, but for the sake of completeness it should be emphasized, that teachers are needed as much in autonomous learning as they ever were in other forms. Their role is not the same, though. While they can still retain their particular expertise in various fields of interests they need to prepare for a role which goes beyond the inculcation of given knowledge, attitudes and skills. Good teaching in developing autonomy may involve none of these. Perhaps teaching is not the best word to use as it has long associations with instruction and didacticism, but there is no elegant alternative: facilitator, the most likely contender, has not been easily accepted in the British tradition of higher education. Facilitation is not the only role of teachers in developing autonomy: they cannot take only a neutral role. They continue to stand for certain values and standards of excellence, but they need to do so in a way which is open to challenge and critical examination. (See the discussion by Heron on this in Chapter 3.)

Autonomy cannot be developed if teachers deny their competence and authority and abrogate their responsibility for facilitating learning. Non-autonomous teachers do not make the best facilitators of autonomous learning.
Although independent learning involves a shift in the locus of control it does not remove the teacher from a position of authority. He or she still remains the representative of the institution and is responsible for providing the best circumstances for the development of autonomy in the students for whom, in this sense, he or she is responsible. The exercise of authority then becomes one of the most sensitive, and possibly contentious, issues (Huntington, 1980). It is not a simple move from an authoritarian position to a *laissez-faire* one. Individual teachers have to come to terms with their new role and explore for themselves the implications for their subject-matter expertise, which still remains, and for their relationships with their students. Such a self-appraisal is possible, as Huntington (1980) and others have shown, but probably only in a context in which the staff of an institution are allowed autonomy in their own work. It would be difficult to imagine teachers who were allowed no initiative in their own work environment being able effectively to assist students who were trying to make decisions of their own.

Finally, there are some institutional assumptions which should be mentioned. This area will be examined in greater detail by Malcolm Cornwall in Chapter 12.

Significant steps can be taken towards developing student autonomy in learning in even the most rigid of institutions. Independent learning does not have to cost more than conventional teaching; the range of costs for independent learning are as great as for conventional teaching and depend on the specific forms and arrangements which are made.

Notwithstanding the caution expressed in the previous assumption, there is ample evidence to suggest that autonomy in learning can be pursued in well-established and conservative institutions. Inevitably the changes there could not be as radical and fundamental as those that are possible in the new institutions, mostly only in the United States, which have been set up specifically for this purpose. Romey (1977) has experienced many of these difficulties in establishing innovative programmes in science and his personal account is a very useful guide for those who wish to examine this area further. The cost factor is one often cited by critics who wish to find some excuse for blocking independent learning programmes, and very often proponents of autonomy for students play into their hands by proposing very staff-intensive courses which place a high load on themselves and their colleagues. It should be expected that in the initial stages of any new course or way of teaching there will be an extra load as the staff concerned work their way into new roles and new procedures, but this need not flow over into the steady state demand if the course is well-designed. Most independent study programmes work on the same budget as conventional courses, purely because they are funded on the same basis: in different circumstances they would cut their cloth to fit. In other situations administrators have found that costs were reduced as staff could be more flexibly deployed and greater use was made of student self-help and non-budgeted persons outside the institution.

Autonomy in practice

The last decade has seen a substantial increase in the amount of attention given to teaching and learning in higher education. There have been many accounts of innovations in teaching and a smaller, but growing number of reports on student learning and how it can be facilitated. The reductionistic approaches of Skinner and his behaviourist colleagues are no longer in vogue and it has become legitimate to look at teacher and student intentions as well as the ways in which their actions can be observed by others. Autonomy, in common with many educational concepts, is not always immediately apparent and has to be inferred from reports from individuals and analyses of their actions. The research which has been conducted related to our concerns has begun to offer insights which are of direct relevance to teachers who wish to plan courses which pursue autonomous learning. The most important of this work has identified various developmental stages which learners pass through from childhood to maturity and on the smaller scale from ignorance to expertise in a particular area of learning. When this research is combined with the thoughtful and perceptive reflections of some of the leading facilitators of learning we have a useful guide for anyone embarking on the path of developing their own courses.

Before we examine this work, it is perhaps worthwhile pausing to consider a paradox in the move towards developing autonomy in learning. As expressed by Little:

> There is no escape from the paradox of leadership — the requirement that men should be *led* to freedom, that students be taught the autonomous style.
> (Little, 1975, p 260)

As will have already become apparent, the stance of this chapter is that it is entirely possible for students to develop the 'autonomous style' given appropriate support from teachers, but I cannot escape the conclusion that teachers can only do so much: they can lead students to self-responsibility, they cannot make them grasp it.

If they wish to do this where can they start? One logical starting point is to examine what is known about how students develop through the college years. Perry (1970) and his colleagues undertook a major study of *Forms of Intellectual and Ethical Development in the College Years*. From a series of intensive interviews with undergraduate students at Harvard he identified a sequence of what he termed 'positions', which represent ways in which students view themselves and their learning. I cannot hope to encompass the richness and variety of response which he describes in his book in a brief survey, but the following extract gives an indication of his findings. The main line of development of his students was as follows:

> *Position 1:* The student sees the world in polar terms of we-right-good vs. other-wrong-bad. Right answers for everything exist in the absolute, known to authority whose role is to mediate (teach) them. Knowledge and goodness are perceived as quantitative accretions of discrete rightnesses to be collected by hard work and obedience (paradigm: a spelling test).
> *Position 2:* The student perceives diversity of opinion and uncertainty, and accounts for them as unwarranted confusion in poorly qualified authorities or as mere exercises set by authority 'so we can learn to find the answer for ourselves'.
> *Position 3:* The student accepts diversity and uncertainty as legitimate, but still *temporary* in areas where authority 'hasn't found the answer yet'. He supposes authority grades him in these areas on 'good expression' but remains puzzled as to standards.
> *Position 4:* (a) The student perceives legitimate uncertainty (and therefore diversity of opinion) to be extensive and raises it to the status of an unstructured epistemological realm of its own in which 'anyone has a right to his own opinion', a realm which he sets over against authority's realm where right-wrong still prevails; or (b) the student discovers qualitative contextual relativistic reasoning as a special case of 'what they want' within authority's realm.
> *Position 5:* The student perceives all knowledge and values (including authority's) as contextual and relativistic and subordinates dualistic right-wrong functions the status of a special case, in context.
> *Position 6:* The student apprehends the necessity of orienting himself in a

relativistic world through some form of personal commitment (as distinct from unquestioned or unconsidered commitment to simple belief).
Position 7: The student makes an initial commitment in some area.
Position 8: The student experiences the implications of commitment, and explores the subjective and stylistic issues of responsibility.
Position 9: The student experiences the affirmation of identity among multiple responsibilities and realizes commitment as a constant, unfolding activity through which he expresses his lifestyle. (Perry, 1970, pp 9-10)

These positions do not reflect a smooth, uninterrupted path from simplicity to sophistication. Students may delay in one position for a year, exploring its implications or explicitly hesitating to take the next step. They may deflect from this path and exploit the opportunity for detachment offered by the structures of positions 4 and 5 to deny responsibility through passive or opportunistic alienation. Or they may become entrenched in the dualistic, absolutistic structures of positions 2 or 3.

Perry does not argue that these are manifest in the students' approach to individual subjects or topics, but rather that they reflect a general approach to knowledge and the world. These positions cannot be simply transferred to a particular course although, of course, they do describe a broad framework through which students see their programme, and it is therefore helpful for the teacher to have in mind that within the same class there will probably be students with radically different outlooks on what is taking place, who will be reacting in very different ways. There are other developmental models which can provide similar insights, but these are not related to students as directly as Perry's work is. Of particular note are the stages of moral development identified by Kohlberg (1972) and those of ego-development by Loevinger (Loevinger, 1976; Head and Shayer, 1980). Loevinger in particular focuses on a stage she labels as 'autonomous'.

At the micro-developmental level, Brundage and MacKeracher (1980) have produced a synthesis of various stage models which focus more clearly on learning activities. This can be applied directly to specific courses and learning projects:

Entry stage: This stage is triggered when a learner enters a situation which has a high degree of novelty, uncertainty, or lack of familiarity, which involves him in personal stress, or in which he perceives a threat to himself. He may perceive himself as disoriented within the situation, may defend himself by using inappropriate behaviour, may feel inhibited in his interpersonal relationships, may act as an observer without making a personal commitment to participate, may appear as if he were dependent or counter-dependent, and may communicate largely through monologue. The learner in the entry stage tends to rely on external standards to guide his behaviour and to make assumptions about his current situation based on past experience which may or may not be appropriate. In the entry stage teachers or others can best support the learner by creating a reliable environment which operates on the basis of standardized and explicit behavioural norms and in which the consequences of behaviour are known.
Reactive stage: A learner moves out of the entry stage and into the reactive stage when he develops a sense of himself as being an individual who is capable of

acting independently within the situation or when he perceives the environment as having become unreliable and unsupportive. The learner may perceive himself as autonomous and independent of the control of others, may work to develop a high degree of self-understanding, and may wish to carry out individual activities within a group setting. Learners in the reactive stage often express negative feelings, engage in conflicts and arguments with others, and express the feeling that the group is disorganized and confused. The learner in the reactive stage is best supported by teachers or others who encourage expressions of individual feelings and opinions and who do not demand strict adherence to standardized behavioural norms.

Proactive stage: When the learner feels confident about himself as an accepted and acceptable member of the group or actor within the situation, he moves on to discover and eventually accept the individuality of others involved. The learner in the proactive stage tends to perceive himself as involved in activities leading to mutuality, cooperation, and negotiation with others in the situation, as searching for an understanding of others in relation to self, and as developing shared norms and values for behaviour within the group. Learners generally use fewer individual activities and engage in fewer arguments. They are increasingly likely to use group activities and engage in dialogues. The proactive stage is often highly productive for the entire group. The learner in the proactive stage is best supported by teachers or others who accept and encourage cooperative and collaborative behaviour in preference to individual performance or competition and who can provide descriptive and immediate feedback about individual behaviour in relation to established objectives.

Integrative stage: When the learner can distinguish between individual others, he moves on to integrate the perspective of others with his own. As a result of integrating activities, he develops a sense of balance between himself and others and between working at group or individual tasks and maintaining interpersonal relationships with others. The learner may integrate perspectives which involve multiple standards of behaviour, multiple interpretations of experience, and multiple sources of information. The learner in the integrative stage is best supported by teachers or others who encourage him to develop internal standards to guide personal behaviour, who openly share information about themselves and their feelings and values, who willingly act as co-learners and value the role of learner for themselves, and who can value and accept individual performance and group activities simultaneously.

In terms of adult learning, these theories suggest that all adults, when they enter a new learning experience, begin with dependent-type behaviours and move first to independent behaviour and then to interdependent behaviour during the course of the learning activities. The progression can be facilitated by a teacher who is prepared to provide some structure and direction at the beginning of the learning activities; to move then to encouraging individual activities; and finally to provide opportunities for interdependent activities within the group and for integrative processes for individuals. (Adams, 1974; Kubler-Ross, 1970; Tuckman, 1965; Hunt and Sullivan, 1974; Gibb, 1964; Schutz, 1967). (Brundage and MacKeracher, 1980, pp 54-55)

These stages are derived in part from the stages of group development as well as those of the development of individuals. It is recognized that teachers can trap learning groups in the early stages of development and block the transition of the group from one stage to another (see, for example, Mulford, 1977). They can also, by appropriate interventions, facilitate progression and assist the group and its members to move from dependence to independence and interdependence. It is interesting to note that the final stage, called 'integrative' by Brundage and MacKeracher, is very similar to those described by many practitioners and called the 'community of inquiry' by Torbert (1976), the 'peer learning community' by Heron (1974), the 'learning community' by Boydell (1976), and the 'experimenting community' by Bilorusky and Butler (1975). All of these teachers aspire to a state in which students are freely interacting with each other, the teacher and others on jointly planned projects and individual projects and are responding to their own needs and those of others in a cooperative and supportive manner.

Stage models are helpful for the perspective they provide on the complexities of learning and on the varying responses of teachers which are required. They are likely to supersede the fairly simple schema which have until now been used in British analyses of independent learning such as that described by Percy and Ramsden (1980):

> A possible conceptualization of the relationship between individualized and 'independent' study and of degrees of student independence (based on Boud and Bridge, 1974) marks out four linked stages of student independence:
>
> 1. *Pace* Student can work at his own pace and choose the times (and sometimes the places) at which he finds it most appropriate to learn. Examples: Keller Plan courses; parts of many traditionally organized university courses (eg essay writing and individual reading); some project and laboratory work.
> 2. *Choice* Student chooses to work or not to work at a course, or at a part of a course. Examples: Keller Plan (to a limited extent); choice between a number of courses offered by a department during an academic year; modular course structures; choice of major and minor options.
> 3. *Method* Student can decide the method of learning he finds most suitable. Examples: independent study programmes; parts of some traditionally organized courses and individualized packages (eg choice between video presentations or texts; choice between different textbooks).
> 4. *Content* Student chooses what he wants to learn according to his own goals and interests. This may or may not imply working within established academic disciplines or structures. Examples: some project work, independent study programmes.
> The notion of student control over content and method in this scheme necessarily subsumes that of control over pace and choice. (p 6)

These focus on the dimensions of freedoms of choice which are available to a student when confronted with a defined course. Such dimensions, when suitably extended, provide a straightforward way of analysing courses to determine the degree of freedom, and thus of autonomy offered to a student. They can be used as a checklist to determine the extent to which autonomy in learning is allowed and thus the upper limit on the amount of independence which can be formally exercised as part of the course.

Perhaps one of the most inhibiting factors in developing independent learning is the fragmentation of subjects which occurs in most tertiary institutions. The progression through stages of learning takes time, and probably occurs separately for each separate component of the curriculum as individual teachers progress at their own pace. Therefore when a large number of subjects are included as part of a course, the time devoted to each decreases, and so the opportunities for students to operate in the proactive and integrative stages is severely restricted, and the students are more likely to be trapped at entry. The timetable arrangements which suit traditional teaching can provide one of the greatest constraints on any new forms which rely on continuity of contact and extended work over time to achieve their ends.

Moving on from stages and dimensions of learning, Boydell (1976) has attempted to summarize the main points made about autonomous learning by some key authors prior to the emergence of interest in stage models. He has assembled these points in a diagram (see Diagram 1), which illustrates his view on the components of autonomous learning and the kind of outcomes to which they lead. Boydell's view is based strongly

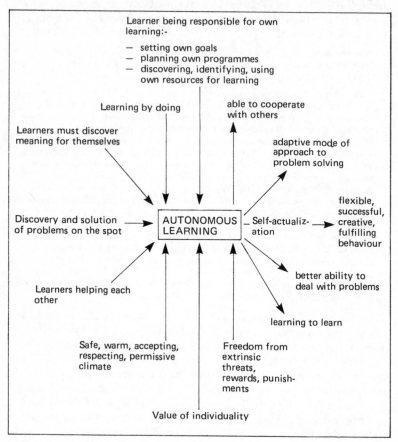

Diagram 1 *Autonomous learning*

(from Boydell, 1976, p 42)

Based upon the ideas of the Association for Supervision and Curriculum Development (1962), Combs (1962), Dewey (1928), Harrison and Hopkins (1967), Knowles (1970), Rogers (1961, 1969) and Wight (1970).

on the work of the early humanistic psychologists such as Rogers and
Maslow and provides a useful representation which strongly emphasizes
self-actualization, experiential learning and personal development, that is
involving all aspects of a person in learning, and which aims to extract the
maximum possible benefit from all experiences.

The components and aims of autonomous learning having now been
presented, the question arises, how can one design learning experiences
which foster its development? Some answers to this appear in the rest of
the book, but there are two other practitioners who have clearly analysed
their own experiences of conducting self-directed learning activities and
summarized the principles on which they are based. Roger Harrison works
within a training context with management programmes and takes an
operational approach. He defines autonomous learning thus:

> Autonomous learning can be said to have occurred in an educational situation
> when it becomes hard for educators to find participants who need a helping hand
> in finding something interesting or productive to do. (Harrison, 1978, p 153)

He then outlines his principles of procedure:

> We give participants maximum feasible choice at all points . . . We try to balance
> structure and ambiguity . . . We . . . reduce anxiety and dependency by providing
> a clearly articulated conceptual framework wherever possible and relating all the
> learning activities and resources to it . . . We try to provide equally valued
> alternatives . . . We try to use the approaches and methods of traditional education
> to support the learner up to the point at which he or she can move ahead
> independently, and then we allow the learner to proceed independently . . .
> We articulate and foster social norms that support individual responsibility and
> independence . . . for example, some useful norms are: it is all right to initiate
> anything, it is all right to withdraw or withhold one's own energy and resources,
> the unexamined activity is not worth doing . . . We try to help participants
> become aware of their own 'learning cycles' . . . the natural process of advance
> and retreat in learning. (Harrison, 1978, pp 161, 162)

It can be seen from this that Harrison and his co-leaders take a very active
stance in facilitating courses. This may be due to the fact that much of his
work appears to be based upon short, highly intensive courses, rather than
the longer time span, low intensity courses which are the norm in formal
educational institutions.

William Torbert (1978), however, has based his analyses on experience
of, sometimes, large classes in traditional universities. He has identified
what he terms 'qualities of liberating structures', that is, characteristics
of the organization of educational settings which enhance student self-
direction. He recognizes the paradox of leadership for self-direction and
adopts a consciously ironic approach. His qualities for liberating structure
are:

☐ recognition that students will, at least initially, view the course
differently from the staff and will need to be introduced to a new
way of looking at learning.

☐ an integration of learning products and learning processes. That is,
setting tasks which cannot be completed without reference to the

processes of learning which are taking place.

☐ planned change to the structure of the course as it progresses so that students take increasing responsibility.

☐ provision of feedback on the course structure and learning tasks so that the process of learning is monitored.

☐ use of the power held by the teacher to support the structure which places increasing responsibility on students.

☐ emphasis on the critical examination of the nature and functioning of the course itself by both teachers and students.

☐ teachers being publicly accountable to their students for conducting the course along the lines which have been agreed and committed to seeking and righting any incongruities which have been identified.

Torbert's prescription is not for the novice. It is a high risk approach which depends on a highly skilled practitioner. That Torbert can make it work with a compulsory undergraduate course with 360 students enrolled does not imply that it is easily transferable. It does illustrate that it is possible to apply autonomous learning principles to courses whose circumstances suggest that they would not be amenable to this approach. An approach applying similar principles to those of Torbert within the context of a smaller course is described by Boud and Prosser (1980).

Carl Rogers is another highly skilled facilitator of learning and it is perhaps appropriate to conclude this chapter with some of his observations. Rogers is probably the single most important figure in the emergence of self-directed learning and his book, *Freedom to Learn*, has been the source of inspiration for many teachers despite criticism by some philosophers of education (Peters, 1970). He summarizes his own guidelines on the facilitation of learning:

1. The facilitator has much to do with setting the initial mood or climate of the group or class experience.
2. The facilitator helps to elicit and clarify the purposes of the individuals in the class as well as the more general purposes of the group.
3. He relies upon the desire of each student to implement those purposes which have meaning for him, as the motivational force behind significant learning.
4. He endeavours to organize and make easily available the widest possible range of resources for learning.
5. He regards himself as a flexible resource to be utilized by the group.
6. In responding to expressions in the classroom group, he accepts both the intellectual content and the emotionalized attitudes, endeavouring to give each aspect the approximate degree of emphasis which it has for the individual or the group.
7. As the acceptant classroom climate becomes established, the facilitator is able increasingly to become a participant learner, a member of the group, expressing his views as those of one individual only.
8. He takes the initiative in sharing himself with the group — his feelings as well as his thoughts — in ways which do not demand nor impose, but represent simply a personal sharing which students may take or leave.
9. Throughout the classroom experience, he remains alert to the expressions indicative of deep or strong feelings.

10. In his functioning as a facilitator of learning, the leader endeavours to recognise and accept his own limitations. (Rogers, 1969, pp 164-6)

Rogers' emphasis is on facilitating group interactions and on a degree of non-directedness which is in contrast to some of the other earlier approaches. This is indicative of the wide range of approaches to the facilitation of autonomy in learning which have been expressed.

Finally, it is in keeping with Rogers' outlook that we end with an issue which is at the core of all approaches, but which he has identified and expressed so well. His overriding contribution is an insistence that what is important in developing student autonomy and in enabling students to take responsibility for their own learning is not any technique or teaching methodology, but an attitude towards students of acceptance and understanding of their views, desires and frame of reference, and the relationship between teacher and students which develops as a result of this acceptance. As Rogers says in the context of therapy, but which is equally applicable to education:

We moved from the *method* to the *attitudes* to the *relationship* as the key ingredient in the [educational] process. (Quoted in Kirschenbaum, 1979, p 202)

2. Changing Basic Assumptions about Teaching and Learning

M. L. J. Abercrombie, *formerly Director, Architectural Education Research Unit, University College London*

Educational assumptions

The argument to be developed in this chapter is based on the belief that much of our behaviour as teachers and learners is non-rational. It is also, of course, sometimes and in part irrational, ie foolish, illogical, or unduly influenced by emotion — the kind we perceive easily in others. The non-rational kind, which we all share, is not so easily perceived either in ourselves or others; however cool, sensible and rational it appears to be, it is in fact influenced by factors which we do not evaluate — they are not subjected to reason. I refer to the basic assumptions, or concepts, or attitudes about education which are so deeply ingrained in each of us as part of our culture, that they are taken for granted and used unquestioningly. They were developed in earlier times in response to needs now outgrown, but because they are not amenable to evaluation in the light of changed conditions they form a barrier to change of behaviour in response to current needs.

Consequently, in much of our behaviour we act as automata, not considering many of the alternatives that could be available to us. A wag has described the human brain as the best and cheapest general computer, assembled by unskilled labour. I would add that even in the cleverest and wisest of us, much of it is *used* by unskilled labour, and that one of the tasks of education today is to help each person to learn to make better use of it, to be able to exploit his own cerebral equipment in more productive and happier ways.

Analogously, in the medical field, people can learn to bring their so-called autonomic nervous systems under control, and can modify, for instance, their own blood pressure or heartbeat, or the state of other specific organs (Luthe, 1971). It is possible that some of the so-called psychosomatic stress-caused illnesses may thus be treated or, better, prevented. Training to control these processes can be facilitated if the physiological changes, of which the person may otherwise be unaware, can be made perceptible to him or her by visual (or other) feedback, though some people do not need such aid. Yogis, for instance, can achieve it through transcendental meditation (Wallace and Benson, 1972). We are only beginning to understand how to manage our own brains.

Each of us needs to become aware of his basic assumptions so that he can evaluate their contribution to his behaviour, and adopt alternatives if necessary. Though it is possible and on occasions convenient to be able to consider assumptions as isolatable units, they are in practice closely related to each other and mutually supporting. Any one person's assumptions together form a tangled, coherent network which is the basis of his personal style of thinking and behaviour. Change in one assumption may affect, and indeed may require, changes in others. Within a person's own frame of reference, the relationships between his behaviour and assumptions are logical, and however ineffective his behaviour is, it does not change unless the relevant assumptions are changed.

In the first part of this chapter I shall illustrate this thesis with reference to some assumptions which seem to form the matrix of our thinking about education. Innovations in educational practice which challenge these assumptions will be indicated. If the innovations prove effective and spread, the relevant assumptions generally held by society will be modified to incorporate the new ideas.

The first part thus deals with basic assumptions which are held with greater or lesser commitment by most of us. In the second part I shall draw on my experience of three attempts to help individuals to adapt their own behaviour to certain specific educational needs by becoming aware, through a process of 'free' or 'associative' group discussion, of their own personal complex of relevant assumptions. Among the assumptions that affect much of our present thinking about teaching and learning the following can be discerned:

The notion is still common that the pupil's state is one of 'innocence' — or that of an empty vessel waiting to be filled. This 'jug and bottle' concept was useful in the early days of universal education, when the chief aim was to teach enormous numbers of children of the illiterate population to read and write. Success was achieved with the majority, and the failures were written off as inherently educationally subnormal. Even at this modest level of teaching, the concept is no longer useful for remedying the present 10 per cent adult illiteracy rate in the UK, and it is certainly not appropriate in higher education. Studies of child development such as those of Piaget give another picture from that of the empty vessel — of a mind that, at whatever level of development and however ignorant of the substance of what is to be taught, is already furnished with ideas or concepts or attitudes, some of which may stand in the way of responding to new knowledge in a simple, open, receptive way. The pupil is not a passive receptacle, but always has to undertake considerable work to rearrange the furniture of his mind to accommodate new material; the difficulties are idiosyncratic and not easily understood by the teacher.

A quotation from R. D. Laing's *Knots* (1970) expresses the consequent difficulties of communication and understanding:

I don't know *what* it is I don't know,
   and yet am supposed to know,
and I feel I look stupid
  if I seem both not to know it
    and not to know *what* it is I don't know.
Therefore I pretend to know it.

  This is nerve-racking
  since I don't know what I must pretend to know.
Therefore I pretend to know everything.

   . . . .

You may know what I don't know, but not
  that I don't know it,
and I can't tell you. So you will have to tell me everything.

The empty-vessel concept was supported by the *telephone exchange analogy* of the nervous system, derived from early studies of reflex action in isolated nerve-brain muscle preparations. Stimuli are sent along well-defined routes (nerves) to the brain and out again and give rise to the appropriate actions. Studies of whole animals show this simple relation between stimulus and response to be only part of the story. Receptors are in fact highly selective, able to pay attention to messages or to ignore them, and further, at later connections in the central nervous system, responses may be inhibited, or augmented, in very complicated sequences of interaction with past experiences. Other perhaps seemingly irrelevant current stimulation may also affect the message; the context is in fact very important in contributing to the response. In human communication the message received may be very different from that intended by the sender. The learner does not necessarily learn what the teacher aimed to teach.

The teaching-learning relationship is one of *authority-dependency*. The biological peculiarity of man which gives him great advantage over other animals is the long period of growth and development preceding the onset of sexual maturity during which, sustained by the social organization, especially that of the family, he is able to learn from the experience of others. Each person develops in a state of crucial physiological dependence on grown-ups who not only feed him and care for his physical survival, but who also instruct him, verbally and non-verbally, in the lore of living and in the social mores. This socially transmitted information is seen as coming always from above downwards, from a big powerful resourceful responsible authority, to a weak and passive dependant. The ways in which a child responds to it, and the form in which it will be stored in his brain to influence future behaviour, will be affected by the emotional relationships between him and the authority figures.

In the small family the child is presented with an exaggerated view of the generation gap, and his experience of the authority-dependency relationship is exacerbated. His infancy will be spent in intimate contact with his parents and he may never see their authority challenged by other adults — grandparents or aunts and uncles as happens in extended family units — nor will he have support in his own littleness from a range of siblings as in large families. This authority-dependency is perpetuated in formal education at school and later, and teacher and pupil tend to collude in it. The furnishings of conventional lecture theatres reify this relationship, the lecturer spatially distanced from the audience, often elevated on a dais, and standing behind a bench or lectern. In conditions of rapid technological change the older generation may not be the main source of new knowledge, and the young must develop new systems of knowledge and skills, learning from people of their own age, or even younger. This may be very difficult.

Some of the innovations which are occurring here and there in educational practice can be seen as challenging such assumptions and helping to correct some of their adverse effects. Perhaps the central change is the recognition that the pupil should be an *active participant* in learning. This has become manifest for instance in the demand for small group discussion methods of teaching. The idea that learning is an active process is extended to the notion that students should learn to manage their own education. Again, analogously in medicine, the possibilities of patients being more active in managing their own health affairs are being increasingly considered (eg Welsh Consumer Council, 1958).

The potentialities of *peer interaction* in teaching and learning are also increasingly being recognized. This entails changes in students' attitudes, eg in the motivation to learn not only to please the teachers, and in feelings towards classmates (of denigration and competitiveness, for instance). The increasing use of small groups in teaching (Abercrombie, 1970) has brought to light the need for teachers also to change their attitudes if they want to encourage student interaction in groups, instead of continuing to use didactic methods to which their own familiarity with lecturing has habituated them (Abercrombie and Terry, 1978b; Rudduck, 1978).

The value of developing *autonomous learning* is becoming increasingly recognized. Carefully designed packaged courses in various media are being made available, at which individuals can work at their own convenience and pace. But the fostering of self-learning involves more than the exploitation of educational technology: it requires also considerable changes in the psychodynamics of teachers and learners.

Alongside the need for changes in the training of professional teachers, the value of *non-professionals* as teachers is being recognized, eg in the very successful use of volunteer tutors in the adult literacy campaign in the UK, or in the teaching of specific clinical skills to medical students by non-physicians (eg Billings and Stoeckle, 1977). Experiments are being reported in which university students undertake some teaching of schoolchildren. Engineering students at Imperial College, as part of the community work in their academic course, teach science to children in local comprehensive schools (Goodlad *et al*, 1978). Both tutors and tutees benefit from this process.

There is another network of assumptions interacting with those indicated above about the *space and time relations* of learning activities.

Formal education is traditionally confined to specific institutions separate from home and work environments, and is limited to the early part of the life cycle and to specific blocks of time (eg a first-degree course in the UK commonly takes three years, no more, no less). The assumption that this must continue to be so is vigorously challenged by the Open University in the UK, and by the lifelong education movement fostered by UNESCO, which recognizes the need to educate for change, and not only to provide cognitive skills but also to further personal and interpersonal development. Cropley (1977) gives a very interesting survey of the psychological changes necessary for the adoption of the policy of lifelong education.

In the three projects to be described next, the essential common feature was discussion in a small group, which was organized with the aim of enabling each participant to become aware of some of the tacit assumptions which were relevant to the topic in hand, including aspects of those mentioned above. The groups (of 6-12 people) would meet for 1½ hours in a series of eight or more weekly meetings. The nature of the discussion was 'free' or 'associative', ie members were free to participate as they wished and to follow up their own and others' associations with the topic. Each participant could see how his past experience and habitual ways of reacting to the context influenced his own processes of perception and interpretation of current events. He could analyse his own reactions in comparison and contrast to the variety displayed by other members, and change if he wished to. Fuller descriptions of the methods used for conducting groups for this purpose are given elsewhere (Abercrombie, 1960, 1970; Abercrombie and Terry, 1971, 1978a).

Seeing and thinking: training of pre-clinical medical students in scientific method

The first project, covering ten years, was concerned with finding ways of helping pre-clinical medical students to improve their scientific skills — to observe accurately and comprehensively and draw reasonable conclusions from what they were examining. Within the general framework set by this aim, the topic of each discussion meeting was given by an exercise taking about 10 minutes, which each participant tackled individually immediately after the group assembled. Examples of the exercises are: to compare two radiographs; to comment on the published account of an experiment; to discuss a passage containing the word 'normal' and to give their own definition of the word; to write notes on 'classification'.

In the discussion which followed, each student was confronted with several interpretations differing from his own, made by his classmates, of the same material. Two points of educational importance are noteworthy. First, the student was not, as is usually the case, comparing his version with a teacher's, the correct one, needing no evaluation on his part, only acceptance, but was forced to consider and make judgement on each version on its own merits, without the guidance of authority. Second, by analysing the various decisions in terms of the ideas that were associated in giving rise to them, it was possible to tease out some of the factors that had caused the differences between the judgements.

For instance, in one exercise based on the report of an experiment designed to test the hypothesis that excess of vitamin A caused diarrhoea in dogs, students were asked to quote a statement summarizing the author's conclusions, to compare it with the observations actually reported, to design an experiment themselves to test the hypothesis, and to say whether they would expect their result to be the same as the author's. The experimental designs were on the whole quite sound, showing that the students had a good grasp of experimental method, but they had come to different conclusions about the validity of the author's claims. Most thought their findings would agree with the author's (the dogs would get diarrhoea), some thought the chances were even, and a few were so scornful of the report they joked that their dogs would get constipated. The students had individually evaluated the evidence in the report before them, and now, in considering the same evidence together, they were to investigate what other factors had contributed to their judgements and had caused the differences between them.

In discussion it became clear that many factors which were strictly speaking irrelevant to the 'scientific' issue had affected the judgements. These factors varied from apparently trivial features of the context (a student said he would be more critical of the article in the classroom than if he had casually picked up the journal in the common-room), to deep-seated general attitudes to human affairs. Different students had different responses to the fact that the author was a woman, and American, and that she wrote from a department of genetics, though the work reported was physiological. They had different opinions about the status of the journal itself and about human nature, eg whether you could take it for granted that researchers would report their work accurately, and that editors would be conscientiously critical.

In the last three years of this ten-year project we gave observation tests to the class. Compared with the students who had not yet taken the course, those who had done so tended to distinguish more often between descriptive and inferential statements, to make fewer false inferences, to consider alternative inferences instead of confining their attention to one only, and to be less 'set', ie inappropriately influenced in dealing with one problem by the experience of an immediately preceding problem (James *et al*, 1956). It seemed then that this eight-week course of associative discussions did help students to make more rational judgements in scientific matters. Some students reported other effects — it helped them to talk (one said he could talk to the vicar now) and some reported that it had challenged their whole outlook or philosophy of life.

Encouraging autonomous learning in students of architecture

A second intensive project on group teaching, this time aiming to encourage autonomous learning, was part of a one-year postgraduate course for the diploma in architecture (Abercrombie *et al*, 1970). This project will be described more fully than the other two, because its objective was more central to the topic of this book, and it has not been reported in book form. Four main aims of the diploma course were: to encourage education for change (Abercrombie, 1966) through autonomous learning; to improve skills in advanced architectural design; to develop effective attitudes to the professional role, and to prepare for team-work in professional practice. We expected that the central problem would be in changing students' very general and basic attitudes to authority. Emphasis was placed on groups and team-work to help them not only to adapt to collaborative professional work, but to replace the support of peer relationships with that of dependency on authority figures.

The intention was to give students much more responsibility than hitherto for their own education by involving them in planning the course, choosing their design projects, and assessing their work. This was in line with trends in some other schools of architecture, and with worldwide demands for changes in education by both students and teachers (significantly the project occurred in 1968-69, during the time of widespread unrest among students and deep-rooted criticism of the academic establishment). The role of the studio teachers (architects) was intended to be participant rather than didactic or authoritarian. Professional consultants (a quantity surveyor, structural engineer, mechanical engineer, building technologist, town planner, sociologist and a systems analyst) were to be available to students at their own request. It was intended that mutual and self assessment should be part of the educational process.

For convenience, the staff planned the first studio exercise and general outline of the course within which the students would choose and plan their own projects. The first exercise, a 'closed' one based on the brief for a current architectural competition, was to provide 24 flatlets for elderly people on a prescribed site. This would be followed by a more open exercise, the general social and ethical problems of housing the elderly which were being studied in North Kensington, a 'twilight area' of London that presents all the urban problems of overcrowding, transport, poverty, sickness, racial strife and delinquency. (This concentration on the elderly could be expected to involve students at a personal level in the 'generation gap' problem.) During the second term, having become acquainted with North Kensington from the angle of concern for the aged, students would individually or in groups choose to work on another aspect of social and architectural interest in the district.

Opportunity was provided for discussion of current happenings in the course of 16 weekly meetings of 1½ hours, conducted by two non-architects (members of the Architectural Education Research Unit which had been working in the school for some years). We anticipated that the main problems of adapting to the changed course would be in the area of the authority-dependency relationship, and that this would face staff as well as students, so the studio tutors attended these meetings with their own students (the class of 24 was divided into two groups).

Evidence from three sources of reactions to the course will be given: how the architect teachers experienced it, how the students reported it, and how the conductors of the group discussions saw it.

The studio teachers found the students enthusiastic about the proposals for the course and in the first three weeks they efficiently completed designs for the old people's flatlets, for which the staff had supplied the brief. Then in preparation for tackling the 'open' project of North Kensington, they formed their own work groups, usually of about four (but one man chose to work alone). They tended to arrange events such as visits to old people's day centres, or to a tower block, in a rather impulsive way, and did not succeed in covering as wide a range of experiences as they might have done with systematic planning such as teachers usually provide. Their products by the end of the first term were mostly unbalanced. For example, some produced detailed socio-economic reports on the area, but with only embryonic design proposals to meet the needs, and others concentrated their efforts prematurely on detailed proposals for particular buildings. One group, however, had made a thorough survey of the problems of old people, nationally as well as locally considered, and had put forward well thought out design proposals.

The second term began with frustration and lack of confidence in developing further studies. Considerable splitting and reshuffling of the self-selected groups took place. Some preferred to work at home, and made little effort to get help from either the studio staff or the consultants. Most markedly, there was great reluctance to participate in mutual assessment of work products. The work presented at the end of term showed even more clearly than that produced in the first term the split between the tendency to extend the professional role far beyond the conventional limits of architectural expertise into political activism, and the contrary tendency to choose a conventional building type (eg swimming pool) and accept narrow architectural constraints (but with the incorporation of personal values). Again, however, the largest and most cohesive group made a mammoth presentation of its work, showing quite radical design philosophies expressed in varying kinds and qualities of design products. One member showed proposals for a mews housing scheme in which the occupiers would choose their own combination of spaces, in line with the principles of 'participant democracy'.

In the third term there was a greater tendency to pursue individual projects instead of work in groups, and to prepare for the examination. This was important professionally, for it offered part exemption from the Part II examination of the Royal Institute of British Architects.

In retrospect, the disintegration of feeling for community in the class that became so clear in the second term and which resulted in rejection of the support which could have been provided by the school and the studio staff and consultants in particular, might seem to be related to the awareness of the threatening approach of the examination. Both students and staff were apprehensive that the somewhat unconventional course had not prepared the candidates appropriately to meet the conventional requirements of an external body. Moreover, the inevitable involvement of the studio teachers with the external examiners as assessors brought them new anxieties about their role, and feelings that the students were alienated from them. This interference of examining with teaching is, of course, familiar to those engaged in liberating students to manage their own learning. Collier (1969), for instance, writes in an article on syndicate methods:

> The final examination was entirely in the hands of the lecturer, and a few students, in their final comments noted the inconsistency between the completely open interchange and collaboration of lecturer with students during the course and the absoluteness of his judgement and authority in the final examination.

Students' observations were reported in dossiers recording personal experiences. As it became clear that some students preferred to work at home independently of the staff, and that in any case what they had learned in the course could not be assessed only on the conventional examination of design products, each student was asked to keep a dossier which could supplement his submission of studio work. Most found this very difficult, because their main medium of expression had previously been non-verbal. References were often made to 'turmoil', 'distress', and 'uncertainty'. One student related this discomfort to 'an effort to let the design conflicts come to a head and to discover the reasons behind them. For the first time I felt that I was left with a fundamental integrity that I could distinguish as being my own and which I could use as a sound basis for designing.' Significant quotations from dossiers include the following:

'I acquired experience in seeking and using well those people whom I thought were in a position to advance my knowledge.'

'I have had the experience of becoming a self-learning person rather than being compelled to absorb certain amounts of knowledge.'

'Much of what I learned in this term was at a rather more abstract level, particularly the problem of acting in a situation where there are no constraints . . . I don't find my ideas in conflict with my wish to be an architect; rather these ideas are beginning to become ammunition for me as a designer! This has not been an easy transition, nor is it by any means complete.'

'I think the course has been professionally-oriented, making students more aware of their education, evaluating their self-education and trying to define their role in society.'

'I began to see clearly other people's as well as the profession's limitations, which in retrospect reflected my own limitations as a designer.'

'I seem to have spent a lot of time in considering what we should be doing, identifying needs, working out our position in society, and in breaking down accepted assumptions that we previously had little time to question.'

'It has certainly brought me down to earth and taught me to be more human. Prior to this, one subconsciously had tended to play "God" and wanted to believe architecture can solve all problems.'

The group discussions were recorded and transcribed. Just as what happened in the diploma course and the school in general reflected what was happening nationally and internationally in the student scene, the discussion groups reflected what was happening in the studio, the school, and beyond. In our architectural students the problems of personal identity, the generation gap, conflicts between wanting to reject authority and yet remain dependent, and the difficulties of becoming responsible authorities themselves, were closely tangled up with problems of becoming professionals, and of designing (Abercrombie and Terry, 1971, 1973, 1977, 1978b).

In the first meeting of the discussion groups, the impact of the challenge to established attitudes to learning that the new course represented was felt (Abercrombie and Terry, 1971). One of the predominant themes was the difficulty of communication between individuals and between groups. This might be expected in a class that was embarking on a course in which human relationships, and especially peer relationships, were being emphasized, but which was itself of diverse origins (two-thirds coming from the same school, but from different cohorts, and the others from various other schools in the UK or abroad). The studio teachers were not well known to the students, and one of the group conductors was new to the school.

At one time the pervasive feelings of isolation would be treated comically, with nostalgic references to the ways the studio had been made cosy in happy days now past, at another tragically, with reference to inter-racial violence in Berkeley, where one student said his room-mate had been shot 'because he was white and they were black' ('and you can't do anything about that' he later added). Another capped this with a story of the dangers of leaving home even in the UK: 'There's an engineer chap who lost his key, and he climbed the drainpipe to get into the window and a cop actually shot him, and today he's lame.' Significantly the students felt that their discomfort was imposed upon them by the school and college environment: 'The refectory over there is just the most disgusting place, I can't think of any reason why anybody should want to go there from choice.' There were social barriers between departments: 'mechanical engineers don't even talk to structural engineers, let alone to anybody else.' Members of the class had not got to know each other because people had tended to work at home on the first project, an individual one, and it did not seem worthwhile coming into an empty studio. This was probably a criticism of the studio staff who had designed the first exercise.

The prevalent mood seemed to be one of depression, loneliness and impotence. In closing the first session I attempted to make use of the themes of the discussion by relating them to the current studio project, the design of homes for old people. Students had been talking about their own relationships with the physical and social environments; my response was '. . . this relates to a thing you have to understand in order to design old people's homes — they will be feeling even more strongly frustration and resentment and anger about being put together or being kept apart by the environment'.

There were sporadic references to professionalism throughout the series of discussions (Abercrombie and Terry, 1973), usually expressing disillusionment with professionals of any description, all kinds of experts, and powerful people generally. In particular, architects were criticized for being out of touch with social needs, eg, 'the whole professional elite has its own way of talking about other people's needs which most people feel has very little to do with other people's needs.' As the approach of examinations became imminent, interest in qualifying intensified and the penultimate meeting was devoted almost entirely to it. Architects were described as being out of touch with reality, unable to see things as they really are, insensitive to social needs, and therefore unable to act effectively. Besides being ignorant, insensitive and ineffective (a wide range of examples from their own experience in practice was given) they were also deliberately deceptive. 'Facadism' was discussed in literal architectural terms — examples were given of designers making the external appearance of buildings belie their inner structure. The rarity of any approving statements about professionals throughout the total of 50 hours' discussion was notable. Their only useful behaviour as experts, it seemed, was when they outwitted their colleagues for ends that the students approved, eg when a lawyer was clever and knowledgeable enough to twist the law on behalf of squatters, or when an architect had provided, in the plans for a single-sexed school, lavatories that could be instantly converted for both sexes when educational policy became more enlightened.

Discussions of the implications of themselves assuming the professional role included the expression of irrational apprehension of losing their own identity, becoming 'fragmented', or 'not knowing where yourself is any more'. The passing of examinations that would qualify them to join what Goodman (1968, in an article a student brought to the class) described as 'the hated system' would be done at the cost of acquiring the skills of alienated, disparaged authorities.

Among the problems of designing (Abercrombie and Terry, 1977) that seemed to be mixed up with the authority-dependency relationship were the resistances that some students felt to suggestions from teachers about changing their designs. 'I know that I have always felt a degree of resistance to having a tutor who comes along and discusses things with me and maybe makes suggestions about a design I'm doing, because I've always felt that I should be able to do things for myself . . . and you resist listening to your tutor and feel your design is being violated if he makes a suggestion which objectively may be quite satisfactory', said one. There was also some resistance to designing as a form of manipulation; students disliked the feeling of power in manipulating the behaviour of old people through the design of their flatlets. They strongly disliked being manipulated and regarded even administrative conveniences (such as our preference for discussion meetings to occur at regular times and in the same place) as manipulative in an objectionable sense.

Among the themes fairly directly related to changes in the authority-dependency relationship (Abercrombie and Terry, 1978b) were the following: the wish to remain dependent, conflicting with the wish to become self-reliant; feelings of impotence, listlessness, apathy, and vague discontent; discomfort due to the lack of perceived authoritarian structure; fears of failure because of not receiving enough help from teachers, and even because of supposed reprisals from rejected teachers; resentment at feeling manipulated and timidity in taking the initiative to manipulate either for themselves or for others. Occasionally there was the exhilaration of feeling emancipated, and of recognizing that it was possible to have and use internalized as distinct from imposed values.

It was hoped that the discussions might give students the opportunity to unravel the tangled web of denigratory ideas associated with professionalism, designing, and the authority-dependency relationship in general. In doing so they might be able to entertain the possibilities of becoming expert but not arrogant, specialist but not narrow, authoritative but not authoritarian, powerful but not insensitive; to be able to perceive differences between people without feeling that communication was impossible; to make good use of other people's experience even across the generation gap, and to be able to commit themselves to a professional way of life without losing their own ideals and their own identity.

The conductors tried to indicate that there might be alternatives to the students' wholesale rejection of authority. For example, with reference to the emotional response to a teacher's advice on design, one said: 'Do you see that there is just as much a lack of liberty in rejecting so much of your tutor's advice as there is in having to take it? . . . A more effective attitude would be to listen to what your tutor says, and decide objectively whether his idea is better than yours or not, which is a very different state of mind from feeling immediately some sort of hostility or rejection just because the suggestion has come from above.' 'Sort of impinging on your divine creativity', another student (the most vehemently anti-authoritarian) chipped in tartly. On another occasion, during argument about a case study which the tutor (reacting against their lethargy) had planned for the students to do, but which they were most reluctant to undertake, Rod, who had hitherto been very quiet, suddenly came in with: 'Is that what we're trying to overcome in this diploma year, to get over this authority? So maybe the best thing we can do, say, with the case study is just not to do it, or change it, and that would be what the diploma year is all about?' There was an explosion of laughter at this, but the conductor said '. . . you could do the case study and make a very good job of it although it has been given to you'. After more laughter, Adam continued 'That would prove your emancipation, would it?' Later Rod said 'That's what we really want, to grow into gods? Ultimately, if I grew into my picture of my god I wouldn't be here, you know, I could leave tomorrow . . . But the thing that we should do in this case study is to take it and do it well', to which the conductor said 'That's equally a matter for your judgement'.

As is to be expected, the tutors also had a difficult time. Sometimes they expressed their discomfort at their ambiguous role — having to remain in authority as was demanded by their official position, but trying to behave in non-authoritarian ways. Early on one tutor said 'I have never really decided what my particular qualification for being here is, and what my role ought to be. At one level I'm just participating on the same level as yourselves, and yet in a way you can do this better for yourselves: you could perhaps structure your own way of working far better than I can, and yet here I am'. The senior tutor was also uncomfortable in the new role (although it was he who had chosen to change the diploma course): 'Whether I open my mouth or close it I'm aware of the fact that I'm being considered as a different sort of guy, and I don't know what to do about this.' On another occasion he said: 'Every so often I get in a real neurotic state because I keep thinking this is just too loose for words. I feel as though I'm shirking responsibility as a teacher. I should add more to these blank programme sheets, put a lot of things in these empty boxes'. Towards the end of the course he voiced his fear of becoming redundant: 'The usual complaint made about it (self-learning) is the fact that the wisdom and experience of the older generation are not used to the extent they should be . . . I'm not saying that I hold this point of view . . . maybe it's connected with the fact that most of the well-experienced people are frightened about growing old and not being needed any more.'

Learning to teach and learn in groups

The account of this third project, on improving small-group teaching in universities, is based on work Paul Terry and I did, sponsored by the University Grants Committee in 1972-75. The work is more fully reported in *Talking to Learn* (1978a). Though within the last ten years more and more teaching in higher education is done in small groups, many teachers do not find it as effective as they would wish. This is often because they were not taught in small groups themselves, and have no model on which to base effective behaviour. The models they automatically use tend to be those whose objectives are mainly the transmission of a body of knowledge — lectures, tutorials, or seminars in which the teacher is didactic and the students comparatively passive. Teachers and students tend to collude to maintain in the group the authority-dependency relationship which is customary in the conventional teaching situation.

We therefore invited teachers from different disciplines and institutions to meet regularly with us in a small group to discuss their current problems in small group teaching. We expected that this would give them personal experience of learning by interaction with their peers instead of from authority figures, and thus would help them to establish different habits of work in their teaching groups. As conductors, our first and most important task was to establish a supportive climate in which participants felt free to talk informally, listen attentively and tolerantly to each other and gain self-confidence in performing in a comparatively unstructured situation. It was reassuring to find that other teachers had so many of the same problems as oneself, in spite of the great variations in institution and subject, not to mention age, status, experience or personality. Different people had different ideas about dealing with the same problems, and after listening to these a teacher could try out new methods in his next class and discuss results in a later meeting. The common problems that were brought up will be only too familiar to teachers and students who have experienced small-group work — how to set the topic for discussion for instance. Often students are asked to do some work beforehand — read an article or a book. They often do not do their homework and usually the teacher fills in by giving a résumé himself. The job he makes of it is so much better than any of their inept, halting, tongue-tied, confused attempts that it seems to them better that they should not try next time either. And his elegant, clear, logical exposition does not encourage them to question, risk a comment, or give an opinion, so the 'discussion' turns into a monologue, the students silent and passively listening (or not listening) to yet another lecture. If there is real discussion, problems of content arise — anxieties about covering the syllabus, or about doing so at the cost of denying a broad liberal education; and problems of control of participation, of how to help silent students to talk, and verbally fluent ones to listen and give others a chance to talk.

Problems of assessment of the work done in discussions took up a lot of time. A discussion on how teachers address students showed an extraordinary range of behaviour, reflecting the recent rapid change in social custom, and illustrating basic assumptions about personal relations with students. Some preferred old-fashioned asymmetry in mode of address, others were for strict equality, whether formal or informal. Some preferred to use first names, others found this embarrassingly familiar; obe teacher never addressed students by name, while another made a point of interviewing each student before the groups started, in order to become acquainted on an individual basis. Some themes of very general interest in higher education were discussed — what should be its aims — to ensure that all students passed the examination with high marks? or to 'develop the whole man'? Personal motivations for teaching were discussed.

Another aspect of our work was arranging for discussions with students and tutors of video recordings of one or two of their small group classes. Perhaps the most striking result of these was the demonstration of collusion between staff and students which defeated their declared objectives. An example is the failure of students to prepare work for a tutorial which resulted in the teacher doing all the work as cited above. When the students saw how this stifled discussion, they decided to make sure that they did do the work in future. It could also be seen how a teacher who thought it important for students to learn to speak in public would encourage a talkative student to engage in a dialogue with him in order to avoid silences, but in so doing effectively excluded the others. Students began to see how *they* could help to control participation by picking up non-verbal clues indicating that a shy student might speak if given encouragement, or maybe only a space in the conversation. Intimate discussion of their own videotapes gave both teacher and students considerable insight into their own behaviour, and increased their ability to manage the conduct of the discussions. The tapes also triggered discussion about the aims and objectives of the discussion classes, and of the course, and higher education generally.

This aspect of the work was self-evaluating, because improvements could be seen in tapes in a series of classes. As to the group discussions, some of the teachers who had attended them answered a questionnaire on their experiences. Of the 58 who responded to the questionnaire, over three-fifths reported improvements in their small group teaching; nearly three-fifths reported changes in other aspects of teaching, half of these in lecturing; over a third reported improved relationships with students, and a quarter with colleagues.

Although free or associative discussion seems to be useful for teachers who want to adopt interactive teaching methods themselves, it cannot be regarded as a panacea. Some people did not like the comparatively unstructured non-directive set-up — they wanted to be taught in a straightforward manner, just as they tended to teach students in their groups. A few people were disappointed because we did not subject them to a frankly psychotherapeutic approach to changing their attitudes, such as is done in 'sensitivity group' methods. Fortunately there is room for many different personal approaches in teaching and learning.

Conclusion

In the projects outlined above, the aim of the free or associative discussion was to help each participant to understand his own behaviour and acquire better control over it. Though the basic principles used in conducting the groups were the same, the areas of behaviour concerned were different in each of the three projects and so were the contexts in which the projects took place. I will now contrast some of the main features of the three projects. In the first project, with pre-clinical medical students, the area of behaviour examined was fairly circumscribed, the specific aim being to improve scientific judgements and the focus of discussion being given by participants' responses to scientific problems. The department in which the work took place had strong interests in the scientific aspects of pre-clinical medicine but there was little relation between the day-to-day teaching and the discussion course. In the school generally, relations between students and staff at that time were fairly formal and many students welcomed the emphasis in the discussion course on individuality and interpersonal relations as playing important parts in scientific behaviour ('we're tickled pink you know our names', one said). Although the discussion course was voluntary, most students attended regularly. The educational scene generally was quiet at this time (1947-58). The questionings of teaching methods that livened the 1960s had scarcely begun and research into higher education was quite rare. Students were very puzzled at my status, finding it difficult to reconcile teaching and research, and to accept that they might learn from a research procedure. Small-group teaching was hardly heard of (when the report of the project was published in 1960 it was mostly the first part on perception that attracted attention, not the main part on groups).

The educational climate of the school of architecture in which the second project took place was quite different. Student unrest was rampant and worldwide, and the architectural students were postgraduates, much less biddable than the medical students of ten or 20 years ago in their first year at university. There had been, in the previous few years, considerable questioning of architectural education in the UK and elsewhere, and in the school itself many innovations had been introduced in the structure of the course. Two-thirds of the class had been through this as undergraduates, and those who had graduated elsewhere had been attracted by the expectation of a new kind of postgraduate course. Small-group teaching was now fashionable, stimulated by the University Grants Committee Report (1964) and students' demands (National Union of Students, 1969), and had been given an extra gloss by the experientialist movement. By contrast with the pre-clinical project, the relations between the discussions and the rest of the course were close, both as to content and personnel. Studio staff participated in the discussions, and the group conductors appeared in the studio, and at class meetings. Consistent with the aim to encourage autonomy, students and staff made what use they wished of the discussions, setting the topics with their own material, current relevant experience and problems, or bringing topical articles or reports that interested them. Problems of assessment, qualification, professionalism and of staff-student relationships, which had not arisen in the pre-clinical discussions, were of major concern.

As to the third project, financed by the University Grants Committee, it came when interest in improving teaching in higher education had been thoroughly aroused, and teachers wanted to get better equipped to teach. Those who came to our discussions felt the need to discuss many aspects of education besides the technique of teaching in small groups, some concerned with the aims and objectives of education, or with their own motivations for teaching. It seemed there was little opportunity for such discussions with colleagues in their own departments, and they found support, relief and stimulation in sharing their experiences with strangers from different disciplines and institutions. They were members of an invisible college, not of the same class as were the pre-clinical and architecture students. Together they were preparing themselves to teach in new non-authoritarian ways by personal experience of interacting with peers about academic matters in the present of non-authoritarian conductors.

In all these projects people were learning to inquire into their own assumptions, attitudes and habits and to modify them if they did not produce the results they intended. In their various ways they illustrate how commonly-held assumptions about education described in the introduction to this chapter can be made explicit and opened to evaluation through discussion of quite specific professional issues. The pre-clinical project for instance, by exposing the subjectivity of scientific observations, challenged the empty-vessel and telephone-exchange notions of how information is taken in and processed. The other two projects, more directly concerned with the relations of teacher and student, challenged the static view of the teacher as authority and student as passive dependant, and offered the alternative and complementary view of education as a collaborative enterprise, involving peer relationships among others.

3. Assessment Revisited

John Heron, *Assistant Director, British Postgraduate Medical Federation, University of London*

Rationality and power

The prevailing model for assessing student work in higher education is an authoritarian one. Staff exercise unilateral intellectual authority: they decide what students shall learn, they design the programme of learning, they determine criteria of assessment and make the assessment of the student. The student does not participate in decision-making at all about his learning objectives or his learning programme, nor in setting criteria and applying them in assessment procedures. He is subject to the intellectual authority of an academic elite who have the power to exercise a very high degree of social control on the exercise of his intelligence and on his future social destiny by intellectual grading.

The issue here is a political one; that is, it is to do with the exercise of power. And power is simply to do with who makes decisions about whom. I have power *over* people if I make unilateral decisions to which they are subject. I share power *with* people if I make decisions on a bilateral basis in consultation with them. The idea of having a rational power over another's rationality involves dialogue, discussion, and reciprocity of exchange, in which each party to the dialogue gives reasons for a point of view and has the inalienable right rationally to assent or dissent from the view put forward by the other party. As a rational being I can only consult with others about decisions that affect the exercise and assessment of their own rationality. Their rationality is impugned if I do not honour it as a party to the decision-making process.

Does the student entering higher education have a fully-fledged rational capacity? If he does not, if he is in some sort of pre-rational developmental stage, then of course I can offer the argument *in loco parentis*: it is my job as staff member to make rational decisions on his behalf that will enable him to emerge from a pre-rational to a fully rational stage of development. I cannot consult him because he is not present with a sufficiently developed intelligence to make an adequate contribution to the consultation. But does anyone seriously hold that the average 19-year-old human being entering higher education does not have fully-fledged rational capacity? Surely not, since it is the general presupposition of higher education that the student has the intellectual competence to

55

acquire a fully rational grasp of a particular discipline or subject area.

How is it, then, that he is not entitled by the prevailing system to acquire and actively exercise a fully rational grasp of his own learning objectives, of the programme that is relevant to achieve them, of criteria of assessment and the actual process of assessment of his own work? He is seen as rationally competent to grasp the discipline taught by his academic superiors and to respond appropriately to their assessment. Yet, paradoxically, he is not seen as rationally competent to *participate* in determining his own academic destiny, nor in assessing his own competence.

The traditional arguments advanced to justify this state of affairs are something like the following. (i) Academic staff are the culture carriers of our civilization: they sustain and develop the values and intellectual standards of our central bodies of knowledge. (ii) Adequately to grasp and learn to perpetuate these values and standards requires a process of student apprenticeship and initiation in which staff unilaterally model, exemplify and apply to students the values and standards. (iii) Only when thus unilaterally initiated can the student himself eventually become a culture carrier and initiator of future generations of students (Peters, 1966).

This initiation model is hierarchical and authoritarian. It does not deal with the argument that if a student is rationally competent to grasp a major discipline at the adult level, then he is competent *ipso facto* to participate in decisions about the educational process whereby he can grasp it, and in decisions about whether he has grasped it; and that if he is not invited to do these things together, his rationality is thereby impugned — and offered a distorted development. The initiation model is a rationalization of the invalid exercise of intellectual power over other rational beings.

I am *not* arguing that if a student is deemed competent to grasp an adult discipline he should also be deemed competent to decide all on his own the best way of going about grasping it or to decide all on his own that he has adequately grasped it. I am not declaring the redundancy of teachers, of academic guides and mentors. I am arguing that for the young adult, three things go together: the capacity to get to know the content of a discipline, the capacity to know how to get to know it, and the capacity to know that he has got to know it. Or put in other words: the capacity to learn, the capacity to know how to learn, the capacity to know that he has learned. For a well-rounded education, these three facts of intellectual capacity need to be developed together. And they can be developed by a significant amount of self-directed practice, facilitated and guided by, and in collaboration with, teachers. The initiation of students therefore needs to be more reciprocal and consultative, with students not simply learning their subjects but also participating in decisions about how they learn them and in the assessment of their learning.

And as we shall see in a later section, I do not advocate that everything about the educational process is to be a matter of negotiation and consultation between staff and students. If absolutely everything is negotiable, then the negotiator stands for nothing, is not committed to any principles or values, in short, is not really educated. For the mark of an educated person, I believe, is that through study, reflection, dialogue and experience he or she has at any given time a considered commitment to certain values which provide the stable ground from which free discussion and negotiation proceed.

What, then, are further arguments against the current system of unilateral intellectual authority exercised by staff over students? In the following section I will present a radical critique in a somewhat extreme form, and will redress the balance toward the end of the section, while retaining much of the force of the critique.

A radical critique of unilateral control and assessment

Staff unilaterally assess students, some of whom then become staff and unilaterally assess more students, and so on. Where did it all start? However much it may be obscured by a variety of other cultural factors, for any domain of human inquiry there is a source point when its originators flourished through self-directed learning and inquiry and through self and peer assessment. These or their successors at some point become the original unilateral academic assessors and commence their role with a significant threefold act of assessment. They assess and continue to assess themselves and each other as competent in having mastered their branch of knowledge through self-directed inquiry. They assess themselves as competent to assess others. And they assess others as relatively incompetent to be self- and peer-assessing and self-directing in learning and discovery. They thus set up a unilateral assessment and education system from which they necessarily exempted themselves, and in the absence of which one may assume their own vigorous discovery, excitement in learning and originality flourished. This is a phenomenon within the politics of knowledge. Knowledge is always potential power. If I am among the first to establish knowledge in some field, I can use that knowledge to establish a power base in the social order, by discriminating unilaterally for or against others on the grounds of my judgements about their relative competence or incompetence. If I can make others, through their hunger for power, collude with my unjust discrimination toward them (even though it may be exercised in their favour), then I have established a new profession, a body of experts, who sustain their power and perpetuate the injustice through the myth of maintaining excellence. The founding treason is that the founders through this professional dominion betray their own origins in self-directed learning, self and peer assessment.

Unilateral control and assessment of students by staff mean that the process of education is at odds with the objective of that process. I believe the objective of the process is the emergence of an educated person: that is, a person who is self-determining — who can set his own learning objectives, devise a rational programme to attain them, set criteria of

57

excellence by which to assess the work he produces, and assess his own work in the light of those criteria — indeed all that we *attribute* to and *hope* for from the ideal academic himself. But the traditional educational process does not prepare the student to acquire any of these self-determining competencies. In each respect, the staff do it for or to the students. An educational process that is so determined by others cannot seriously intend to have as its outcome a person who is truly self-determining.

Authoritarian control and assessment of students breed intellectual and vocational conformity in students. Given a pre-determined syllabus, learning in a way dictated by others, taught by those who make the continuous and final assessment often according to hidden and undisclosed criteria, the average student has an understandable tendency to play safe, to conform his thinking and performance to what he divines to be the expectations of his intellectual masters, to get through his final exams by reproducing what he believes to be staff-approved knowledge and critical judgement.

But there is not only conformity in terms of the intellectual content of the students' work. There is a subtler, more insidious, more intellectually distorting and durable conformity. For the student absorbs the whole authoritarian educational process, and those students who go on to become future staff reproduce the unilateral model with remarkable lack of critical acumen and awareness. It is notorious that academics, who normally would pride themselves on their ability critically to evaluate the assumptions on which a body of theory and practice is based, are so uncritical and unthinking about the educational process which they mediate.

The authoritarian educational model is thus an agent of social control at the higher education end of the spectrum of conditioning procedures to which the person is subjected in our society. It precipitates into the adult world a person whose intellect is developed somewhat in relation to the content of knowledge, but truncated, distorted and oppressed in relation to the politics of knowledge, the process of truly acquiring it. A general social and political attitude of conformity and a relative sense of powerlessness is reinforced by a partial sort of intellectual competence: 'To survive I must go along with the system and divine what is expected of me. I must accept the fact that I am here so that other people can do it for me and to me and tell me whether I have made it or not. And if I subscribe to all this with sufficient intellectual application I may if I am lucky arrive at a point where I can dictate the system that other people have to conform to.'

Unilateral control and assessment of students by staff generates the wrong sort of motivation in students. They tend to become extrinsically motivated to learn and work. The degree is a ticket to status, career, and opportunity in the adult social world; it is designed by others, awarded by others and withheld by others, according to criteria of others. The student's intellectual masters manipulate his motivation without ever involving him as a self-determining being. External rewards and punishments tend to motivate learning rather than intrinsic factors such as authentic interest and involvement in the subject matter, the excitement of inquiry and discovery, the internal commitment to personally considered standards of excellence, self- and peer-determined debate, dialogue and discussion.

Such extrinsic motivation to learn can breed intellectual alienation: the student becomes habituated to exercise his intellect in a way that is divorced from his real interests, curiosities and learning needs. The acquisition of knowledge loses the excitement of discovery and becomes the onerous assimilation of a mass of alien and oppressive information. Such alienation during the learning process while acquiring knowledge and skills, can extend after qualification and graduation, into vocational alienation: the person exercises his vocational role in a way that is cut off from his real needs, interests, concerns and feelings, and hence uses the role in his human relations with his clients somewhat defensively and rigidly. There are two extreme variants of this: the professionalization of misfits and the misfit of professionalism. The former occurs when the extrinsic attractions of a profession's power and status seduce into it those whose real interests and abilities lie elsewhere. The latter occurs when the professional blindly and unawarely tries to close the gap between self and role by compulsively and inappropriately 'helping' his clients.

An authoritarian educational system is only able to focus on intellectual and technical competence, on the cultivation of theoretical and applied intellect. Personal development, interpersonal skills, ability to be aware of and work with feelings — all these are excluded from the formal curricular educational process, since an authoritarian system represses — in staff member, in student, and in the relation between them — the kinds of autonomy, reciprocity and mutuality required for the building of such development, skills and ability.

The roots of this situation lie deep in the philosophical past, but a past that is still present with us in a very pervasive way. Our educational system rests on an ancient, hierarchical view of the person. In Aristotelian terms, intellect is that which supremely differentiates man from animals, and the cultivation of this prime differentium, in its purely theoretical form, is that which constitutes the highest virtue. In Platonic terms, intellect rules over the nobler emotions, which under the guidance of intellect rule over the baser passions. This authoritarian, hierarchical role anciently ascribed to intellect is with us still today.

The prevailing norm about feelings, in our educational culture and indeed in our culture at large, is that they are to be controlled. The message is unmistakable, coming over in all kinds of tacit and explicit ways: the intelligent, educated adult is one who knows how to control feelings. But if control is the *only* guiding norm, it can rapidly degenerate into suppression, repression, denial and then blind displacement of feelings. The authoritarian academic projects unawarely his denied feelings on to the students: hence academic intransigence about reform, for if academic control of students is a way of acting out denied feelings within, it will not lightly be given up. Only significant personal development among staff can liberate them from this particular compulsion.

The unilateral model of control and assessment in education is a form of political exploitation, of oppression by professionalism. The academic maintains the myth of superior excellence and educational expertise from which the student is necessarily debarred and which it would be irresponsible and dangerous for the student in any degree to practise. Thus the academics, by the control and assessment system they run, condition students to see themselves as inadequate and dependent with respect to all major decisions about the educational process (learning objectives, programme design, assessment). So staff maintain their power as a privileged elite to determine unilaterally the future social destinies of their dependent students. Psychodynamically, the academics deal unawarely with their own distressed dependency needs by conditioning students to be dependent on them. The result is that students are oppressed and manipulated by educationally extrinsic factors, by being assessed and graded — all in the name of 'higher' education.

Finally, of course, unilateral assessment methods are notoriously unreliable. Different examiners marking the same scripts show significant variability; the same examiner may vary considerably the stringency with which he marks on one occasion compared to another. All this adds up to a very palpable injustice — so long as the assessment is unilateral. The only way to avoid such injustice is to make the student party to the assessment procedure, and hence party to the general unreliability. I cannot cry injustice when I have been a free negotiating participant in the assessment of my work.

The whole of this radical critique as presented above is something of a caricature. It overstates the case. So I will briefly mention some of the main considerations which countermand it and present a more balanced view.

Academics do continually engage in a variety of informal and more formal equivalents of self and peer assessment, if not with students, then at any rate amongst themselves: in offering their written work for comment and judgement from their peers, both before and after its presentation or publication. And this at least provides a model for students in their professional work after graduation.

The traditional educational system has produced and continues to produce persons who may be to a greater or lesser degree self-determining. This is not least because, whatever its defects of method, central to its teaching is the importance of rational critical thinking, of assessment of views and of evidence. So the central precepts which it teaches may survive, more or less impaired, the methods by which they are taught.

And the corollary, of course, is that some academic tutors do genuinely seek to elicit in their students sound reasoning, judgement and critical appraisal, and do genuinely rejoice in students who exhibit originality, intellectual competence and independence of judgement.

An increasing though still relatively small number of academics are becoming critical of the assumptions underlying the traditional educational process which they are mediating to students. Staff development and innovation is a growing movement in higher education.

Despite the rigidity of the educational system, both staff and, to a lesser extent, students can become intrinsically motivated and committed to pursue standards of excellence in pursuing their disciplines. And some tutors do exhibit great sensitivity, skill and humanity in dialogue, both intellectual and personal, with their students. Not all academics or professionals use their roles defensively.

The positive account is therefore not inconsiderable. But in my view the general thrust of the radical critique prevails and requires an alternative model of the person, a redistribution of educational power, and a new approach to assessment.

An alternative model of the person

The hierarchical, authoritarian model of intellect-in-charge referred to above has served its historical and cultural purpose. The time is ripe for an alternative, democratic model: that of equal human capacities which mutually support and enhance each other — intellectual capacities for understanding our world and ourselves, affective capacities for caring for and delighting in other persons and ourselves, cognitive capacities for making real choices about how we want to live, relate to others and shape our world. On this model, intellectual competence, emotional and interpersonal competence and self-determining competence go hand in hand. You cannot properly cultivate any one without at the same time cultivating the other two. Single-stranded development necessarily involves distortion of that strand.

Staff-student collaboration and consultation about the educational process — that is, with respect to objectives, programme design and assessment — require, for all concerned, the exercise of discriminating choice, the cultivation of intellectual grasp, awareness of and skill in managing feelings, and other interpersonal skills. Thus it honours the alternative, democratic model of the person.

The democratic model also generates a more sophisticated set of guiding norms for the management of feeling. It proposes not only conscious control of feelings of all kinds when appropriate, but also spontaneous expression of positive feelings when appropriate; conscious, intentional discharge or abreaction of distress feelings at appropriate times and places and with appropriate skills; the transmutation of tense emotion through art, meditation, symbolic imagination and related methods.

The ability to work with feelings in this comprehensive and flexible manner is a precondition of political liberation. The interlocking compulsions to oppress and wield power, and to be powerless, dependent and helpless, are rigidities of character structure which each person needs to dissolve in himself by uncovering and dispersing the hidden effect that holds them in place. To exercise power *with* others in collaborative ways requires the ability to be aware of and take charge of feelings — to dismantle tendencies to act out denied feelings through politically oppressive or submissive behaviour. Skills in control, expression, catharsis, and transmutation are the intra-psychic pillars of political release.

The redistribution of educational power

The redistribution of power in educational decision-making is what is at stake: who decides what about whom, with respect to all the many and varied aspects of the educational process. The main parts of the process are well-known to all of us. I enumerate them here as a reminder that there is a very wide canvas on which to experiment with different decision models. (1) Objectives: (i) outcome objectives relating to what knowledge, skills and attitudes students and staff are to acquire from a course; (ii) process objectives relating to what sorts of behaviours and experience are to go on during the course to achieve intended outcomes. (2) The programme: which puts together (i) topics; (ii) teaching and learning methods; (iii) time available; (iv) human resources; (v) physical resources. (3) Assessment: of student performance, continuous, periodically through the course, final at its end. (4) Evaluation: of teaching and of the course as a whole, again both continuous and final. Ancillary to the educational process as such are: the selection of staff and of students; the administrative structures that support it; and the underlying philosophy and principles which it exemplifies.

Elaborating a point already made in the opening section, it is absurd to suppose that everything on this list must be a matter of staff-student negotiation and consultation. It is absurd for two reasons, a strong and a weak one. The strong one stems from the fact that staff are permanent members of the educational institution; students are transient members. If staff have really thought through the matter, there will be some parts of the educational process which will be non-negotiable because they exemplify principles to which staff are committed. These parts define the sort of educational institution that staff are dedicated to realize. It may be that students are to be significantly self-assessing, or self-pacing or whatever else. These parts, stated in the course prospectus, constitute the non-negotiated educational contract to which prospective students are invited to subscribe, and which defines the lesser, negotiable contracts — the way in which decision-making about the educational process is to be shared by staff and students. Of course, any such initial contract need not be totally rigid, but sooner or later the full-time educationalist, *qua* moral being, will stand for principles, values and their concomitant procedures which are *necessary conditions for entering into* collaboration and negotiation with other staff and students. They may change and develop as a function of interaction with past students, but for the prospective student they are a given, which define the culture into which he is entering.

The weak reason is that the transition from authoritarian control to collaborative control needs to be gradual. Conditioning induced by the

traditional model is not undone in one term, one course or even one
decade. And there is scope for a great deal of variety and experiment in
effecting the transition. Thus if we consider the main parts of the
educational process — objectives, the programme, assessment, evaluation —
then within each of these with their many components, and as between
each of these, decision-making can occur according to one of seven basic
models:

1. Staff decide all (educational process issues)
2. Staff decide some   Staff with students decide some
3. Staff decide some   Staff with students decide some   Students decide some
4. Staff decide some   Students decide some
5.   Staff with students decide some   Students decide some
6.   Staff with students decide all
7.   Students decide all

On the left are unilateral decisions by staff, on the right unilateral
decisions by students, in the middle collaborative decisions. Model 1 is
the traditional unilateral control model. Model 7 would make staff
redundant or at most resource persons waiting to be called on by students
on terms unilaterally determined by students. Model 6, I have already
suggested, is the absurd one: if everything is negotiable, then staff do not
stand for anything, have nothing on offer. The most comprehensive model
is model 3; and within itself it can encompass the widest range of
alternatives along a spectrum from staff control to student control
(Heron, 1979a).

All this, I am sure, is a necessary precursor to looking at issues of
assessment. Assessment is the most political of all the educational
processes: it is the area where issues of power are most at stake. If there
is no staff-student collaboration on assessment, then staff exert a
stranglehold that inhibits the development of collaboration with respect to
all other processes. Once varying mixtures of self, peer and collaborative
assessment replace unilateral assessment by staff, a completely new
educational climate can be created. Self-determination with respect to
setting learning objectives and to programme design is not likely to make
much headway, in my view, without some measure of self-assessment.

Self and peer assessment

What, then, is assessment for? Traditionally it has had a two-fold purpose.
First, to provide the student with knowledge of results about his
performance with regard to the content of the course; this is an aid to
revising past learning, and to preparing future learning. This purpose is
fulfilled by assessment of student work during the course. Secondly, it
awards the student a certificate of intellectual competence, theoretical
and/or applied, which accredits him in the eyes of the wider community
to fulfil this or that social or occupational role. This purpose is fulfilled
typically by the final exam. Nowadays continuous assessment often
contributes a significant percentage to the final assessment, as well as the

final exam — in which case the second purpose pervades the whole course. But the traditional focus in both purposes is entirely on what the student does with the content of the course.

If the student is seen as a self-determining person, and thereby significantly self-assessing, then assessment will include the process of learning as well as work done on the content of learning. Thus if — to whatever degree — I set my own learning objectives, devise my learning programme, set myself and perform appropriate tasks — then I can assess my objectives, the way I have put the programme together, how I have worked, as well as the work I have done. We are therefore immediately presented with the importance of process assessment, as well as content assessment. Assessing *how* I learn and *how* I provide evidence of what I have learned is really more fundamental than assessing *what* I have learned. The shift to self-direction and self-assessment starts to make process more important than content. Procedural competence is more basic than product competence, since the former is a precondition of providing many good products, while the latter is one off — each good product is strictly a witness only to itself.

Next, a self-determining person can only be so in appropriate relations with other self-determining persons. Persons are necessarily persons in relation and in dialogue, where each enhances the identity and self-discovery of the other. On this view, self-assessment is necessarily interwoven with peer assessment. I refine my assessment of myself in the light of feedback from my peers. My judgement of myself is not subordinate to that of my peers. Rather, I use what my peers say to acquire the art of balance between self-denigration and self-inflation. A just self-appraisal requires the wisdom of my peer group.

In a self and peer assessment group each person assesses himself before the group (using common or autonomous criteria — see below), then receives some feedback from members of the group on whatever it is that is being assessed, and also on the self-assessment itself. The process can also occur reciprocally in pairs, but a group of six or eight gives more scope for peer impact. The person receiving peer feedback is invited to use it discriminatingly to refine his original self-assessment. On one model there is no negotiation with peers about a final agreed assessment: the primacy of self-assessment is affirmed, together with the assumption, elegantly borne out in practice, that a rational person has no interest in deluding himself about his own competence and will use the insights of his peers to attain a just self-appraisal. On another model self and peers negotiate until agreement is reached about a final assessment.

Of course to participate effectively in this process requires a measure of affective and interpersonal competence. I must be willing to take risks, to disclose the full range of my self-perceptions both positive and negative, to confront others supportively with negative feedback, to discriminate between authentic peer insights and unaware peer projections, to trust others, and so on. Hence the importance in practice of the alternative, democratic model of the person mentioned earlier, in which intellectual competence, emotional and interpersonal competence, and self-determining competence go hand in hand.

The student *qua* self-determining person, then, engages in a combined self and peer assessment procedure that looks at both the process and the content of learning, but gives more weight to process than content. The purpose is threefold: (i) to raise awareness of, and improve mastery of, the process of learning in all its many aspects; (ii) to raise awareness about the range of, and to improve mastery of, content; and (iii) at some appropriate point along the road to accredit himself or herself in association with the wisdom of his or her peers as competent to offer this or the other service to the wider community.

I have used this self and peer assessment model for one or other of the three purposes mentioned in a variety of continuing education settings, such as co-counselling teacher training courses, and in-service courses for a variety of different professional groups. These courses are run as peer learning communities (Heron, 1974) in which I function as facilitator and participant, but in neither case do I have any special role as staff assessor. My function as facilitator includes, *inter alia,* enabling the group to work through an acceptable self and peer assessment procedure. These courses are obviously not within the aegis of the traditional undergraduate and postgraduate educational bureaucracies: they are not awarded degrees and are not subject to unilateral assessment by staff and external assessors. Hence they have provided a very useful crucible for important innovation and experiment, using an experiential research model (Heron, 1979a; Reason, 1977-79), in which everyone involved is both student and subject on the one hand, and tutor and educational researcher on the other, thus combining within his own person a fundamental dialogue and a collaborative inquiry, as well as engaging in a collaborative inquiry with his peers.

A fundamental extension of the model takes it into the heart of professional life. Self and peer assessment is in my judgement the central way of maintaining and developing standards of professional practice. A group of professional peers meet to pick out the central procedures of their daily practice, to determine criteria for performing those procedures well, and to devise some form of self-assessment whereby they can sample their own daily work and assess it in the light of the criteria. They then go off and apply the self-assessment format to their daily work; and meet together at a later date to take turns to disclose their self-assessment findings to their peers and receive systematic feedback on the disclosure. Such peer review audit of professional practice has a strong if not exclusive emphasis on process assessment — hence the very great importance of building up skills in such process assessment from the very beginning of professional education and training. I have introduced peer review of this sort to doctors and dentists (Heron, 1979b) and to teachers, researchers, managers and others.

Sometimes I use a truncated version in which the self-assessment is done mentally and retrospectively on past practice, then shared with peers:

in this way the whole procedure can be done at one session. The full-blown model can run through many cycles of individual work and self-assessment, peer review, individual work and self-assessment, peer review — and so on. As such it is an educational model, a professional development model and an action or experiential research model in which the procedures of professional practice are developed through action and review and the criteria for assessing them are likewise developed. There is clearly an important future for this approach.

I wish now to mention briefly the four parts of the assessment process itself. First, there is a decision about *what to assess*: whether process or product and then which bit of process or which product. Secondly, there is the all-important phase of deciding *which criteria to use* in the assessment. Thirdly, there is a decision about *how to apply the criteria*, whether individually and serially, whether collectively and simultaneously; whether to weigh the criteria equally or differentially; whether to have pass/fail results only or whether to have a range of qualitative or numerical grades. Fourthly, there is *doing the assessment itself*: applying the criteria and coming out with the result. If what is being assessed is the assessment process itself, then we have a fifth part.

The most critical part other than doing the assessment itself, is deciding which criteria to use. Because of the prevailing authoritarian system, people are not used to criterial thinking. Some staff in traditional institutions have difficulty: they do not make the criteria which they unilaterally use explicit to themselves and each other, let alone to their students. So an important part of facilitating self and peer assessment groups is consciousness raising about criteria and criterial thinking. I have explored two alternative strategies about criteria with these groups. One is to start with each person generating criteria and then, through sharing and discussion, move on until there is an agreed set of criteria to which everyone subscribes, and which each person subsequently applies in his self-assessment and which all use in the peer feedback. The other strategy is for each person to generate, say, three primary criteria; these are then shared, and each person in his self-assessment uses any three from the total list — he may retain his own and others', or use others' criteria entirely; peer feedback is given in terms of whatever criteria he has used on himself.

The first strategy emphasizes common standards, the second strategy emphasizes autonomous standards, which also have the benfit of the pool of peer wisdom. Which emphasis is appropriate depends on the sort of group, on what is being assessed, and on the purposes of assessment in relation to the wider community. In my judgement, common standards are more appropriate when technical issues are the focus of assessment; whereas autonomous standards are more appropriate when personal and interpersonal issues are the focus. Again, common standards are more appropriate when there is a high level of accountability to the wider community for the provision of technical, expert services; autonomous standards apply more when accountability is primarily to oneself and one's intimates for personal values being realized.

Collaborative assessment

Collaborative assessment I see as an important intermediary stage between traditional unilateral assessment of students by staff, and the sort of self and peer assessment model I have used in continuing education. In collaborative assessment, the student assesses himself in the light of criteria agreed with his tutor, the tutor assesses the student in the light of the same criteria and they then negotiate a final grade, rating or judgement. This model can be introduced and applied quite quickly to students' course work by staff working in the authoritarian system — although it then stands in somewhat glaring contradiction to the model applied in final examination assessment. Still, if course work counts for some percentage of final marks, then the student has had some small say in his own degree award.

Typically, in the current educational climate, collaborative assessment is made on students' work. It could, however, even within the traditional system, be about process issues: thus the assessment could be about how the student plans his time, paces himself over time, uses available resources (library, lectures, seminars, his academic tutor, other students), takes notes, reads books, writes essays, and so on. Indeed it is typical of the restricted educational awareness that widely prevails in higher education that so little attention is paid, relatively, to how students manage their end of the learning process. But it is probably best to start practising collaborative assessment on students' work handed in. There is a weak model and a strong model.

The weak model applies where criteria of assessment are already laid down, made explicit to staff and written out, and where the system does not allow for any current modification of them either by staff or students. In this case the tutor can make the following moves. (1) Inform the students of the criteria and explain that they are non-negotiable and why. Share your own views on both these matters. Agree with students on the most acceptable interpretation of criteria that you and they find problematic or objectionable. (2) If a rating or grading method is laid down for how to apply the criteria, then discuss this with students and seek to reach agreement on the most appropriate way of using this. (3) Invite the student to assess his or her work using the criteria and the agreed method of applying them. He can do this first mentally and then verbally. (4) You then assess the student's work using the criteria and the agreed method. Compare, contrast and discuss the two assessments. (5) Negotiate and agree a final assessment.

The strong model applies where there are no criteria of assessment laid down, and what they are and how they are used is left to staff discretion. There is usually some sort of grading system, so whatever the criteria are, their application has to be fitted into this. But there is space here to launch students into criterial thinking, to encourage them to start thinking about setting themselves standards of excellence by which to assess their own work. In this model stage (1) is different, but stages (2) through (5) are the same as in the previous model. There are also at least two alternative versions of stage (1): (1a) Where students have great difficulty in thinking in terms of criteria, present them with your own list, ask them to discuss each item, to seek clarification on it, to raise arguments for and against it, to propose modifications, deletions or amendments to it, to raise issues about the list as a whole — any items not included that should be included — and so on. Continue until there is general assent. (1b) Where students are better able to think in terms of criteria, invite each one to work out his own list, have the students share their lists and then share yours with them. Collate all the lists, continue discussion and debate until there is general assent to a final composite list.

What are you to do if students insist on criteria that you find totally unacceptable? There are three basic solutions. (1) You can set the thing up so that you have final powers of veto. It is important to tell students in advance about this. (2) You can reason with them until they grasp and are persuaded by your arguments about the irrationality of their criteria. (3) You can invite them to use the irrational criteria in assessing their own work and so discover by experience whether they really believe in them and want to use them. In my judgement this is the best strategy. It means of course that you and the student will not be using identical sets of criteria in assessing the student's work. But this can be interesting too.

In my experience of using collaborative assessment in one-to-one tutorials on undergraduates' essays, there is a definite tendency — not large, but noticeable — for students to mark themselves down. This is not surprising, given that years spent at the receiving end of unilateral assessment make for a somewhat negative self-image. But once the process is under way, students show an authentic conscientiousness and thoroughness in the way they handle it.

For the future, I see collaborative assessment as the next step forward, first with respect to students' course work, then with respect to final essays and examinations. As more contract learning comes in and students start to determine their own learning objectives and learning programmes to a greater or lesser degree, then collaborative assessment will tend to have as its primary focus *how* the student is handling the whole learning process as distinct from *what* it is that he has learned, although assessment of products will presumably always be relevant and important.

Collaborative assessment between staff and student can also be interwoven with a variety of self and peer assessment procedures on the student side. Thus a student can first go through a self and peer assessment exercise with his fellow students, then take the assessment that emerges from the exercise into a collaborative assessment session with his tutor. A more adventurous model involving greater staff-student parity is one in which the tutor participates directly in the self and peer assessment session between the student and his fellow students, and the tutor, the student concerned, and his peers negotiate together until an agreed assessment is reached.

Part II Case Studies

4. Reducing Teacher Control

J. P. Powell, *Acting Director, Tertiary Education Research Centre, University of New South Wales*

Introduction

When I began my career as a university teacher, I was fortunate in being required to give only one lecture a week; most of the rest of my time was devoted to reading and preparing material. As a result I learned a great deal about the subject but all that most of the students did was to listen for an hour, take a few notes, and perhaps spend a little time reading. At first I saw nothing odd in this but gradually the absurdity of teachers learning more than students became clear to me. The way in which teaching is organized in higher education ensures that the greatest beneficiaries are the teachers. A consequence of this is that students become dependent upon their teachers to such an extent that they cannot envisage learning very much without them. The evidence for the truth of this lies all around us and one illustration must suffice here. One winter evening in Manchester I watched a small stream of MEd students arrive at the university, many of them having driven perhaps 30 miles after a day's work, to be greeted by a notice which announced that Dr Smith was ill and his 7pm lecture was cancelled. After reading it they returned to their cars and set off for home. It seemed that they were helpless without Dr Smith and unable to learn anything together except under his personal direction. The whole of their previous experience of institutional learning had been such that they had become totally dependent upon being taught.

It must also be said that most teachers are similarly dependent upon students, in that they see their job as being essentially to tell or show things to other people; which they equate with learning. They may complain about heavy teaching loads but are often remarkably reluctant to reduce them and allow students greater opportunities to learn outside the classroom.

A somewhat extreme response to this situation is to remove teachers from classrooms altogether and in 1962 I did this by beginning a series of experiments with tutorless groups. These shifted on to the students all the responsibility for learning and group organization. They also created opportunities for learning which were simply not available in conventional lectures and tutorials. More recently I have been seeking ways in which

71

teachers can effectively contribute to learning in small groups without always being in the centre of the stage and in control of virtually everything which takes place. In 1976 I had a chance to organize an entire course along these lines. It was part of a master's degree programme designed to increase the educational expertise of experienced teachers of the health professions. In what follows a description of the development and outcomes of that course will be offered.

Information about the progress of the course was gathered from several sources. After each class I attended a de-briefing session with two colleagues which usually lasted for about 30 minutes and was tape-recorded. During these sessions I gave an account of what had happened together with my reactions and feelings, and responded to questions and comments. At the end of each class the students reflected, in writing, on what took place during the meeting and tried to relate this to what they felt they had learned. There was also an end of course evaluation but, unfortunately, only four students completed that. All these data sources have been drawn upon here.

Aims of the course

The 'official' outline of the course was as follows:

> This course will focus primarily on theoretical and practical aspects of human learning. Recent research on skill and concept acquisition, problem-solving, memory, and motivation will be reviewed. Consideration will be given to the effects of cultural and emotional factors in learning. There will be an emphasis throughout on the skills required to identify and analyse the differences between individuals in their approach to a variety of learning tasks. A secondary focus will be the nature of the connections between learning and teaching and the development of an ability to devise teaching procedures and environments which are appropriate to specific learning tasks.

This was produced in order to satisfy university requirements for a course description and mainly comprised the 'official content' of the course. When teaching began I was far from clear about the 'real content' of the course or the form it would take. What I was clear about was a determination to keep my own contributions at a low level in an attempt to transfer responsibility to the students. There is no ready-made vocabulary with which to describe the kind of course which I had in mind for this purpose. It was to have less 'structure' than most conventional courses — the meaning of which can best be made plain by looking at conventional courses. In these the teacher prepares a syllabus detailing the content to be covered, assembles all the material to be taught, produces booklists and hand-outs, controls the process of class sessions and usually monopolizes their verbal content, specifies the number and nature of assignments to be completed, and determines assessment procedures. A course which is completely structured would be one in which the students play a passive role with respect to all these activities. A totally unstructured course would be the reverse of this, although it is doubtful if any examples could be found in institutional settings. Most university courses exhibit a very high degree of structure with perhaps some scope for choosing areas of content specialization and assignment topics. My aim was to maintain the educational values of the course with the least possible structure without producing undue anxiety in the students.

A course, however, has to be 'about' something: what was it that the students could be expected to learn? As has already been said, this was not a question which I could have answered, except in the most general terms, before the course began: the details of the answer only emerged clearly as we went along. The major foci of attention would be the power and authority of the teacher and the effects of this upon learning, the role of the student and the ways in which this interacts with that of the teacher, the significance of individual differences, the influence of the milieu within which learning has its setting, and the place of the emotions in relation to learning. More important, however, was the manner in which this material was approached and handled. These topics together with the events and processes which occurred in the classroom made up the real content of the course. Some relevant information could probably be gleaned from the psychological literature although I was very sceptical about the value of what could be learned from that source and in that fashion. I therefore intended to make the immediate, and the recollected, experiences of learning of the students form the bulk of the content of the course with the 'official' content serving only as a series of starting points.

There were thus an 'official' course and a 'real' course developing in parallel week by week as we examined what we were doing and analysed the many ways in which this influenced what was learned. The official course was a necessity because without it there would be no raw material to which we could respond, and it was the analysis and exploration of those responses which the course was really concerned with. It must be stressed that the nature and significance of this distinction only became completely clear to me as we went along and I was thus unable to make use of it to give a convincing outline of the course to the students when we began.

Adopting this approach had the great advantage of allowing me to shed all responsibility for being familiar with the literature and for preparing material for classes. If anything were to be done in those areas it would have to be done by the students. My own contributions would be limited to commenting upon classroom events and encouraging discussion of their significance for learning. Prior to the first meeting, however, it would still be necessary for me to plan sufficient of the official material and activities for the real course to get off the ground.

Events prior to the first class

There were 11 students: three were full-time and came from the Pacific region and the remainder came from Australia and were part-time, returning to their own professional responsibilities after each class. Most had postgraduate qualifications in their own specialities but none had any formal qualifications in the field of education. The part-time students were also doing another course in the degree programme and were thus extremely busy and very much aware of the demands being made on their time. The overseas students had also made considerable personal and financial sacrifices in order to enrol in the programme. They were all highly motivated and anxious to gain skills and knowledge which they felt would be immediately applicable to their own professional work.

A week prior to the first class there was a meeting of all staff and students. This was primarily a social occasion but it was also an opportunity for staff to give an outline of what their courses would be about. I said that I had no very clear idea of the content of the course and that we would develop it as we went along. I also indicated that the course would have some experimental aspects. This limited amount of information accurately reflected the state of my own planning and preparation activities. It had already been determined that there would be one weekly class lasting for two hours and that performance in each course would be determined on a pass/fail basis.

Although I undertook few of the usual preparations for teaching a course, some preliminary work was unavoidable. I made a list of half a dozen books, which I felt would be useful for people to read if they wished, and I planned some activities for the first two meetings. As soon as possible I hoped that students would take over the classes by presenting material on topics which were of interest to them, but it would obviously take some time for these topics to be identified and for the material to be prepared. It proved rather more difficult than I had anticipated to avoid the preparatory work associated with conventional courses: so strong is the force of habit that at times I made some notes almost inadvertently. I also experienced a good deal of anxiety and had serious doubts about my ability to manage a course of this type successfully.

The progress of the course

During the first meeting I gave a brief sketch of the course and the way in which I proposed to conduct it, and again stressed that I did not know very much about the subject-matter and had no intention of remedying that deficiency. We then tackled some problem-solving games so that we could discuss the various ways in which solutions were sought and evaluated. The first meeting of any class is of great importance because it tends to set the tone for what is to follow and, in a small group, reveals something of each member's interests and personality. The students' written reflections at the end of the class indicated that some of my disclaimers had not been taken at face value. They also showed some anxiety about lack of direction associated with the unfamiliar role adopted by the teacher. Some of their comments included:

...disappointment that the teacher did not indicate what to expect from the course.

...intrigued by lecturer's style: a bit like the magician whose act is to appear unprepared and lacking in skill but still manages to get the rabbits out of the hat on time.

...felt frustrated that I was not going to achieve anything substantial from this course because of the vagueness of the introduction, but the penny dropped and later I felt more enthusiastic.

I felt that the teacher was inventing a lack of preparation as an example in promoting dissatisfaction.

I was wondering if you had really given the course much thought and my feelings were that you were filling in until next week when something more concrete would develop.

...characteristics of some of us: some like it structured, others do not.

...lack of structure and direction; too theoretical; discussion of semantics boring.

This final point was made fairly often and it should be mentioned that my own background is in philosophy and I am therefore naturally inclined to show a keen interest in definitions and conceptual issues. It seems clear that I sometimes took insufficient care to suppress my own predilections.

Two further points merit comment. The first is the wide range of reactions to the degree of structure which a course exhibits: one of the students remarked on this and it is a serious difficulty when there is a considerable mis-match between expectations and reality. The second is that the style of teaching which is required for a course of this type keeps the teacher very busy monitoring and managing the discussion and this can lead to the error of supposing that all the students are also very actively involved when in fact they may be feeling that the discussion is dragging itself along.

In the second and third weeks games and problem-solving activities, many of them provided by the students, continued to be used as the raw material for discussion in order to provide time for presentation topics to be identified and prepared. The written reflections of the students continued to show an extremely wide range of reactions. After a class, one remarked that it had been one of the most significant educational experiences he had ever had, while another said that it had largely been boring and a waste of time! Such dramatic differences in response to what is often taken to be a shared experience pose a great challenge to teachers, especially in universities where it is commonly assumed that individual differences can largely be accounted for by variations in degree of idleness.

Another major difficulty which became apparent at this stage was the inability of many students to shift the focus of their attention back and forth from the official content to the real content. This was a much more difficult task than I had anticipated and it became apparent that insufficient opportunities to practise shifting focus had been provided during the first couple of meetings. Many of my comments were interpreted as being either irrelevant or as resented intrusions into what was perceived as the 'real' discussion. This came out in some of the reflections:

... satisfaction at successfully solving problem but frustration at wide-ranging
   discussion of irrelevant concepts: I want to get stuck into narrower field of
   exploration.
... sometimes frustrating because some people cannot see things which are pretty
   obvious to me.
... frustrated at times by what I felt was irrelevant discussion.

At this point I became increasingly concerned with the need to complete
arrangements for the students to take over the running of the classes by
contributing material, in pairs, on topics of interest to them. This was,
admittedly, a highly unoriginal way of doing things but it was all that I
could think of at the time and it had the advantage of exposing a variety
of teaching styles and personalities which we could then examine in
relation to our own learning experiences. I was also beginning to feel that
I could not continue running the classes for very much longer without
doing a good deal of preparatory work. A difficulty with the transfer of
responsibility is that the 'housekeeping' tasks associated with it inevitably
take up a good deal of class time and this can be resented rather than
viewed as an important part of learning.

In the fourth week I began by giving a short lecture which attempted
to pull together some of the earlier discussions by giving a more systematic
analysis of the concept of learning. This provoked a variety of responses.

Too much time spent discussing definitions: need more intervention and
   explanation by the teacher to make atmosphere of the class more orderly.
I felt good about the whole session in that we explored people's ideas and
   allowed free discussion of these.
People talk for the sake of talking, often about things that are obvious.
I understood better some aspects of conducting group discussion. Felt impatient
   because I feel we are standing still because I feel I have worked through these
   conceptual areas already. Not as good a session as some that have gone before:
   not productive for me.
I am enjoying the course very much, perhaps more than any other educational
   activity I have so far taken part in.
Lectures can be really boring.

The lecture was not very well received, partly because an expectation had
been created that none would be given. It was also, of course, unprepared.
It may be that very well-prepared lectures block discussion in that they
leave no loose ends which students can seize upon in order to unravel the
whole. All one can do is applaud and go home. A tightly-constructed
lecture also seeks to impose upon students the teacher's ordering of the
material and this may prevent the learner from making a meaningful
approach to the content. You either take it or you leave it. There is no
psychological space within which the individual learner can move and seek
to get to grips with the material in his own way.

The remainder of that session was spent in allocating responsibility for
topics and arranging the order of presentation, and for the next few weeks
we listened to and discussed the contribution of each pair. The following
are fairly typical comments on one of these sessions:

> . . . challenged my previous ideas rather than taught me anything.
> A very structured and frustrating session because the two leaders insisted on
>   sticking to their prepared material and did not encourage free thought.
> Felt that the presenters did not seem to understand some of the theories they
>   were discussing.
> I become confused when the presenter lectures and when he or she is also
>   confused, ie when there is no discussion. I was angry at being lectured to
>   and felt rejected and unfulfilled.
> I felt relaxed and enjoyed it all. Pity there was no time to complete what we
>   wanted to do. (A presenter)

I continued to make pedagogic comments as opportunity offered but felt that I was not making anywhere near enough of them and that the official course was supplanting the real one. The last of the above quotations, for example, should have been discussed in relation to some of the other comments indicating that there had not been enough time for discussion. My reluctance to intervene was partly based on a fear of diverting interest away from the students' concerns towards those of the teacher. Teachers have the power to do this and students are usually unable to resist. Instead of struggling with their own problems and ideas they are constantly forced to confront those of the teacher. In this course, however, it was essential to intervene frequently in order to focus on what the course was really about and so make it possible for the students to make interventions of the same character instead of continually returning to the official content.

A significant event occurred in the sixth week: unable to inform the students that I had influenza I failed to turn up for the class. The meeting went ahead as planned but I was unable to discover very much about what happened beyond the fact that the group had experienced a crisis of some kind revolving around discussion of the tendency of some members to monopolize the meetings and make leadership bids. Several people doubted the explanation for my absence and suspected that I had deliberately stayed away in order to see what would happen. This reinforced my view of the importance of the first meeting of any class. The impression that what I said could not always be taken at face value, which had been formed during the first meeting, had apparently remained.

At about this time I was also concerned with the issue of how the students were to be assessed. I had raised this briefly at the beginning of the course but it failed to generate any interest. In the eighth week I expressed my concerns at some length and said that I felt it was important for everyone to produce a fairly substantial piece of written work. Several students were concerned that I should be worried about this and said that they were willing to help me by writing something, although another said later that he suspected that this was yet another pedagogic move on my part. Nobody seemed to be worried about assessment and a quite clear assurance must have been given at the beginning about this, although I have no recollection of giving it. One student wrote at the end:

> The freedom from worry about a summative assessment on the course and
>   relief of anxiety about passing or failing was a major contribution to learning
>   for me. To be able to undertake the major assignment out of concern for

John Powell's needs rather than from a need to pass or fail made a difference to the sort of effort that went into it. I am sure it added to the quality of the work, because it became an assessment of me by myself — and I was not satisfied with it when completed, where I suspect an external examiner would have been.

After the completion of the presentations there were still three weeks to go to the end of the semester and I was unsure what to do with this time and the group was slow to come forward with suggestions. One week was spent considering a document which I had distributed and which set out some of my own reflections on the course, and then things ran downhill. I was in the same position as most of the students who in their presentations had shown that they should attempt to 'cover the ground' even though we could not identify anything which we wanted to go over. If this had been faced squarely then the time could have been used to examine in detail the nature of what had been learned.

What did the students learn?

It is not easy to answer this question because I unfortunately failed to require the students to provide a written account of their reactions to the course and what they felt they had learned from it. Only four evaluations were completed, one of them a year later. With hindsight, it would have been extremely useful to have spent the last two weeks in a detailed analysis of the course with special attention being given to factors and events which had helped or hindered learning. Some useful information, however, can be gathered from the weekly reflections and the four final evaluations. The latter each yielded a summative comment:

My main conclusion was that real learning is not possible without meaningful involvement in the teaching-learning process. I very largely abandoned my previous almost totally content-oriented attitudes to learning . . . (what matters is that) *I* feel that *I* learned something which had significant influence on my views and attitudes to life and education.

This course has positively identified in me the urge to generate change in my teaching methods — to foster a better learning system for my students. This is the most valuable contribution to one who has taught for 15 years non-stop.

The dawning of many understandings have flowed from all the sessions . . . The understandings are neither complete nor simple and I find them continually affecting all the facets of my life and knowledge as I continue to reflect on them.

The ultimate benefit of this course (for me) will only emerge in time as I cope (or try to) with the difficulties of 'teaching' my students attitudes and interpersonal skills. I am sure that there are real benefits to come.

These are all rather vague statements, although it must be admitted that it is extremely difficult to state explicitly what one has learned from a course. They tend to focus on attitudes and to look forward to possible future effects of these on professional practice. Those who felt that they had gained little from the course were probably too polite to say so.

One of the most striking features of the comments made in the weekly reflections on the course was the frequency with which feelings were mentioned, eg disappointment, frustration, enjoyment, enthusiasm, annoyance, resentment, interest, anger, rejection, anxiety, irritation, fulfillment. The emotions play an important part in all teaching and learning situations yet their role is rarely openly discussed. It seems likely that most of these students gained a greater appreciation of the role of the emotions in learning.

There was also quite frequent mention of the gaining of insights related to group processes: understanding others' viewpoints, the need to feel a sense of group coherence, the influence of the teacher's style, the uneven contributions made by members and the difficulties of involving non-contributors, and the problem of keeping discussion relevant. All this could be considered as part of the content of the real course. Surprisingly, the official course material was not often mentioned and this suggests that I may have overestimated the extent to which the students were involved in it.

There were many comments on the need for leadership, more structure, a sense of direction and points of departure. As one student put it:

> I do not feel that I am an expert and I require a start or need to start in some direction before I can operate. This would make me dependent on direction or on a need to work on a particular problem or need.

The relative lack of these was seen by many as an obstacle to learning and there is little doubt that for some this unfamiliar situation created an insuperable barrier which they never managed to overcome.

What did the teacher learn?

At the end of the course I was convinced that, despite all my efforts to the contrary, I had learned a great deal more than the students. On further reflection, however, this seemed a rather simple-minded conclusion. When a course is being taught for the first time it is quite likely that the teacher will learn more than the students: there is much truth in the saying that the best way to learn something is to teach it. But with practice this effect vanishes and everything becomes routine and familiar. This explains why teachers tend to become bored with repeatedly offering the same course. Enthusiasm and interest can then only be maintained through variations in the mode of presentation or by the introduction of new content.

In the course which has been discussed here I was learning how to teach that particular course. Naturally I learned much more about this than the students because they were concerned with quite different problems. Prominent among what was learned was the importance of distinguishing clearly between the official course and the real course, and establishing from the outset the skills and procedures required for the latter. Almost as significant was perceiving the central importance of fully exploring the interests and concerns of the students so as to ensure that any gap between these and what the course offered was not dangerously wide.

This raises a major problem. Some students do not wish to accept more responsibility for their own learning. They prefer to cast the teacher in the role of expert and are quite happy to do little more than take notes and read books as directed. The analogy with doctors and patients is quite strong: we even 'prescribe' texts. How far should one go in respecting and making provision for such preferences? If one adopts the neutral role of facilitator then the problem does not arise although there is still the difficulty of attempting to satisfy what may be a very diverse set of preferences. A teacher, however, has an obligation to try to ensure that certain things are learned and this responsibility cannot be abdicated in favour of leaving everything in the hands of the students. To do this would be to give up the very idea of teaching.

The role of the teacher is crucial in creating, from the beginning, an atmosphere of trust and confidence within which the learners are able to feel free to exercise their independent judgement and pursue their interests within a fairly loose framework of content and procedures. The teacher must give a lead by providing starting points without subsequently transporting everyone to a pre-determined destination.

The reduction of teacher control as a means of fostering independence involves the creation of a role for the teacher which lies outside the experience of most students. They are thus apt to reject it and exert pressure intended to compel the teacher to behave in a more conventional manner. This must be resisted without alienating the learners or provoking disabling anxieties. There is a very strong case for introducing some courses of this type from the beginning of the undergraduate programme. Delaying until it is believed that students are more 'mature' or 'expert' will not work because each experience of a conventional course only locks them more firmly into a passive and dependent role. Primary schools have long allowed and encouraged a high degree of independence in learners: universities should display the same confidence in their students.

Note

For an account of the subsequent development of this course and fuller discussion of some issues which have only been hinted at here see the author's 'Helping and hindering learning' in *Higher Education* (in press).

5. Independent Study: A Matter of Confidence?

Harry Stanton, *Director, Higher Education Research and Advisory Centre, University of Tasmania*

Introduction

It has long been accepted that no one 'best' way to learn exists for all students under all conditions. Traditionally, however, institutions of higher education have behaved as if this were not so, using the lecture format, supported by tutorials or laboratory sessions, to the virtual exclusion of other approaches. In this chapter, one possible alternative will be explored, which emphasizes independent work undertaken by the student on an individual basis. Under such an approach, contact with the lecturer is minimized, and it is assumed that a student is capable of assuming a considerable degree of responsibility for his or her own learning.

The theoretical basis of such a learning method is outlined, drawing on the principles of humanistic psychology. A case study involving an actual course in educational psychology conducted according to these principles is described, and is discussed in terms of students' willingness to assume responsibility for their own learning.

The latter part of the chapter is devoted to the description of a particular method for helping students develop more confidence in their own ability to work independently. Drawing heavily on a therapeutic framework, this approach involves relaxation, positive suggestion, and success imagery. A number of empirical studies attesting to the efficacy of this approach are presented, and the link between improved student self-confidence and improved capacity to undertake independent study is elaborated.

The nature of the course

Some years ago I designed a rather 'freewheeling' course. My aim was to encourage students to take more responsibility for their own learning. Entitled 'Psychology and Education', this course was taken by Diploma of Education students at the Flinders University of South Australia over a period of one semester. During the four years of its life, the course underwent certain modifications but the basic elements, as set out below, remained unaltered.

The first element, *content,* centred on eight topic areas:

☐ humanistic approaches to education
☐ groups
☐ motivation
☐ behaviour modification
☐ instructional systems approach to education
☐ theories of learning and instruction
☐ factors facilitating learning
☐ programmed instruction and computer assisted instruction.

Obviously this list is only one possible sample of topics which could be included under the label 'educational psychology'. If a student, therefore, did not wish to concentrate his major effort for the semester on one or more of these topics, he could discuss alternatives with me. As an important principle upon which this course was based involved the concept of meaningfulness, I considered it essential that each student should have the opportunity to study something within the context of educational psychology which he found personally significant. If, for a particular student, my initial choice of content failed to provide such a topic, it became necessary to expand the list to meet his needs more satisfactorily.

Teaching method, the second element, was a combination of lectures and student reading for the first three weeks. Four lectures were presented. These provided an overview of the eight topics, emphasis falling upon stimulation of interest rather than upon the provision of information. These lectures, the only ones given in the course, served as an introduction to give students some idea of the material encompassed by each topic. In addition, they were to read two key books in each of the eight areas. I encouraged skim reading at this point, for my intention was to have students overview the material rather than study it in detail.

After the three-week period, students saw me, or my tutor, on an individual basis. At this interview, the student was expected to reveal his familiarity with each of the eight topics, demonstrating that he had actually completed the set readings. Discussion then centred upon which area, or areas, appeared most meaningful to the student. He was free to select any number, ranging from one to eight. A reading list comprising a minimum of 20 items was available for each topic, and the student who opted for depth study focusing on one area only was expected to read everything on the list. Those who preferred more breadth made up a composite reading list drawn from asterisk-marked items on the individual lists.

Voluntary group tutorials were provided on demand. Students who wished to clarify points which had emerged from their reading placed their names on the sheets outside my office. For each topic, there was a separate sheet. I checked these lists daily and when five or six names appeared under a particular topic a tutorial was arranged. Students could come to as many tutorials as they wished. As one would expect, considerable variation existed, with some students attending frequently, others occasionally, and some not at all.

Individual tutorials were also available. Students could arrange to see either my tutor or myself at a mutually convenient time. Approximately 75 per cent of students enrolled in the courses did make use of this opportunity for personal discussion. Time consuming it was, but it certainly helped me to establish a closer rapport with my students than had been possible under the lecture dominated method I had used previously.

The third element, *assessment*, presented something of a problem. Although I felt that self-evaluation was an essential element in helping students take more responsibility for their own learning, I was unable to resolve the essential dilemma posed by this concept. My experience (Stanton, 1978a) has been that self-evaluation is of immense educational value to students. Through consultation with their lecturers and tutors about their self-assessments, students learn how to evaluate themselves realistically. By so doing they also learn a great deal about themselves as individuals.

Yet, the university is held responsible by society for assessing its products. If it permits students to assess themselves, and they do so unrealistically, the university is seen as turning unqualified people loose on the community. Thus it is open to the criticism of shirking its task, of abdicating from its responsibility to place its stamp of approval upon the students it graduates.

I talked over this problem with the first group of students who took the course. A conventional examination, common to all, was obviously inappropriate, for no two students would necessarily be pursuing the same course of study. The alternative at which we arrived was to set 6000 words as a reasonable requirement for a half-year course. How these words were presented was up to the individual student, who could, if he or she wished, submit a single essay. Just as acceptable would be a number of shorter essays. Choice of topic was the student's responsibility. I made it clear that should he or she be unable to think of something personally meaningful I would, as a last resort, provide a specific title, but no one made use of this 'service'. A deadline date was set. If students so desired, they could submit their 6000 words before this date. This procedure carried with it the advantage of a rewrite should their first effort be deemed a failure.

Criteria for making such a judgement were again clarified in discussion with the students. First, the students had to make it clear to me that they had read the material on the reading lists and, I hoped, other books and articles followed up on their initiative. Secondly, this material, as far as possible, was to be expressed in the student's own words rather than in those of the various authors consulted. My feeling is that if a person cannot express an idea in his own words, it is unlikely that he actually understands it. Similarly, I encouraged the student to draw on personal experiences to illustrate the general theoretical points he made, for use of ready-made examples from the literature seems to suggest a lack of understanding of the concepts involved. After all, these students were writing about educational psychology, about learners and learning. They were learners so their own experience was clearly of greatest relevance.

So far I have outlined the main elements of a course which could be labelled 'independent learning' or 'individual learning'. I have not, however, outlined the reasons why I chose to set up a course in this particular way. This I shall now attempt to do.

Rationale

I see teaching as the facilitation of learning. It is warranted insofar as it makes learning easier and/or more efficient than it would otherwise be. If, through his exposure to a lecturer, a student learns something better than he would have done alone, the teaching is of value. If no such facilitation takes place, I cannot see any real justification for teaching. As I considered my own teaching in this light, I had certain doubts about my value to my students. Like the majority of my colleagues, I 'taught' by means of lectures and tutorials, giving out information by 'telling'. Underlying such a procedure is the assumption that students learn by being 'told' things. Yet my own experience as a learner and my reading of the literature relating to how people learn would suggest that such an assumption is incorrect.

I do not see learning as primarily a process of accumulating information which is then stored for use on later occasions. Something more is needed which involves the student as an active participant rather than a passive recipient. As Combs *et al* (1971) put it:

> Learning is the discovery of meaning. The problem of learning, modern psychologists tell us, always involves two aspects: one is the acquisition of new knowledge or experience; the other has to do with the individual's personal discovery of the meaning of information for him. The provision of information can be controlled by an outsider with or without the co-operation of the learner. It can even be done, when necessary, by mechanical means which do not require a person at all. The discovery of meaning, however, can only take place in people and cannot occur without the involvement of persons. (p 21)

If this definition of learning can be accepted, it would seem that in our lectures, and perhaps in our tutorials, we concentrate unduly on Combs' first aspect, that of information transmission. We tend to neglect the second aspect by failing to create an environment in which students are encouraged to find personal meaning in the avalanche of material with which they are presented.

Thus, dissatisfaction with lecturing as a method of facilitating students' search for meaning lay at the basis of my change in course design. Also, I had confidence that a viable alternative was available. In his book *Freedom to Learn*, Rogers (1969) has pointed out that the traditional approach to teaching is virtually guaranteed to reduce meaningful learning to a minimum. This it does by prescribing that all students should follow the same curriculum, write similar assignments, listen to the same lectures, and be assessed by the same examination. To change this state of affairs, Rogers has suggested creation of a learning environment involving a largely self-chosen curriculum, student-generated assignments, a relative absence of lectures, and a reduction in the importance of grades. If a teacher is able to provide such an environment he will, according to Rogers, help students find the relationship between the material they study and the personal significance it holds for them. A lecturer cannot do this learning for his students, but he can make it easier for them to do so themselves. Gibran (1926) puts it beautifully when he says of the teacher:

> If he is indeed wise he does not bid you enter the house of his wisdom but rather leads you to the threshold of your own mind.

Assessment of the course

My course, then, was an attempt to put into practice some of the principles of humanistic learning propounded by Combs and Rogers. In terms of process it was a very rewarding experience for me, and also for some of my students. They put a great deal into it, reading widely, attending group tutorials, talking with me, and writing superb essays, ranging in length from the 6000 words set to well over 12,000 words. It was not only the length of essay which was so impressive — the content was often very moving. A number of students re-evaluated their lives in terms of self-concept theory, or applied the principles of behaviour modification to their family situation, or attempted to formulate a mode of education which would be superior to one which they had experienced. From such writings it became painfully obvious that many of our best students were completely alienated by the education they had received at school and university.

Comments such as the following were not uncommon:

> I think this has been the most relevant assignment that I have done this year — it's been a piece of work in which I have really discovered and not merely regurgitated masses of material which we have had to read in order to fulfil someone's requirements. It's been a refreshing change and, I think, one of the rare instances of real learning in my whole time at this University.

In fact, a consistent thread running through many of the anonymous responses made by students on the end of course evaluation questionnaire was the contrast between the sense of personal discovery in this course and the complete irrelevance, in terms of relationship to important life issues, of their other university courses.

Heady stuff this, but the observant reader will have noted that I said *some* students found the course a rewarding experience. Others obviously did not. Despite initial enthusiasm for a course which actually gave them the freedom they said they wanted, many students, approximately one-third of the class, did very little work at all. They dashed off their essays as just another meaningless academic exercise to be disposed of with as little effort as possible and with a minimum of personal involvement. This attitude disappointed me greatly, but that was my problem. Probably I was quite unrealistic in expecting all my students to respond to the type of course I had provided. In fact, I was forced to reassess a basic assumption which had guided much of my effort to provide enhanced learning experiences for my students.

Like many of my colleagues I believed, perhaps naively, that students at a university were there because they wanted to learn. Where my experience indicated that they were not learning, I attributed this to poor teaching methods or to an irrelevant, pedestrian curriculum. The evidence produced by the humanistically based course which I have described, however, made it difficult for me to continue to explain student indifference in this way. Some students obviously do want to learn; many others do not. No matter how a course is designed, it will not, I believe, encourage more than a certain percentage of students to actually learn.

Perhaps I am overstating the case here, my view being distorted by my definition of learning as a two-stage process involving both information acquisition and the discovery of personal meaning in that information. If my definition was restricted only to information acquisition, then many more students could be described as learners. Or could they? Our usual measure of learning is examination performance, and it is no great task for students to pass by feeding back the lecturer's own words. These words, though, are frequently quite meaningless to the student and have to be learned by rote, almost like nonsense syllables in a psychological experiment. Such 'learning' is likely to be of a very short-term nature.

My feeling that a sizeable proportion of our students have no real desire to learn has been confirmed by others. Many journal reports of educational initiatives bear eloquent testimony to the lack of student interest and response, even when these experimental methods directly incorporate the features students claim they want most (eg Goldman *et al*, 1974; Paskow, 1974).

Before I commenced my own experimental course, I asked several Diploma of Education classes whether they would prefer it to the more traditional course they were at present taking. Something like two-thirds of these groups expressed a preference for the unstructured, 'freewheeling' course. However, over three-quarters of these favourably-inclined students doubted their ability to handle such a course. The idea appealed to them but they had little confidence they would actually complete the work without regular compulsory tutorials, or assignment deadlines. That is, they felt unable to timetable themselves, unable to take responsibility for their own learning without someone to force them to do so. One student summed up the attitude of many of his fellows when he said:

> Without constant compulsion and supervision I wouldn't do any work. Going to lectures is the easy way. The lecturer does all the work and all I have to do is sit there and copy down as much as possible of what he says. Then I give it back to him in an examination. No sweat at all.

Remember that these students were graduates. Already they had spent three, or sometimes four years, at a university one of whose avowed aims was to encourage students to take increased responsibility for their own learning. A very depressing situation, surely, one which certainly drained from me much of my enthusiasm for modifying learning environments.

If students showed so little interest in managing their own learning why should I bother? Yet something continued to niggle at me. Was it simply that students did not want to take responsibility for their own learning, or was it that they lacked the confidence in themselves to do so? In so many of the comments made by the students, the theme of self-doubt emerged, taking the form of a negative attitude towards anything which required real effort. Alexander Dumas summed up the effect of such an attitude in these words:

> A person who doubts himself is like a man who would enlist in the ranks of his enemies and bear arms against himself. He makes failure certain by himself being the first person to be convinced of it.

I hypothesized, then, that if I could find some way of helping students to increase their self-confidence, this might effect a change in their attitude towards independent study. Instead of doubting their ability to undertake such courses, they might be able to attain an expectancy of success. As Gindes (1973) has pointed out in the context of psychotherapy, the patient who expects to get well is likely to do so. Perhaps this concept is generalizable to the educational environment.

In fact, there appear to be many similarities between teaching and therapy (Stanton, 1978b), for both involve learning. With the course I have described earlier in this chapter, I was attempting to establish an environment in which students could learn meaningfully and in a way which was significant to them. I hoped that they would be helped to discover meaning in the material encountered so that their potentialities as human beings might be more fully realized.

My work as a psychotherapist embraces the same principles. I do not think I can cure anyone, nor can I do a student's learning for him. However, what I can do is help patients to cure themselves by helping them to discover meaning in their own lives, in the hope that through this contact with me they may learn how to organize their lives more successfully (Stanton, 1979). Similarly, I hope I can help students learn more effectively than they otherwise would.

As I considered this basic concordance between therapy and teaching, I speculated that the method I had been using in the former context might apply equally well to the latter. This method, comprising a combination of three elements, relaxation, suggestion and imagery, has proved most successful in helping people lose weight (Stanton, 1975a), conquer insomnia (Stanton, 1975b) and stop smoking (Stanton, 1978c).

Three or four treatment sessions were used, the same general procedure being followed on each occasion. First, patients were helped to relax. A variety of means was used to achieve this end, including deep breathing, counting, fixation of eyes on a bright object, muscle heaviness, and mental visualization of a pleasant scene. Possibly the last of these proved to be the technique most consistently successful in inducing a state of deep physical and mental relaxation.

Once the patients had allowed themselves to 'let go', I talked to them quietly, employing a series of positively worded suggestions designed to produce ego enhancement. These pertained to increased energy, improved health, ability to cope with problems, increased calmness, personal well-being, feelings of contentment, increased self-confidence and improved concentration. Details of a comprehensive script suitable for use in a wide range of therapeutic situations may be found in a previous article (Stanton, 1975c).

It would appear that when a person relaxes, the normal critical 'watchdog' faculty of his mind becomes less marked, permitting easy acceptance of suggestions which are in accordance with his wishes. People cannot, of course, be made to do things they do not wish to do, nor can they be given abilities they do not already possess. However, they can be helped to gain confidence in their own power to change themselves in ways in which they want to change and to transcend the often unreasoned limits they have tended to place upon themselves.

Particular emphasis, then, was placed upon the way in which the patient's confidence would increase as he realized the power he had to control his own life. This emphasis was achieved both through verbal suggestion and through encouraging the patient to think of himself the way he wanted to be. For example, the person wanting to lose weight would mentally visualize himself standing on a set of scales showing the weight he wanted to be. Also he would see himself looking the way he wanted to look when he was that weight.

My first attempt to generalize this relaxation-suggestion-imagery (RSI) technique to an educational context was directed towards the reduction of test-anxiety in primary school children (Stanton, 1977). Test anxiety, operationalized in terms of scores on the Test Anxiety Scale for Children (Sarason *et al,* 1960) was considerably reduced for an experimental group as compared to a control group which experienced no RSI treatment ($t = 22.57$, $df = 49$, $p < 0.001$). These gains were maintained in a subsequent test administered six months later.

When the RSI technique was used with student teachers feeling anxious about their first teaching practice, similar positive results were achieved. The measuring instrument used was a self-report confidence scale on which students were asked to rate their confidence in themselves as teachers (see Figure 1).

I have employed this type of scale in most of my studies into self-confidence enhancement. In so doing I have been greatly influenced by Allport (1960) who maintained that the most effective way of finding out what a person is like is to ask him. This view he contrasted with that propounded by the advocates of projective and disguised purpose testing who, he felt, needlessly complicated a relatively straightforward issue. Combs and Snygg (1959) have made the same point:

> . . . it is a person's perception of his personality that would seem to be more important than some 'objective' personality, discoverable only through projective measures which deceive the respondee over the true purpose of the test. If a person thinks he is highly anxious, his behaviour is likely to reflect this personality trait.

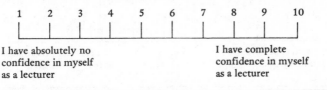

Instructions
Each person has a picture of himself or herself, usually reflected in terms of common personality characteristics. The scale set out below is an attempt to translate one such characteristic into measurable terms. What we would like you to do is to circle the number on the scale which you feel would provide the best description of your level of *confidence about yourself as a lecturer*.

For example, you may feel that the statement: 'I have complete confidence in myself as a lecturer' describes you very well, so that in this case you would circle 10. Alternatively, you may feel that you are neither 'completely confident' nor 'completely lacking in confidence', but that you are closer to the former description than the latter. In this case you might circle 7 or 8. Try to be as frank as possible for there are no right or wrong descriptions.

```
 1     2     3     4     5     6     7     8     9     10
 |__|__|__|__|__|__|__|__|__|__|
```

I have absolutely no   I have complete
confidence in myself   confidence in myself
as a lecturer   as a lecturer

Figure 1 *Confidence scale*

Whatever the particular personality trait might be, if a person believes he is anxious, or lacking in self-confidence, or anything else, he is likely to behave as if that perception were true. Therefore, if he can be helped to change his perception, there is a strong possibility that his behaviour will be modified accordingly.

In the student teacher study there was no measure of behaviour change. However, of the 18 subjects who experienced four RSI treatment sessions, 13 improved their score on the confidence scale. Further studies using matched pairs of Diploma of Education students and tertiary level teachers drawn from universities and colleges of advanced education produced favourable results. In all cases, the RSI treatment enabled subjects to report themselves as feeling more self-confident.

An indirect measure of behavioural change was then added to the experimental programme. In an attempt to discover whether improved teaching performance resulted from increased self-confidence, students evaluated a group of lecturers both before and after they experienced the RSI treatment on a simple rating-of-performance scale (see Figure 2).

I reasoned that if students rated a particular lecturer at the same level on both evaluations, this would suggest the RSI treatment, though effective in helping a person feel more self-confident as a teacher, was not effective in actually modifying his or her teacher behaviour. However, if a lecturer was rated more highly after treatment than before, this would indicate behavioural change in a positive direction.

Of the 20 experimental group subjects, 11 improved their scores on the student evaluation scale. No member of this group recorded a lower score on the post-treatment measure than he did on the pre-treatment measure. Students had no knowledge that these particular lecturers had been undergoing any special treatment, and the evaluations were carried out as part of institution wide surveys.

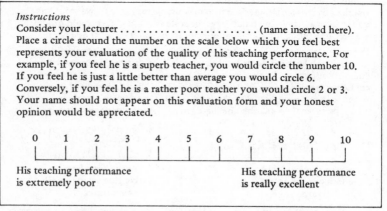

Figure 2 *Student evaluation of teaching scale*

These positive results encouraged me to investigate whether the RSI procedure could help students to feel more confident in their ability to study independently, and to take more responsibility for their own learning instead of relying on a lecture-imposed structure.

From a class of 128 Diploma of Education students, 40 were selected at random. They were matched in pairs on the basis of their scores on a structure of course scale which is set out in Figure 3.

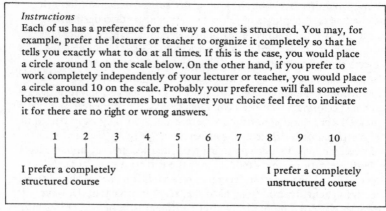

Figure 3 *Structure of course scale*

One member of each pair became a control and the other, allocated at random, experienced three RSI sessions. These sessions were spaced at weekly intervals, the first of them being of 50 minutes' duration. This time was used in the following way:

☐ Fifteen minutes spent in the establishment of rapport, the answering of questions, and the inculcation of a positive expectancy of success.

☐ Twenty minutes spent in the induction of a relaxed state, the delivery and reception of ego-enhancing suggestions, and the creation of success imagery. This involved subjects visualizing themselves organizing their time, reading attentively, participating informally in discussion with peers, writing essays well before due dates, and covering a lot of material effortlessly and with enjoyment.

☐ Five minutes of discussion with me relative to their feelings and thoughts during the 20-minute RSI treatment.

☐ Ten minutes of further RSI activity.

The two succeeding sessions were of 25 minutes' duration. Each involved an initial relaxation period, reception of ego-enhancing suggestions, and creation of success imagery. After the first induction, virtually all subjects achieved relaxation very quickly so they had ample time for very specific visualizations.

The attitude of the experimental group towards independent study as opposed to a tightly structured lecture course in which virtually everything was organized for them was measured by the structure of course scale. This scale was administered before and after the three RSI sessions, as was the confidence scale mentioned earlier in the chapter. This same measurement procedure was adopted with the control group which received no treatment. They did, however, discuss, for a comparable period, the advantages and disadvantages of independent study relative to highly structured lecture courses. This discussion was rather anecdotal, involving the exchange of experiences in differing types of courses. The role I adopted in the group was that of moderator, although I contributed information about my own experiences, both as student and teacher.

A comparison of experimental and control groups on the structure of course scale scores revealed a marked difference. Naturally the two means (3.7) were similar on the pre-treatment measure, for this score was the basis on which the groups were matched. However, after the three RSI sessions, the experimental group mean was 6.3. That of the control group, tested at the same time, was 3.5. This difference was highly significant ($t = 11.1$, $df = 18$, $p < 0.001$). Of the 20 subjects in the experimental group, 18 recorded an increased score of at least one point in the structure of course scale while two remained the same. Comparable figures for the control group were three improvements, four decreases, and 13 remaining the same.

A similar result was produced by the confidence scale where the post-treatment difference in means between the two groups was again highly significant ($t = 6.9$, $df = 18$, $p < 0.001$). Seventeen members of the experimental group showed an increase of at least one point while only four members of the control group showed a gain. No experimental subject recorded a lower confidence scale score, whereas four control subjects did so.

Developing Student Autonomy

A very pleasing aspect of this investigation was the six-month follow up which involved a further administration of the two scales. At this time, the gains of the experimental group over the control group were still maintained. Earlier studies had indicated that the RSI treatment produced gains enduring beyond the actual experimental situation and the results of this investigation confirmed this finding.

One further study has been conducted with senior secondary school students who were to be offered the choice between a conventional teacher-dominated course and a more loosely structured course in which they were to receive greatly reduced guidance. In this latter option, the teacher was to act as a resource person. When requested to do so, he or she would provide assistance but basically students were to be furnished with a list of objectives, a comprehensive reading list and a sample examination paper indicating precisely how they would be assessed on the work done. They were then allowed to achieve these objectives in their own way. Working in pairs or groups was encouraged.

Of the 74 students given the choice of the two options, only 21 preferred the independent study programme. In an open discussion on what their choice revealed, students admitted to a lack of confidence in their ability to handle the freedom. They felt they would let down both themselves and their teacher, and did not wish to take the responsibility of organizing their own study. However, after these 74 students experienced the three RSI treatment sessions, 53 decided they would tackle the independent study option.

This study, and the one described previously, do seem to indicate that the RSI treatment will help students feel more confident in their ability to handle an independent study programme. However, the question remains as to whether this increased confidence will enable them to actually achieve the success they now believe is possible for them. On this issue, I have no hard data, for I have not been in a position to conduct another course on the lines of the one I described at the commencement of this chapter.

Fortunately some anecdotal evidence is available. The teacher who proposed the two-option course to his senior secondary students was delighted with the results achieved. Actually, this was his third attempt to encourage his students to take more responsibility for their own learning, the first two having produced a very disappointing outcome. This time, he felt the majority of the students taking the independent study option had worked really well. This effort was reflected in excellent examination results which compared more than favourably with the group taking the teacher-dominated option. Both these groups sat a common examination. Although one cannot discount the teacher's bias here, for he wanted the 'independents' to do well, the fact does remain that they performed far more creditably than had the students in the two previous attempts. An added bonus was the positive attitude of most of the 'independents' at the end of the course. They had demonstrated to themselves that they could organize their own learning and this contributed to a marked increase in self-esteem.

I would not claim, of course, that every one of the 53 students taking the independent option showed this improved self-concept. Despite their initial confidence that they could take more responsibility for their own learning, 17 students found performance did not match intent. With the best of intentions, they were unable to timetable themselves or to discipline themselves to work without close supervision.

Somewhat the same proportion, approximately one-third, behaved in this way when the Diploma of Education students referred to earlier undertook an independent study course. According to the lecturer in charge of the 40 members of the experimental group, 28 performed well. This compared quite favourably with the control group, of whom only 12 were considered by the lecturer to have put any real effort into their work.

These anecdotal reports suggest that the RSI treatment does not only help students to feel more confident in their ability to cope with independent study but also to perform in accordance with this belief. As attitude change is so difficult to achieve, it is most encouraging to find that a method as simple as RSI should be able to produce the effect it does. This is particularly so when it is realized that the actual time involved is only 100 minutes.

The RSI method has other advantages, too. In itself, it is an enjoyable experience. People like the feeling of relaxation, of 'letting go'. They feel good about the control they are able to take over their own lives, for the effect of the RSI treatment extends far beyond that of helping students feel more confident about their ability to study independently. It results in a general increase of confidence so that people feel more competent to transcend the limits they have been placing on themselves. Schwartz (1971) put it neatly when he said:

> You are what you think you are.
> Think more of yourself and there is more of you.

Through the RSI technique people can, it would seem, be helped to think more of themselves, to feel competent to cope with situations which had previously overawed them. More specifically, it would appear that RSI offers a reasonable prospect for helping students to handle independent study courses more confidently and, perhaps, more successfully.

6. One-to-one Learning

David Potts, *Department of History, La Trobe University, Melbourne*

Introduction and background

In 1973 I began a series of workshops in a history-sociology course at
La Trobe University, Melbourne. They were 'workshops', as opposed to
one-hour tutorials, in that they each ran for three hours of varied learning
activities. In them I tried to integrate academic learning with a growth in
self-confidence, self-knowledge and enjoyment and identity with the
group. All this both implied and led to autonomy. The main method I
used — and this is a central theme of this article — was what I call one-to-
one discussion, something like an application of co-counselling techniques
to academic work.

Some of my ideas for these workshops sprang spontaneously from a
long standing interest in learning innovation, including experience as a
schoolteacher and, more recently, study for a degree in tertiary education.
However, the big fillip came when my department and the university
allowed me to look at tertiary learning experiments overseas. In 1972, in
London and New York, I experienced anything that I thought might
expand my sense of how people learn in groups. I went to teachers'
conferences and training programmes, kindergartens, schools, universities
(especially New York experimental colleges), humanistic psychology
groups, communes, and religious sect meetings; and I talked to anyone
anywhere. Out of the vast flurry of experiences and ideas, and nights of
restless excitement, I gradually concocted plans for my workshop
programme.

The one-to-one discussion technique that was central to these plans can
best be described from a set of narrative accounts of how I came by the
idea. The first, and most important experience for me in this respect, was
what was called an 'Enlightenment Intensive'. I attended a group run along
these lines by Jeff Love, through Quaesitor, at a farmhouse in
Worcestershire, England. Here, the whole experience was based on paired
learning. The 20 people who attended were split up into ten pairs,
scattered throughout a large room. They were instructed to sit up alertly
and face each other, then one asked the other, 'Tell me who you are'.
The speaker had seven minutes to work on the question, while the
listener, always paying supportive attention, would not interrupt in

any way. The roles would then be reversed. After 42 minutes, that is, after three talk periods for each partner, everyone got up, formed into new pairs, and repeated the process. Occasionally there were short breaks for exercise or light meals, but basically the one-to-one talk pattern was maintained over an 18-hour day, for three days.

The object was to formulate a simple answer, to convince oneself and not be dissuaded by the group leader. No one reached this point until the third day. But it was the experience of exploration, not the answer itself, that mattered most. Even those who at the beginning were self-denigratory (such as a drug addict who said he was 'fucking nothing' and spent most of his time silent or weeping) eventually battled through, with nothing but the space provided by attentive listening, to a position of huge self-affirmation.

Those who formulated answers satisfying to themselves went on to other questions, such as, 'What is another?' and 'How is life fulfilled?' Particularly from these latter questions I became inspired with ideas for adapting self-enlightenment to other forms of enlightenment. The 18-hour day of effort also fascinated me, in the fact that people could pay attention so long if given a 50-50 chance for self-expression.

Next, I discovered various forms of co-counselling, and I came to see further advantages of uninterrupted talking-through. Jerome Liss gave me a paper in which he argued as follows:

> People in their daily lives are too often interrupted and not permitted to complete their thoughts. Direct interruptions, meaning one person speaks while the other is still talking, can block one talker's mind if he does not finish his say ... Repetitive interruptions not only chop up the ongoing stream of thoughts and feelings of the moment, but the two-person pattern is internalised and repeated by the interrupted person's mind when alone. Thus, people who feel 'blocked', 'stuck', 'bogged down' or 'hemmed in' have been stopped by others from unravelling their thoughts and feelings and are plagued by self-interrupted thoughts when alone.

From this, it struck me that students' experiences of traditional tutorial discussions are more of interruption than self-expression. A dozen students at a one-hour session mostly average only a couple of minutes of talking time each. This gives some chance for a fruitful clash of competing ideas already formed, but not for careful and individual development of ideas. In my experience, students trying to work up their ideas are quickly attacked on any weaknesses, weaknesses they could have corrected themselves given more space. They become frustrated and defensive, and few I think try later to work it all out. Most give up before they start under such conditions, and simply listen to two or three leaders being herded along by the tutor. It is inadequate practice for the personal articulation of thoughts, and this shows up in poor written work.

I went on to discover more about co-counselling (from Harvey Jackins, John Heron and others), particularly about blockage in rationality through emotional tension. Any learning is about the processing of experience, and is generally inadequate if initiated and consolidated under stress. Yet students start at school and tertiary institutions with self-doubts about their worth and ability, and this may be added to by the pressures of competition with others and the judgements of authority. I came to believe that they need structured space in which to explore ideas, without criticism or other interruption, to assist them to feel values, to clear blockages, and to learn to think both freely and, from that, rationally. It was to create such a space that I decided on the three-hour workshops with extensive one-to-one talking.

When I returned to Australia I began to plan workshops in more detail for our course in Mexican history-sociology. I designed these around a few major principles. First, for a tertiary course of somewhat conscripted participants, I made the one-to-one talk periods briefer and more varied than in Jeff Love's enlightenment intensive, not to make things too tough. Secondly, even academic questions were worded on the Zen-like principle that the process of exploration is more important than the answer. For instance, I preferred 'What is the Mexican Revolution?' to 'What caused the Mexican Revolution?' It is more inexhaustibly explorative. I especially eschewed anything as potentially factual as 'How was the Mexican Constitution formed in 1917?' I believed open-ended questions would give students more chance to work from limited information and to develop more autonomy. Thirdly, I decided to include activities to build self-confidence and self-knowledge, group identity and so on, as steps towards other learning, but they were to remain steps and not become prime objectives; I decided I would always try to integrate them with coursework and make links apparent. Fourthly, I sought, and was thankfully granted the right, to have the course non-graded; anyone would pass as long as they attended and did a set quantity of written work (quality judgement was not to be a control). And lastly, and quite as important as all the other aspects of method, I decided to demand a weekly written statement or 'journal' from students on their workshop experience, to consolidate learning, to help develop writing skills, and to give me feedback.

My feeling that Australian university students would respond positively to all this was, of course, quite untested. Several colleagues condemned the programme. Some, for instance, said students should not be made to talk, and that it could not be done anyhow; others said I had no right to tamper with psychology and navel-gazing. I argued vigorously. Eventually the chairman, with many regrets, quietly gave me permission to try.

The first workshop and the course in general

At the beginning of the academic year, in the first lecture on Mexican history, a first-year course, I called for volunteers for the experimental workshops. Out of 130 students I was able to form two groups which stabilized out after a week at one of 15 students and the other of 16. We were given a professor's large room to work in, with a carpeted floor and a scattering of ordinary chairs (which allow people to sit up alertly). Altogether, I had just what I wanted.

I planned the first workshop in detail, and this is outlined below. The one-to-one partnerships are presented in shorthand form. For instance, one pattern reads: 'One-to-one: "What is fact?", A 3 min, B 3 min; A 3 min, B 3 min'. This means that each partner talks twice for uninterrupted times of three minutes. Students were always instructed to address their partner by name in asking the set question, and to thank each other by name at the end of each partnership. I regard these courtesies as very important. All timing was done with an oven-timer and I took part in the pairs where there were unequal numbers of students. The numbers in the left-hand column are the hours and minutes of the start of each section, from 0.00, at the beginning, to 3.00, the end of the third hour. Note, too, each stretch of uninterrupted talk time is short, for these first experiences. Later I expanded them to 3 to 6 minutes and set more repetitions.

1. Plan of first workshop
(As adhered to and with some additions to what actually happened.)

0.00 Loss due to delays

0.10 Introduction: Express pleasure that the group has formed. Broadly explain the one-to-one method, something of my experiences and the general philosophy behind it. Ask students to keep in mind for immediate purposes that the listeners are serving the speakers; their job is (a) to pay alert attention and (b) not to interrupt in any way. Answer questions, but suggest main discussion should come after experience.

0.30 *Getting to know each other*
One-to-one: 'Tell me something about yourself.' A 2 min, B gives résumé of what A said (purely an attention test) 1 min; B 2 min, A résumé 1 min. Change partners: A 2 min, B 2 min (ie this time. no résumés).
Group (everyone in a full circle): comments, complaints, attitudes to non-interruption. Group (making sure no one is sitting next to either of his or her previous partners): Turn by turn going around the circle, each person to identify himself and each of the two people who partnered him to give one or two sentence comments on what was remembered as most interesting, everyone constantly naming each other, eg, A, 'I'm Joan'; B, 'I'm Harry. I listened to Joan, and what I found most interesting was that Joan was brought up at Apollo Bay and she has a pet magpie'; 'I'm Pat. I listened to Joan, and . . .'. In this process everyone is eventually named several times, at dispersed intervals. At the end of it call on volunteers (everyone forewarned) to name the group one by one till everyone can do it.

1.20 Filling in departmental record sheets.

1.30 *History method*

97

Purpose: to discuss distinction between 'fact' and 'interpretation'.
Brief discussion in group to set up problem.
One-to-one: 'What is fact?' A 3 min, B 3 min; A 3 min, B 3 min.
Describe each other's face in factual terms (as near as you can):
A 2 min, B 2 min; A and B (open discussion) 2 min.

1.55 Group: one volunteer to attempt to describe someone's face
factually, followed by group critical discussion of the exercise.
Students are shown a large photograph, unlabelled (it was of
Zapata); each write (a) a short factual description of the face, and
(b) an interpretative description. General discussion of the exercise
including my reading some of the written observations and asking
for comments, and my leading individuals into difficulties over
justifying their interpretations.

2.15 Individual: reading of a short document (a mainly narrative
description of a hacienda), 5 min.
One-to-one: 'What parts of the document are factual *v*
interpretative?' A 2 min, B 2 min.
Individual: reading of a second document (an interpretation of an
Indian's attitudes of mind in his response to a flogging), 5 min.
One-to-one (new partners): discuss second document. A 2 min,
B 2 min; A 2 min, B 2 min.
Group: sharing of main conclusions on the two documents, 7 min.

2.45 *History content* (preparation)
One-to-one: 'What is Mexican?' (Instruction: if you are short on
information, discuss it as a *type* of question.) A 2 min, B 2 min;
A 2 min, B 2 min. Change partners: A 2 min, B 2 min; A 2 min,
B 2 min.

2.55 Instructions for next week:
(a) We will continue with 'What is Mexican?' and introduce 'What
is revolution?'
(b) Suggestions for reading.
(c) Journals: to be about 500 words, as a recollection of your main
learning experiences in the workshop; any emphasis you choose but
I would appreciate some comment on each of the three major
sections and the general learning method. Keep carbon copies.
Original copies to be handed to me as soon after the workshop as
practical.

3.00 Conclusion: express pleasure that we have shared our first workshop;
thank everyone for participating.

In the opening sections of this first workshop I felt awkward and anxious,
while putting on a bold front. Students sat in silence while I explained the
method. The whole idea began to overwhelm me as ridiculously contrived;
16 blank faces watched me as I talked. Then I had to give the orders: pair
up, await further instructions. An endless five seconds followed before
anyone moved; gradually they found partners, shuffling into position.
I gave the instructions: face your partner, introduce each other; decide

who is going to talk first; listener, address your partner by name and ask him, 'Tell me something about yourself'; remember, listen attentively and do not interrupt in any way; start now. As I actually spoke the words I felt an immense inner wave of insecurity; what if my colleagues were right, what if they wouldn't talk? Pause. Then began a faint surge of speech. The exercise staggered under way. That was the worst moment. Thereafter energy and enthusiasm picked up all round.

The other most intense emotion for me in the first workshop, and for several other workshops until I was used to it, was a strange sense of loss of role and authority as a teacher. Once people were paired up they were on their own. Sitting back to take it in (where I was not in a pair if there were even numbers of students) I watched animated faces and gestures, heard bursts of laughter, saw pained expressions and noted moments of silence. The arguments might be wrong; someone might need encouragement; someone might need prodding. But it was all beyond my influence. The oven-timer ticked away as a watchful guide over the protected space; no directing, no judging. What was happening out there? I could only find out, roughly, in a chosen set of confidences, when the journals came in a day or so later, though I learned a little along the way, from a few people in group discussion. For the great part, however, the immediate experience was, as I said, one of lost control, lost authority. Colleagues have since had similar experiences.

From here on I continued to plan each workshop to the last minute (drawing on direct experience and on criticism from journals). However, in practice I treated the plans rather flexibly. As the students in the workshops were volunteers from the main lecture and set-reading course, a formal academic structure was always there for them to use. The one-to-one questions were broad enough for them either to do the reading as set or to develop their own lines of inquiry and find their own reading.

The assessment of the workshops which follows is based mostly on students' journals, and each student comment is identified by the author's first name and a bracketed number indicating the week in which it was written (over the 13 weeks of the course).

2. The journals

In the workshop groups students were under constraint to produce a 500-word journal each week or else they would have to do a final examination. I prewarned them at the end of each workshop, and sometimes we made brief notes on the main structure of the three hours, as a memory guide. Apart from that, they were instructed to write as they wished on what they wished, as long as it bore some relation to the three-hour session. Given the large range of issues touched on in workshops, that gave a lot of scope for variety. I did not correct the journals in any way or comment on them or return them (students kept copies for themselves). I felt that any opinions would be prescriptive. As a requirement, journals were in excess of the traditional essay work and other exercises on which I did offer criticism, so they could safely be left as a learning rather than a teaching tool. All I did was comment at the next week's workshop on problems raised or on questions of general importance to the group and so on, often primarily just to assure students that the journals were always read.

As a task for me, even when I had 60 students in workshop courses in later years, I did not find reading journals a chore. It took only a couple of minutes to read each one and my incentive was always high because they were a continuous reflection on my role as a teacher, whether they were very specifically on history problems, or on the impacts of methods, or about personalities and personal problems or perspectives. Some were very moving, insightful, passionate; some were highly skilled and perceptive pieces of history; some were very funny or creative (dialogues, mock biographies, narratives, comic form, paste-ups . . .); and one or two from year to year were utterly exhausting in their personal abuse (a Maoist woman, for instance, attacked me regularly as a 'bourgeois individualist shit'). Throughout it all I remained silent. If students wanted to discuss something, they had to see me personally. Journals were to be unjudged, a sort of natural extension of one-to-one.

As a task for students, attitudes to journals varied. Nearly everyone submitted them regularly without trouble, and many wrote well beyond the minimum required length. Different people had different ups and downs about the writing. Some took to it immediately. Some had periods of alienation and got over them. Many pushed me with questions about what I wanted; what 'should' they write about. I kept telling them to make their own choice, to discover their own areas of interest from their own issues raised in one-to-one. A growth of autonomy in this respect is reflected in the following pair of comments from Marylin: '[I find writing the journal] annoying . . . I'm just filling up a gap of 500 words' (week 4). Then, 'I found that by writing the journals regularly I have lost the hang-up completely of writing them. It is no longer a dread to write a journal, in fact it gives me a little satisfaction'(6). Paul (13) discovered 'The best way to write journals is to write them to yourself and not to David or history department heads or to anyone else.' A couple of students regarded journal writing as a chore from beginning to end. But these were clearly exceptions. I think it was a measure of students' learning to express themselves in journals, and to value the experience, that a few began to write them in other subjects.

For my own part the journals were invaluable. They gave me a deeper sense of contact with everyone, which one-to-one did not allow. They helped me to meet problems as they arose, or even reduced problems in themselves as they seemed to give the students a cathartic sense of release from lows (as well as a consolidation of highs); they gave me insights into what was happening in group discussion that I could never judge from the dominant spokespeople; they were inspiring in showing what people could write from their own drive and interest, from prior articulation; and they gave me both tremendous confidence to judge the value of particular exercises and questions and a flood of ideas towards planning each coming workshop.

3. The one-to-one method in general

Students mostly felt very uneasy about one-to-one at first. They claimed to feel 'strange' (Robyn), 'defensive' (Betty), 'frightened . . . nervous' (Gary) and 'shy' (Doris). John, a very sociable 28-year-old ex-truckdriver, said, 'I felt some unease at being drawn, nay forced, into conversation with a total stranger . . .'. At the personal level, however, John found the 'barriers quickly came down'. Students were generally thrilled at getting to know each other so well within the first workshop. On the method itself for general purposes, week by week, they had most difficulty with non-interruption. I had to be strict about this, moving across the room to ask the student not to interrupt if I saw him break the rule, and spending several moments of group discussion over various weeks to look at problems with the technique. Students came to accept it. They did, however, ask for a pattern of open discussion at the end of one-to-one rounds, and this procedure I adopted more and more frequently for later workshops. Thus a likely pattern on a given question would become: A 3 min, B 3 min; A 3 min, B 3 min; AB 4 min (the 'AB' indicating that cross-questioning and argument were allowed). Another complaint was against the oven-timer. Some people objected that it cut them off at a peak moment of insight, and so on. But no one could think of a way round it if each talker's space were to be clearly delineated and if the whole group were to be working on the same time-span for changes of partners and questions.

Another problem caused by the system of partners was the formation of favourites or complaints about partners who had not prepared properly. My main response to complaints was to try to persuade the members of the group not to let the partner establish a tone, or style, for the whole partnership. I reminded them that they were not engaged in a discussion but that they were each working for himself. Too often, I argued, people were accusing their partners of sins they themselves were committing (being repetitive, off the question, or overgeneralized). If they looked to themselves they had plenty to work on. They could provide a service to their partners by self-improvement and good example; and they could use their listening time to try to think out what explicitly bored or troubled them with their partner's observations — to raise their own consciousness of how they could improve themselves. In sum, my message was: you cannot, and should not try to, assume responsibility for your partner; but you can and should assume responsibility for yourself. This message got through to some.

By and large the problems, even if not resolved, were outweighed by the successes. My main expectations of one-to-one were confirmed. First, students felt they became more articulate, both in their pairs and, from there, generally; Gary (2), 'I felt . . . my ability to express my thoughts had been improved'; Paul (13), 'because the one-to-one established an open casual atmosphere, small and large group discussions became easier'; John (4), 'I am finding it easier to engage in conversation about any subject I am doing'. Secondly, they felt the method generally boosted their confidence to tackle ideas: Kevin (13), 'It was very big to know you could throw it in and kick it around and not get shouted down. Maybe it is real security blanket stuff, but it certainly encouraged some original thought.' Jeff (later in the year, from a report to the sociologists): '[In one-to-one] . . . the talker can "confront" the listener with ideas of his own without fear of being knocked back or laughed at (and thus becoming defensive), reaching conclusions he may not have otherwise reached.' And thirdly, the method led people to new incentives to read. Doris (3) summed this up: 'As usual I came away from the workshop stimulated. I want to bury myself in books and read as much as possible . . . There is far greater desire to read when attending the workshop when compared with other formal tutorials. I feel I gain so much more from talking to other students that it would be positively immoral for me not to be as well-informed as they are. Also, this constant interaction breeds new concepts which I feel I must follow up by more reading and further discussion.'

In relation to learning to talk more structurally, I began to receive comments on the value of non-interruption such as the following: James (5), 'I agree a person must not be interrupted . . . I was interrupted very gently but I realized later that I had forgotten to say some of my main ideas as a result'; and Linda (13) who for several weeks had attacked one-to-one and had preferred group discussions: 'With regard to the one-to-one discussions I considered this approach to have been most beneficial . . . [Non-interruption] did prove quite frustrating at times . . . however I also discovered that if my partner interrupted my discussion it generally destroyed my train of thought or forced my pattern of conversation to change. Thus in general I consider the idea of non-interruption to be a valuable approach to analysing and articulating one's ideas.' Indeed students got so used to one-to-one space they began to resent group talk as 'drifting', or, as John (5) put it, '[in group] . . . ideas that are aired are not given time to settle before we are off on a different tangent listening to someone else'.

Another major benefit of one-to-one which seemed more marked for the students than I originally expected, was that it taught them to listen to a partner. Many students raised this point, for example Jenny (13), '[One-to-one] helps the listener discipline himself to *hear*'. Some students referred to an overflow beyond university life; one, for instance, to better relations with his girlfriend, from giving and expecting more attention.

For all this, my biggest effort with one-to-one, my attempt at its most sustained use towards the greatest autonomy for students, met only with ambiguous moments of success. My central scheme was to keep the students, after a couple of introductory weeks, to two main questions, week-in and week-out, for six weeks. I intended a variety of other exercises, but the two key questions would always be tackled. These were to be 'Tell me something about yourself' and 'What is the Mexican Revolution?'. I held students to the personal question in the hope that they would explore different ways of perceiving and presenting themselves in the university environment. And from the second question, I hoped students would develop their own approach to history.

Types of reaction to both questions, and the times at which they surfaced, varied tremendously, but by the fourth week the honeymoon period seemed to be over for a significant number of students. I began to receive such complaints as the following: Lyzbeth (4), 'I am bored with what I say . . . similarity in the answers . . . a lot of repetition . . . cannot seem to break through into new areas'.

In response to this barrage I discussed the problems with the group. I tried to persuade them that if they were bored, they were boring themselves, and that they should and could do something about it for themselves. I stressed that in answer to 'Tell me something about yourself' they could project themselves in much richer and more challenging forms than by merely presenting a superficial life history (most had talked of schooling, domestic situation and so on — safe public information). We suggested different types of personality projections. Some students took a lead in opening up, which encouraged others to follow. But still the complaints remained. Many simply would not make a choice and continued to take the question at a peculiarly unsatisfying sort of face value. It struck me that the very people most dissatisfied with their self-projection to the set question were the ones least confident to make a choice to change. Had I felt I had an open mandate to help in human relations, I might have kept on the pressure for them to solve the problem themselves. But, as I was running a history course, I decided to back down. I shifted off the ongoing self-presentation question on to varying ones, starting with 'What are your main life values?'. A general sigh of relief followed. Even students who had been prepared to battle on with the original question expressed satisfaction at having something more specific to follow. The new question invited more openness, and the less confident students found it easier to work under that sort of direction.

Meanwhile, I continued for a further couple of weeks with the broad history question, 'What is the Mexican Revolution?' — in the teeth of continuous protests from several students. It seemed to me more important to stick at this one, if students were to develop academic self-confidence, their sense of self-discovery of what history is about. I argued: 'If the question is monotonous, form interesting sub-questions; if you are bored with being too general, be more specific; if your approach is colourless, colour it; if you are being repetitious, read up on the subject and present new and varied content.' This was to little avail. There were students who continued to complain of being 'bogged' and so on. Linda (4) was most outspoken when she insisted she could not shape her own sub-questions, that they were 'only useful when introduced by another person', that with the current question she felt 'discontent and hostility'. She asserted flatly to me, 'so much for your theory'. For all that, the next week she came up against a partner who impressed her with his formation of sub-questions, and she said she began to 'wonder' what her 'inability to explore different angles means'. Others like Gary (5) accepted that 'the answer lies within the group — so stimulate their own interest'.

And Ronis, who had dropped out from Monash University in the previous year, was one who continuously expressed support for the open method: 'I enjoy not being told what to read but I'm still having trouble finding my resources. I'm used to being told what to read and am enjoying the confidence I feel someone (I guess David) has in me . . . Got really mad at everyone for wanting more direction, and didn't feel very much a part of the group. Felt that people weren't making the most of what I thought was a terrific opportunity.'

The problem for me about whether to stick to 'What is the Mexican Revolution?' was that week by week, for every couple of people complaining, there was one making some sort of breakthrough. There were people like Linda, as above, being jolted into some form of self-recognition, starting to wonder, to choose. Several went flat and then began to lift themselves, using phrases like the following from Doug (5): 'Improvement because I wanted it to be' and 'thought-provoking. . . I was determined to get something out of it'. Several simply continued the whole way through using their time to their own satisfaction. For instance a few were referring through weeks 4 to 6 to reading whole major historical texts, sometimes even two or three. Such free reading, taking pleasure in historical research and follow-through is, in my experience, very rare amongst undergraduate students.

Finally, however, I decided to tighten things up. There was, in any case, a natural tightener in the set essay, in its submission and discussion. And I became concerned towards the end of term about a number of students who were doing very little work. I felt that we should drive the Revolution study through to some sort of conclusion. So for weeks seven and eight, having warned everyone beforehand (and a number bustled into a new burst of reading) I presented the students with a grinding run of specific historical questions on the Revolution. Many immediately liked this, as a big lift in purpose and direction. Some spoke of the sessions as 'exhausting' but 'exciting' or 'deeply satisfying'. But Ronis (8) solidly reminded me that I had deserted the cause of students finding self-responsibility. She wrote, 'I was angry at the heavily directed history questions. I am not able to research things my way. Also I am not motivating myself. We now have to do what teacher wants.' So, not unusual in the workshops, I had fallen between two stools, or rather, in response to majority pressure, I had deserted a minority by opting for the stool of more direction.

I still believe that the intensified approach to one-to-one has enormous potential. However, it can also be extremely difficult, even painful, especially in the extreme form I had experienced in the London group. Its benefit, even for a history question, would come from students driving themselves into corners. From there they would need to build up self-initiative and will to pull themselves out. I believe everyone would be able to do that eventually, and that all would be joyous and fulfilled in their victory, but it would only come after a lot of agony about being in a corner. Anyone aiming for the fullest potential of one-to-one should at least consider it in such an extensive form. Out there lies the chance for students to achieve true autonomy. However, it took more courage, determination, and force of personality than I was able to muster at the time. I also felt that history, in a rather standard course, should be more enjoyable than that, and the achievements not necessarily so high.

4. Variations on one-to-one for academic questions

For basic history purposes I settled in to a variety of one-to-one questions, interspersed with other learning techniques. I now wish to refer briefly to the more successful of these patterns.

One technique was to mix one-to-one with lecturettes. I would set up a question and let students discuss it one-to-one, and then I would give them a five-minute lecturette to remind them of basic content and to raise problems or suggest various perspectives, and then I would let them return to one-to-one discussion. I was a bit concerned lest I dominated students' thought patterns, but overall the responses suggested a large degree of independence from my opinions yet some interest in them. After I had overcome my hurt pride at not having my penetrating insights widely applauded, I decided to feel pleased.

The most direct teaching I did was through essays, but here too I tried to reduce the authority of my opinions. There was no grading but three sets of comments were given on each essay. Students made two photocopies of their essay; one went to each of two pre-selected partners, while I took the original. At the following workshop they received my written comments on their essay as well as discussing it with each of their partners in turn. Nongrading, I believe, helped in this exercise. All I insisted on was that an essay of a certain length be submitted by a certain time. Simon actually asked me if that meant he could turn in something copied from a telephone directory. I said yes. (It seemed worth a risk.) In fact, he wrote an essay of first class honours standard. In general, the release from formal grading did not result in any loss of incentive. As Marylin (6) put it, 'It was quite strange writing this essay. I knew it was not going to be marked, all I had to do was hand it in, yet I think I put more work into the essay than I have previously where my work has been marked.' Indeed, nearly everyone worked hard, and only a couple failed to get their essays in on the exact due date. And overall, though the quality of individual essays still varied from poor to excellent, I thought the standard higher than in the traditional tutorials. Students learned a lot, too, from criticizing each other.

Several other patterns of approach to weekly history reading proved effective. I led into some historical problems with perceptual ones. For instance, before tackling a critique of the revolutionary government, we worked on 'What is democracy?'. Students were excited by that question. I also varied the structure. For instance it could be tackled as follows (all on the question of democracy): Group: warm up, pooling of variety of initial ideas, 5-10 min. One-to-one: A 3 min, B 3 min; repeat. Threes-or-fours (no one with his original partner): each in turn, summarize your own and your previous partner's ideas, discuss generally, 15 min.

Group: discuss results, 10 min. If the energy was good, I might even conclude with a one-to-one for all students to articulate their own conclusions.) Another structure I used which generated enthusiasm was this: One-to-one: 'Tell me what you would do if you were president of Mexico in the 1920s.' A 6 min, B offer criticism 4 min, AB 4 min; reverse roles. Such variations, including interspersals of source material from documents or lecturettes, are endless. And they always involve effort by and for each individual student.

The most distinctive use to which I put one-to-one for history purposes was to set patterns of questions that could lead from self-understanding to historical understanding. In some ways connections between personal and historical questions were made by some students very quickly, even where I had not clearly set up an association. For instance, Mike (2): 'The two questions "Who am I?" and "What is Mexican?" did seem relatively close. Why? Both required meticulous sifting of particulars, yet one could not discard any, rather all the particulars . . . established a character.' Illustrative of my deliberate mixing of the two perspectives are the following questions, one after the other for students to try in rounds of one-to-one talks: 'What are your main hopes and expectations?', 'What were the hopes and expectations of the Zapatistas?', 'What are your main hopes and expectations for the Mexican Revolution?'. Moving towards my intentions behind this chain of questions, Marylin (8) wrote: 'It made it easier to talk about the revolutionaries. I felt I had understandings of their feelings.' But she did not simply stop at attributing to others what she felt for herself. She began to contrast her own emotions and incentives with those suggested by the statements and behaviour of the Mexicans. She went on to say, 'It was not until I said what I wanted for the Mexicans that I realized what I had said was really what I wanted for myself.' By that realization she was better able to understand the Mexicans in their own context.

5. One-to-one and personality questions

My first personality question, 'Tell me something about yourself' had been loosely conceived as helping group members to enjoy each others' company and to talk more easily, to develop social incentives to attend the workshops. Gradually I came to realize I had broached much more important issues of self-confidence and self-projection and how they affect learning in general. When I tried to persuade students to be more open on their personal life (such as to include feelings), a lot of bugs crawled out of the woodwork. For instance, Jan wrote, 'I cannot discuss my personal self. . . . Things close to me will always remain for a few trusted people.' So I talked with the group as a whole about taking risks to share, about self-trust, and so on. Perhaps they just learned from experience, but either way, three weeks later Jan wrote, 'I now feel able to be frank in my discussion with any member and I no longer have a preference whom to talk to.' Similar shifts occurred for others. I feel sure it freed them to tackle the academic questions more confidently. And similarly I began to discover that the academic purpose of the course gave students a focus for the development and use of self-confidence (or a retreat from being personal when they needed it). The two sides of the workshop seemed to help each other more than I had expected.

As the workshops went on I began to tackle the personal aspects of learning problems more directly. For instance, I used one-to-one for students to discuss their attitudes to criticism (to try to distinguish the legitimate response of a peer from deeply antagonizing ancestral voices from afar postulating shoulds and shouldn'ts). I also used personal questions to generate incentive for our work. One set went as follows: 'How is life fulfilled?', 'How is life best fulfilled?' and 'How can I best fulfil myself in these workshops?'. Lastly, I plotted some questions in response to journals when I found that a few students were casually accusing themselves of being 'not too bright', of having 'limited intelligence' or 'poor capacity for attention', and so on. In week 5 I tried, 'Tell me how intelligent you believe you are and how you came by that belief'. That sparked off some valuable reactions. So the next week I tried a chain of questions to seek to promote a positive self-image (or at least a recognition of the arbitrariness of some of the self-denigration). We did two main one-to-ones: 'Tell me one good thing that happened to you this week' and 'What are your greatest joys and abilities?'. (For the latter I suggested they elephant-shit, not just bullshit). Then I set up a little exercise: people faced each other in pairs while I recited three phrases for each person to say to his partner, one after the other with the partner looking him straight in the face and replying 'I agree'. The phrases were 'I am a warm loving person', 'I am a very talented and intelligent person', and 'I am a very *very* magnificent person'.

With all personal questions I took care to explain what I had in mind. If anyone wished to opt out, they could do so. Everyone was encouraged to try, just to see what if felt like, without necessarily implying support for my intentions. Of course, a question like the last one generated some deep emotion. A few students were very angry that I should encourage self-praise; they said the exercise was 'embarrassing' or 'pointless'. But some of these critics were the most affected, bit by bit, towards a more positive self-view. For instance, one who said in week 6, 'It makes no sense big-noting myself', said in week 12, 'The personality questions helped me in that by telling myself I am better or more so that I thought I was, I started acting that way (and consequently am) . . . I found this immensely useful.'

Many students exuded enthusiasm for personality questions from the start, and typical of the responses to the self-appreciation questions in week 6 were these words: 'jubilation' (Frank), 'really stoked' (James), 'peachy-keen' (Mike), 'tremendous' (Jenny) and from Linda, the sometime cynic, 'stimulating . . . perplexing . . . wonderful . . . entertaining . . . revealing'. Overall, I think the wider scope of learning induced by the personality questions contributed as I had hoped to students wanting to attend the workshops. As Ronis (7) put it, 'It's getting to the stage for me

107

that I just have to go along on Thursday morning [to the workshop] to be with the people and talk a bit and I feel good.' So, people kept coming. The attendance rate was well above the minimum requirements, and I had no drop-outs.

By the end of the course, in summing up their responses, students strongly backed the personality questions as an important part of the workshops. Typical comments were: Linda (3), 'I was more-or-less learning about the people involved and applying those discoveries to a better understanding of people in general', and Paul (13), 'I have enjoyed the workshops very much. It has been a completely new learning experience . . . joining the social and learning aspects of education.' In fact, a number of people said we should have done more personality questions and more with them: Gary (13), 'On personality questions . . . there should have been a lot more . . . we could have learnt more about ourselves (and I was learning more about myself) . . . and been more able to identify where we stood in relation to the subject', and Kevin (13), 'It could be that understanding people is the key to history . . . I think because we did stress this aspect we were really able to get to the personalities concerned . . . understanding others through understanding self comes in here. I don't think we went far enough on this.'

6. *Two responses to the course in general*
Below are two quotations from others to sum up the Mexican history course. The first is part of a student's final journal, and it does, I believe, reflect on issues of autonomy without the writer having that in mind. It is by a woman not previously quoted in this article.

> I would like to give my impression of the workshops . . . The stuff about one-to-one I feel is very important. I like being able to have an uninterrupted space in which to express myself; and I can't help feeling that this is universally important, if the space is to be used constructively. I like being able to pause and think about using the most appropriate word etc, knowing that my expression cannot easily be cut off by interruption from the other person. The listener is forced, to a degree, to take in a *wholeness* of information and vibes, and I've found this to be valuable both as a listener and as a speaker. There also seems to be value in a spontaneous reaction from the listener which can only occur in open discussion. Thus, I think a blend of the two approaches as we have mostly been doing lately, is a good compromise.
>
> The concept of the workshop as a personal and group exercise in learning made it seem important to study the characters and events of the Revolution in a real way — not just in order to be able to regurgitate facts and figures to pass an exam or to write an essay. Reading and discussing historical issues which are seen as personally important leads to an increase in perception of the reasons behind historical happenings. In turn, the new perception can be applied critically to current situations . . . In summary, it seems that the workshops are extremely important in allowing and encouraging a *real* work effort, but that other factors such as pressure of other courses and lack of time retard their better use.

The last quotes are from a colleague in the School of Education who wrote a paper on the workshops from an independent reading of the journals:

On teacher direction: a few students did mention they'd have preferred a bit more structure, for example weekly assignments — but the journals of about half the students showed that they were using these for just that kind of task, working through the history learned during the sessions and from reading and reflections between sessions: there was no clearly discernible common 'line' in the history (which one might expect from a group of students heavily influenced by a particular tutor).

... A fairly common pattern was an early dissatisfaction with David for offering too little guidance — students' worry about not being 'right' initially inhibited them from expressing their opinions freely. All but two of the students seemed to me to exhibit a marked growth in self-direction and confidence as the semester progressed.

... The students mostly showed an awareness of bias and selectivity in historical writing, their own as well as authoritative sources, and of the need to evaluate evidence in the light of this; they did not seem to mind risking their own opinions, which were quite diverse.

Repercussions

I had started my workshops at the beginning of the Australian academic year, in March 1973. Later that year two other colleagues set up their own style of workshops, based more on an encounter approach. The next year we gave papers on what we had done, and several others began experimenting with related structures. As of 1978 about half our department (of over 50 members) have adopted some aspects of the original workshops.

The profusion of workshop techniques has proved to be a two-edged sword. Few people apart from me like using one-to-one, yet so many of the other aspects of workshops are correlated to it that selectively to exclude it creates new problems. While the good teachers continue to be good, and develop their own approaches according to their own personalities and objectives, and while others miss the best opportunities of a technique but do well enough, some have turned everything into a new and increased set of burdens and dissatisfactions.

For me, one-to-one is the most exciting learning technique I know. Something of its potential for autonomy lies in the nature of the questions, but by and large, whatever the question, the structure alone guarantees autonomy; as people develop their sense of the technique they realize that they have space and support to do with a question whatever they like — even entirely reverse it or ignore it. Yet it is a very difficult technique, very demanding. Students (like myself and others at Jeff Love's group) need firm direction to get into it, yet paradoxically the firmer the control the greater the freedom. I think the only justification for it, as a highly structured format, is that it works.

The confidence I evolved that it would work, and how, came from my direct experience of it in Worcestershire. For many of my colleagues, any confidence at all in it comes only from articles and from recommendations by my ex-students. Backed only by such second-hand experience they approach the method diffidently, in a spirit of trying it on. Often they do not explain the concepts behind it; and no one that I know of, in trying it as a teacher, has been firm about its practice (alert postures, direct facing, clear set-up of questions and use of names, strict non-interruption, partners thanking each other, clear delineation of time spans). Often, too, their questions are not adequately conceptual. So, loosely faced with a technique that is both difficult and embarrassing, students opt out of it. Most do not try hard, but await a chance for complaint and release because they sense (or know) the ambivalence of the lecturer. This is to be expected, surely — much the same as they would opt out of any difficult written task, like an essay, if they were invited to see how they liked it and given the choice not to proceed with it. As workshops proliferated I have had students come to me in their third and fourth years who have experienced attempts at one-to-one in other groups and deeply disliked it, only to find, if properly introduced, encouraged and protected in it, that it could prove exciting.

Some teachers hold one-to-one together as a form of paired discussion with open-ended time. I recognize that such discussion does have a value of its own; clearly it allows better space for the development of a type of competitive articulation than is available in strict one-to-one. But it is a very different technique; and it misses out on a lot of the benefits of one-to-one. In paired discussion people can deplete each other's energies by interruption as much as they might build them up; if one person initiates non-directed and personal chat, his partner can confirm him in this (whereas the responsibility in one-to-one is more clearly on the individual to do useful work in his given space); the theory of rationality as expounded at the beginning of this paper receives no chance; and judgements (rather than self-judgements), put-downs and manipulation can occur.

The worst problem, however, lies with teachers who go halfway and then give up. In a spirit of enterprise they set up two-hour or three-hour 'workshops', but then rather quickly abandon either one-to-one or small groups as a main technique — perhaps because they feel uncomfortable or out of control. They then come to rely overwhelmingly on the traditional full-group discussion. Old patterns occur, with teachers talking most of the time, or with directive chairing, with selective approval and disapproval, and the shunting of students through hoops towards ends very few contribute towards or understand. The tedium of one-hour tutorials now becomes extended over two or three hours. Consequently some students have become bitter about the whole process.

Lastly, the potential of journals is easily destroyed if they are converted (as has happened frequently) into simply another directed writing task. As I saw it, they were extra work over set requirements, so there was no need to labour them. They were to be spontaneous feedback on individual one-to-one experiences, something where students could enjoy writing and in which they could vent their emotions — especially criticism of the learning methods. I never liked being abused, but in another sense I appreciated the open information as part of knowing what were the various realities of workshops for all students. And I accepted, too, that discharge of personal problems might be important to students, and for me to recognize what was affecting their approach to academic work. Some teachers, however, made journals a specific academic task, for instance a summary of set reading with later additions according to historical understandings gleaned in group work, all followed up by the return of the journals with judging comments. There were students who used this system well, but others, already on the lower rungs of academic achievement, found it a troubling chore and a further contribution to their sense of inadequacy. Several students, then, have cursed me for the introduction of the idea of journals, occasionally for the way I use them, but overwhelmingly for the more rigid use of them by some other staff.

Out of all this, especially on how the groups are run, I have come to believe that staff need experiential training in various experimental teaching methods. The chances of effective change from reading articles, especially with a technique like one-to-one, seem to me rather low.

Conclusion: on autonomy

To discuss adequately either the possibility or the value of autonomy in tertiary education would, I believe, necessitate starting with issues like free will and determinism and going on to what I would want to achieve for myself, for my students and for society as a whole. It is all too difficult to explore briefly here. However, I have a few simple guiding prejudices.

First, I have come to believe that, for myself at least, it is wrong to ask students 'What do you want to do?' as a starting and controlling point for a learning programme. They are either too inexperienced or too conditioned for that to be liberating. I believe that by putting on a course I have a responsibility to lead and to use my abilities and experience to offer valuable material and ideas.

Secondly, students cannot know without training *how* to do something. It is not giving a person autonomy to throw him into water without teaching him how to swim. Such an approach grants him neither success nor satisfaction. Skills are most rapidly learned where most conscientiously taught, and where structures are set up to allow for their practice.

Thirdly, however, there is a dilemma. I believe the acquisition of knowledge and skills under imaginative leadership gives great joy to students. Most are happy to be led, if where they are led is satisfying. And if they want to be, teachers can easily be alert and sensitive enough to set up interesting coursework. Nevertheless, I believe teachers have a responsibility to themselves, their society, and their students' long-term interests, to tackle the harder task, to generate autonomy. I want students to become self-aware and honest, able to confront the world adequately, to make their own judgements, and to recognize and respect their own considered (not manipulated) needs. And yet again, I do not want that autonomy to lead to arrogance or rampant individualism. I want it to be

111

wed to sensitivity to others and willingness to cooperate and assist.

There is no simple position to take on all this, either philosophically or practically. I keep being trapped into wanting students to have autonomy but to adopt the values I believe in. Even, for instance, an attempt to generate autonomy in people who do not want it illustrates one of many paradoxes in the education game. What I sit back on is some sort of intuitive balance. Perhaps it is like Freire's idea that the best environment is one in which in the final achievement no one has taught another and no one is self-taught. I believe that workshops with one-to-one and open journals can be one way of creating such an environment.

7. 'Parrainage': Students Helping Each Other

Professor Marcel Goldschmid, *Chaire de Pédagogie et Didactique,*
Ecole Polytechnique Fédérale, Lausanne, Switzerland

Introduction

A number of attempts have been made in the past few years to counteract
some of the problems the typical modern university is faced with: large
classes, lack of contact among students and between students and faculty,
passive teaching methods and inadequate study methods.

Peer counselling programmes in particular (eg Gentry, 1974; Wasserman
et al, 1975; Wrenn and Mencke, 1972), have emerged, whose objective is
to enhance the affective climate and enable students to be assimilated
into the university. One could also argue that in order to improve
instruction in higher education, it is essential that students be trained in
a variety of specific learning skills to enable them to participate effectively
in innovative as well as traditional forms of instruction (Goldschmid and
Goldschmid, 1976a).

I should like in the following article to describe a peer-counselling
programme which we call parrainage. It aims to develop both a favourable
climate in the university and students' learning skills.

Origins and objectives of the parrainage

The parrainage was initiated by a professor of mechanical engineering
and myself in autumn 1973 in the mechanical engineering department
(Goldschmid and Burckhardt, 1976).

In this programme, more advanced students act on a voluntary basis as
counsellors to first year students in a variety of areas. For example, they
offer their assistance in practical matters, such as questions of housing,
transportation, stipends and loans, as well as academic problems, such as
study skills, curricular choices and vocational orientation. More generally,
the objective of the parrainage has been to help incoming students adapt
to their new environment and provide them with a favourable climate at
the beginning of their studies.

The assignment of *parrains* (the term used for third and fourth year
students) to small groups of three to four first-years, was based as much
as possible on their nationalities, mother tongue and regional origins in
order to facilitate the first contacts. The parrains had offered their help

spontaneously, although as it turned out later, it was possible to offer them a small stipend at least during the first two years of the programme.

Once the parrains were recruited, the *filleuls* (first year students) invited and the counselling groups formed, the two academic staff members met regularly with the parrains (about once or twice a month) in order to discuss their experiences and problems with the students they were counselling. During these meetings the parrains also indicated situations which they felt were beyond their capacity to deal with, ie either complex personal problems of their counsellees or serious difficulties the students had encountered with their teachers. In such cases, the professor of mechanical engineering would talk to either the students or professors concerned in order to try to remedy the situation. The parrains also wrote monthly reports about their meetings with the filleuls in order to inform us of the progress being made.

The first encounters with the newly enrolled students (about once a week) were usually initiated by the parrains and were devoted to practical problems, such as the functioning of different student services and the library. Numerous problems of adaptation were identified in the meeting and the records kept by the parrains during this phase clearly indicated the importance of a counselling scheme. The students, often being away from home for the first time and, in many cases, having come to a foreign country, were disoriented and unaccustomed to the structure and working methods encountered at the university. The large classes, in particular, created a feeling of impersonality and difficulties in establishing personal contacts. The academic backgrounds of the students also represented a factor of uncertainty and anxiety, many wondering whether they were sufficiently well prepared to meet the demands.

One of the tasks of the parrains consisted of offering reassurance and practical help during this difficult period. Another was to provide information about their field of study. Although the students had enrolled in mechanical engineering in line with their preference, they often had only a vague idea about the profession. In fact they were rather disappointed by the apparent lack of relationship between the courses they were taking in their first year and their perception of the work of a mechanical engineer. The senior students, who had been confronted with the same problems earlier on, were able to orient the new students, for example by telling them about the courses they were taking and the projects and fieldwork they were presently involved in.

These first group meetings which had been organized by the parrains were gradually replaced by more spontaneous and informal contacts. In fact, later on the parrains frequently met with their filleuls upon their request, often on an individual basis when personal problems were revealed. As it turned out some of these 'personal' problems were shared by other first year students and could therefore subsequently be discussed in the group.

First results

In general terms, the monthly meetings with the parrains and their reports clearly confirmed the need for such a programme and demonstrated the effectiveness of the parrains' interventions. More specifically, one could cite the improvement in the affective climate and the contacts among students (much as Heiney, 1977, had found with a peer-counselling programme in psychology), as well as the resolution of a number of practical problems, such as housing or transportation.

Based on the parrains' reports, the professor of mechanical engineering was able to intervene successfully with some of his colleagues in matters of teaching as well as with individual students who had motivational or academic problems. Occasionally, the parrains also addressed themselves directly to the tutors in order to remedy a specific problem, such as the lack of instructional materials or consultation time with teachers in certain courses.

Another area where the more senior students were able to help their younger colleagues concerned working- or study-methods. Examples included more effective use of the library and preparation for exams, as well as more efficient note-taking. In fact, the parrains' reports revealed that a majority of students were at first unable to take notes which they could use later in individual study.

We also attempted a statistical analysis at the end of the first year by comparing the grades in mechanical engineering at the end of the first semester for three consecutive years (the two preceding ones without parrainage), in order to determine whether or not the parrainage had an effect on the freshmen's academic performance. The results turned out to be quite favourable to the scheme: the grade point average was higher and the number of drop-outs smaller in the year with parrainage. Furthermore, the number of failing grades (below six in a 10-point scale) was considerably lower (4.6 per cent for the year with parrainage and 15 per cent and 12.5 per cent respectively for the two preceding years). Nevertheless, it should be pointed out that these statistics do not necessarily indicate that the improvements were due to parrainage. In view of various grade fluctuations in other departments, one cannot exclude the possibility that other factors might have contributed to these changes.

Finally, it should be mentioned that the parrains had identified several cases of students who had been so discouraged that they were thinking of dropping out, but who with the encouragement and assistance of the parrains and the professor were able to persevere and pass the exams successfully. These observations are in line with the results obtained by Brown *et al* (1971) who were also able to help potential college drop-outs through a peer-counselling programme.

In view of the positive outcome, the department of mechanical engineering decided to continue the experiment with another professor and a new group of first year students and parrains in 1974-75. The structure and procedure adopted were much the same, but in addition, a short guide with practical recommendations for the parrains was prepared by two parrains and one filleul of the first year (Audemars, Borel and Jacot, 1977).

After the first and second years, we conducted a survey by means of a questionnaire in order to ascertain the reactions of both parrains and filleuls (Brun, 1976). The parrains (23 of 24 responded) felt that the parrainage had helped them improve their interpersonal relations, gain a sense of responsibility, become more conscious of first-year problems and acquire a better perspective on their studies. The parrainage was thus clearly perceived to be helpful to the parrain as well, not just to the filleul. The literature on peer teaching (Goldschmid and Goldschmid, 1976b) supports this finding: the student counsellors benefit themselves considerably, ie peer-teaching is by no means a one-way 'philanthropic' exercise: all the parrains indicated that parrainage should continue. Among the problems, they thought that information about the parrainage given to new students was inadequate, and that the programme started too late.

A majority of the filleuls (49 of 84 responded) also reported great satisfacton in the affective area. Most of them acknowledged the help they had received with regard to practical problems, study methods and information about the school, the professors and vocational questions. Relatively few (less than 20 per cent) stated specific complaints: some wished for more contacts with the parrains and others felt that the parrainage could have been more efficient (eg started earlier, better information, etc). Only 6 per cent of the first year students said they would *not* be willing to be a parrain in their fourth year.

Evolution of the parrainage

In view of the general satisfaction of the students in mechanical engineering during the first two years, the student association (Agepoly) decided to extend the parrainage to all departments of the university. They also insisted on operating the programme themselves without the help of the professors. In 1975-76, the Agepoly was able to recruit over 70 parrains in eight of the nine departments and in principle assign every first year student to a parrain. Unfortunately, because of a lack of cooperation among the students, various delays and organizational inefficiency, the parrainage did not function adequately in all departments. Some of the freshmen, for example, had not been informed of the parrainage and some of the parrains were not properly instructed as to their role. It was obvious that such a large enterprise involving several hundred students strained the organizational capacity and manpower of the student organization.

Our third survey (Chaire de Pédagogie et Didactique, 1976a; Champagne, 1976) which was carried out in all departments concerned (filleuls: N = 338, respondents = 105 or 31 per cent; parrains: N = 76, respondents = 46 or 61 per cent), nevertheless revealed that a large majority (80 per cent of the filleuls and 70 per cent of the parrains) felt that the parrainage met a real need at least among a portion of the first year students, especially those from abroad and other regions in Switzerland. A number of respondents also indicated that it was not necessary to assign a parrain to each new student, ie that it was sufficient to make a parrain available to those who wanted one. (This was in fact the procedure which was adopted in the fourth year.) Among the most serious problems the survey pinpointed was the late start of the programme. Many respondents felt that the parrainage was most useful at the very beginning, ie in the first weeks, and much less needed later on. Furthermore, both parrains and filleuls complained about the infrequent contacts between the two groups, leaving the new students with doubts about the efficiency of the programme and the parrains with considerable frustration and disappointment since their services were apparently not wanted. A third deficiency in the new structure was the relative lack of direct interventions by the class counsellors (one professor in each department) who had played such an important role in the first two years of the programme.

Another set of questions in the survey concerned the students' attitude to study methods (Chaire de Pédagogie et Didactique, 1976b). A large majority (81 of 105 first years and 31 of 45 parrains) stated that the university should offer the students the opportunity to improve their work and study methods. Among the *subjects* which many would find most useful (in decreasing order of frequency) were the following: how to write a report, how to carry out a project, how to present a report, developing study skills, memorization, documentation, public speaking, and preparing for exams.

As to the *form* of this training, by far the largest number (close to one-third of the respondents) would prefer to have access to a manual on these subjects. Close to one-fifth would prefer an information centre; somewhat fewer would prefer regular courses; and about 10 per cent each, seminars, mini-courses and workshops.

Finally, in the fourth year (1977-78) the parrains were only assigned to those first year students who had indicated that they wanted access to a student counsellor. Again the student organization was largely responsible for the information and orientation of both incoming students and parrains. The results as indicated by a fourth survey (Talbot, 1978) were similar to those obtained in the third year, when the parrainage was first generalized to the entire university: organizational problems and infrequent contacts were listed most frequently among the problems, but again a majority indicated that the parrainage was useful and those who participated were satisfied with the results, especially in the affective area.

Conclusions

This programme of peer counselling has now been running for several years and has been regularly evaluated. On the whole, it appears that the parrainage meets the real needs of a sizeable portion of first year students,

117

in particular at the very beginning of their studies. Besides improving the social climate and contacts among the students, such a programme can contribute to the solution of practical problems, such as housing, transportation and social services. It can also enhance the development of study skills and working methods. In short, the parrainage constitutes an effective self-help organization directed at getting students off to a good start. It is also an inexpensive operation, an advantage which, in a time of budget constraints in higher education, is by no means negligible. Successive student groups can — on a voluntary basis — serve as student counsellors, after having benefited perhaps from the help of older colleagues when they began their own study. Each generation then in turn assumes the responsibility for helping the other. The parrains also profit from the experience and besides establishing better personal relations, further deepen their understanding of their subject matter and future profession.

Our experience also showed that close cooperation between professors and students in the running of the operation greatly enhanced its success. In fact, without institutional resources and connections, the programme's reach is very much curtailed and its continuity in fact questioned from year to year. It is necessary, therefore, to strive for a delicate balance between student initiative and responsibility on the one hand, and the provision of sufficient institutional structure and support on the other.

8. Student Autonomy in Learning Medicine: Some Participants' Experiences

Barbara Ferrier, *Professor of Biochemistry, McMaster University, Hamilton, Ontario*
Michael Marrin and Jeffrey Seidman, *medical students, McMaster University*

Introduction

One of the stated objectives for students in the McMaster University MD programme is 'to become a self-directed learner, recognizing personal educational needs, selecting appropriate learning resources and evaluating progress'. In order to graduate, students must meet this as well as the other objectives; student autonomy in learning is therefore not an option but a requirement. The objectives were developed to ensure that the school's graduates would have the qualities, knowledge and skills necessary to provide them with the flexibility, awareness, and attitude to learning thought to be necessary to meet future health care needs. The programme is based on an interdisciplinary problem-based method in which students work in a sequence of small groups throughout its three-year (31 months) duration. It is of considerable complexity and cannot be fully described in this article. A rather comprehensive description of it at an early stage was published (Journal of the Royal College of Physicians of London, 1972), and aspects of its subsequent development and of some particular features have been described in many publications (Neufeld and Barrows, 1974; Barrows and Mitchell, 1975; Sweeney and Mitchell, 1975; Hamilton, 1976; Ali *et al,* 1977; Ferrier and Hamilton, 1977; Barrows and Tamblyn, 1977; Pallie and Brain, 1978; Sibley, 1978; Walsh, 1978).

Since the emphasis is on small group learning, the students must not only be able to direct their own learning, but to do so in a way which is compatible with the learning objectives of the group and its other members. They must also accept responsibility for facilitating the learning and evaluating the progress of their peers. Thus, the autonomy which they must acquire is a conditional one. They cannot allow their own objectives to interfere with those of the group, and collectively the group must ensure that all its members meet the programme objectives.

These programme objectives are general and descriptive. They specify no core content or factual requirements. The programme is divided into sequential segments which last for periods of up to ten weeks, and which have conceptual objectives. For each segment students are allocated to new tutorial groups consisting of five students and a tutor, and each group has to decide what methods, models, examples and strategies they will use to allow its members, individually and as a group, to achieve the objectives. In each segment, problems in various formats, clinical experiences and a variety of resources are offered from which students may select. They may also identify other problems, negotiate other experiences and find their own resources. Thus the students have some minimum objectives to achieve, but how they achieve them is their responsibility. They may also add to these objectives. Evaluation of progress towards meeting the objectives is finally the responsibility of the tutor, but students are expected to share this responsibility and actively assess their own and their peers' performance during the programme. The written summary of student performance, which is done on completion of each segment of the programme, is a summary of observations made by all participants on the level of performance in tutorials, associated activities and problem-solving exercises.

An attempt is made to select students for the programme who will perform well in this setting (Ferrier *et al*, 1978). As well as appropriate personal qualities and academic ability, potential in problem-solving ability and self-directed learning is sought. There are no course prerequisites for admission and nearly all students have completed at least three years of university undergraduate education before entering. The very small number of exceptions to this are students who are at least 24 years old who have demonstrated adequate performance in university extension courses and have shown evidence of creativity and leadership in community service.

On entry into the programme, students have to adapt immediately to an educational system which is strange to many, and to a complex organization involving several hundred faculty members, many of them in different hospitals. To help them to adapt, three days at the start of the programme are devoted to orientation, with emphasis being put on key aspects of the system. Students from the second year plan these events in the light of what was, or would have been, useful to them. These students also take on most of the tasks of introduction and familiarization during the days of orientation. Different sessions are devoted to group learning, problem-based learning, and self-directed learning.

The text of the session on self-directed learning is given here (I) and it will be followed by a commentary by two second-year students (II). One of these students had no prior experience of programmes which required self-direction in learning. The other had had a considerable experience and his remarks will therefore relate to the specific problems of adapting this style to medicine and to the McMaster programme. As a conclusion, a summary of some graduates' perceptions of their skills will be given (III). Explanations given in italics are additions made for clarification for the present purpose and were not part of the original talk.

I. On self-directed learning and setting personal goals: a tutor's view

(A tutor is assigned to a group of five students for each unit of the programme. The tutor is responsible for guiding and evaluating the work of the students in that unit.)

When the students planning orientation asked me to talk to the new class about setting objectives, personal goals, and personal assessment, they asked me to do so as someone who had tutored for several years in Phase I *(initial 10 weeks of the programme)*. I agreed to do so on that understanding, and what follows, therefore, is my opinion only, based on my experience and not on any educational theory. You will all find it obvious. I hope you will find it acceptable and useful.

In the programme you have just entered, you will be expected to get involved in your own education, and that of your peers, at a very personal level. You will have to make major decisions about the design, the style, the implementation and the evaluation of the programme you follow so that you can get the most out of it. The involvement of each of you as a person rather than as an intellect is inevitable for several overlapping reasons. First, the school's objectives require this. This is put explicitly in the objective which requires that you 'recognize, maintain and develop characteristics and attitudes required for a career in a health profession — these include: (a) awareness of personal assets, potential, limitations, and emotional reactions; (b) responsibility and dependability; (c) ability to relate to and show concern for other individuals.' This objective is taken up in the Phase I objectives which include the need 'to develop competency in . . . self-directed learning, small group learning . . . to develop a self-awareness of and ability to cope with individual strengths, weaknesses and emotional reactions'. This means, bluntly, that if you do not meet these objectives you will not be considered to be suitable to graduate. A second reason for your personal involvement is the fact that the emotional climate dramatically influences the effectiveness of learning. If you cannot assess this and, if necessary, change it, you will not have the best conditions to work under. The third reason is that you will find that the personal interactions in the small groups, in which you will work, will become intense.

Self-directed learning

You are now largely responsible for your own learning progress. One very important aspect of self-directed learning is the development of self-evaluation skills. There are three components to self-evaluation: you need to be able to assess where you are when you begin a task; you need to be able to monitor your progress as you proceed; and you need to know when to stop. I want to look at each of these components in a little more detail.

Starting condition. Assessment of your starting condition should review your knowledge, skills, attitudes and personality traits. Your pre-existing knowledge should be relatively easy to assess. For those of you without a biological science background, you may feel this is glaringly obvious, but I suggest that everyone has knowledge gaps that should be identified. You may not have had an introduction to the behavioural sciences, or you may have no awareness of the historical, social, political and economic realities of health care. Many people tend to underrate themselves in the area of their knowledge, especially those who do not have a science background. Perhaps this is because they are reluctant to apply knowledge from life experience to 'scientific' or 'medical' situations. One student who had no science background before studying medicine, when faced with some simplified problems of measurement of rate and flow in the cardiology-respiratory unit, hotly denied the ability to solve them. Yet, when translated into problems of driving a car or filling a kettle, the solutions were obvious. In this case, the knowledge lacking was the knowledge that what was already known was validly applicable.

Assessment of your learning skills is important because many of you will be faced with the task of re-organizing your methods. What worked for you in the past may not work in medicine. You will have to cope with vast areas of knowledge and vast areas of ignorance, and methods of presentation which may be verbal, photographic, diagrammatic, schematic, mathematical, or any mixture of these. Some of the questions which you can ask yourself to help define your skills are given in the Phase I manual as *Inventory of Learning Habits*. In this inventory of questions, Phase I tutors have rated the possible answers from undesirable to highly desirable to give you some guidance about what they have found to work well. Assessment of your attitudes should particularly include those towards group learning. Your past experience in this will no doubt have influenced your attitudes and this influence should be identified.

Personality traits are often said not to be relevant to education. But I suggest that in all education, including the isolating and structured programmes which many undergraduates experience, final achievement, even when represented by numerical grades, is very greatly influenced by personality. Emotional stamina would be one such trait, compliance would be another. In the small group learning setting here, the importance of personality in learning is magnified. For example, inflexibility will not only limit your experiences and impair your learning, but it will impair the atmosphere of the group, and hence the learning of the other group members. Virtually all aspects of your personality will become relevant considerations.

Measuring progress. Measuring your own learning progress will be new to many of you, who have been able to rely on external judgement in the past. I would like to emphasize that self-evaluation does not have to mean evaluation carried out alone. It means that you are to be responsible for gathering the necessary information on which you will make a judgement about your performance. There are a variety of tests available for you to use to assess your knowledge. You should also use your tutor, your peers, your student adviser (*an adviser is assigned to each student on entry, and is responsible for monitoring the progress of the student through the entire programme*), and your senior mentor. (*A senior mentor, a selected second year student, is assigned to each tutorial group in Phase I. The role of the senior mentor is to help the new students adjust to medical education at McMaster and to assist in the successful operation of the Phase.*)

Students are, perhaps rightly, very conscious of what they do not know, and what they have not managed to do, but all too often they do not realize what they do know and what they have accomplished. It is important to register your development so that you do not get disheartened. As well as keeping fact-files and notes and references, you should try to record your acquisition of skills such as mastery of a new vocabulary, and changes of attitudes. Think about your experiences both good and bad and try to analyse what you learn from them. Remember that you can learn a lot from bad experiences so try to be resilient without losing sensitivity. This advice to be analytical could lead you to be too self-conscious so try not to lose your spontaneity either.

In assessing how well you are doing, you need to be able to accept and respond to criticism, the most important type of which in this context is self-criticism. If you find something in yourself which you genuinely criticize, or if you can accept criticism from others without making excuses or being defensive, you should consider this to be a sign that you have a good sense of your own worth and that you therefore have an acceptable base on which to work in this respect. You should all believe that the school has already judged you worthy of being given this chance. You are not here by mistake.

As well as monitoring your own progress, you have to be able to generate your own satisfaction, since the rewards in this system are largely intrinsic. Those of you who have been high grade achievers in the past may miss this more than you now suspect. If rewards for performance are not institutionalized, the positive regard of your peers becomes very important. It is therefore important for you to express this regard when you feel it. There is a danger in this system, I think, of students over-reacting to what they take to be negative signals from faculty members. Like everybody, faculty members can be moody, distracted and forgetful. In spite of that, I believe that you should trust that faculty members are well-intentioned towards you.

Knowing when to stop. The problem of knowing when to stop will remain with you all your lives, because you will always have access to more information than you can cope with. The strategy to adopt is not to aim to become super-efficient information processors, but to develop confidence in selecting problem-specific information. At first, many of you will find it impossible to be confident in stopping work in an area where it is all too obvious that you have left much undone. You should rely on others to help you: your tutor, resource people (*experts in relevant disciplines who are assigned to be available for consultation by tutorial groups or individuals*), student adviser and senior mentor can all be consulted. Your peers in your tutorial group should also be involved in developing a consensus of what is a right amount of any subject for the group members to know at any time. Since group members have different academic backgrounds, the appropriate amount of knowledge for all members will not be uniform. You will find that if you work with all these people you will gradually develop a sense of what is enough 'for now'. It is important to keep reminding yourself that problems will recur in slightly different forms throughout the programme, and your clinical life. You will have the opportunity to increase what you know at each recurrence.

In relation to the problem of knowing when to stop, you should adopt a pragmatic use of time. Set goals for what you want to achieve with your available time, even quite small blocks of study time, and try to stick to your plans even though great areas of your ignorance become apparent in the course of your work. You should also resist the temptation to re-allocate time to esoterica.

Learning in a small group

The setting of your own goals and the monitoring of your progress which are components of self-directed learning, have to occur in a situation which has its own constraints. The education programme which you are entering requires you to work as a member of a small group. This will provide a wide variety of benefits, but will add to your responsibilities. As I have already said, your goals must be compatible with those of your group, and you will be expected to accept responsibility for the learning of the other members of your group as well as your own.

For groups to be functionally effective, the members must be challenging and critical of each other, as well as being supportive. Criticism can only be usefully exchanged when there is an atmosphere of trust, and it takes time for most groups to develop this trust. This happens more quickly when group members are concerned not with the question, 'Can I trust them?' but rather with the question, 'Am I behaving in a way that shows they can trust me?'.

Trust must go beyond the group however. You will be happier and more successful if you trust the intent of the people who run the programme. Great efforts are made to help students in any kind of difficulty. However, the school has a responsibility which overrides its responsibility to its students. Its graduates must not fail in their competence, reliability and honesty, as they deliver care in the future. Of course, any medical school has this responsibility, but here you are asked to share it, and you should not condone or ignore incompetence, unreliability or dishonesty in your peers.

As a member of a group, you will almost certainly find yourself sometimes behaving in ways which do not help the group's functioning. Even the most skilled and experienced group members have lapses. You will find yourself being defensive of your ideas and of yourself. Of course, there are many ways of expressing defensiveness. Sometimes it takes the form of immediate counter-attack. 'I don't agree with you' quickly becomes, 'You're wrong' and then, 'So what's your problem?'. A more muted counter-attack is the affected surprise, 'Nobody ever told me that before'. The defence of prior knowledge becomes, 'I knew you were going to say that'. You may meet people who will tell you that their angry and argumentative response to criticism is due to former experience in 'academic debate'. You may find it difficult to resist the temptation of bolstering your apparent strength by showing up others' weaknesses and avoiding your own areas of weakness. Common ways of doing this are to ask questions which demonstrate knowledge rather than a desire for knowledge, and to project an image of composure which is a veneer on confusion and trepidation. I believe that it is impossible for most people, students and faculty members alike, to avoid such behaviour completely. But you should try to minimize it and be alert for when it happens, so that you can try to identify the reasons for it and ask yourself why it was necessary for you to behave in that way.

You will share the responsibility of evaluation of all the members of your group. It is sometimes said that evaluation by peers becomes too personal, and a matter solely of liking or disliking. You should remember that performance is being measured, not the person. However, the school's objectives require an evaluation of some aspects of performance which are very personal, and discussions of personality often become inevitable. Degrees of liking and disliking among group members are not relevant issues for evaluation, but the attributes of both the observer and the observed which are the basis for these feelings are relevant. A form called Individual Group Member Assessment is included in your manual to guide you in assessing your own and your peers' performance. The roles of the student, tutor, and senior mentor in relation to evaluation are also given in your manual.

Formerly, if you worked as individuals, nobody else suffered if you were unpunctual or irresponsible in any other way. Now your group will be directly affected by such behaviour. The demands of responsible professional conduct apply to you now as a result, and you cannot look on your time in medical school as time to make gradual adaptations in behaviour. If you were formerly unpunctual or unreliable or uncooperative in any way, you will be expected to change rather abruptly.

Setting goals
By being here you have all accepted the school's objectives, so the goals I am talking about are those which go beyond, or are additional to, these. Any individual goals will have to be compatible with those of the school and of the tutorial group you are working in.

When you think about this, try to think about all areas of your life; about how your being in medical school will affect your family and your friendships. Do not minimize the stresses which will be put on them: start now to plan how you are going to protect what is important to you.

I would urge you not to get totally immersed in the world of medicine. If you are to meet the school's objectives you will have to be able to sense the needs of the community. You will not be able to do this if you are out of touch with all but the medical community. You should also be sure to safeguard time for mental and physical recreation. Students here work very hard, even compulsively, and 'time off' all too often disappears. Self-directed learning can turn into an enslavement by one's own demands and fears.

Sometimes it is easier to make a start by setting negative rather than positive goals. Most of you have probably seen things you did not like in the health care system, or if you have not you certainly will. From your experiences you can probably identify behaviour you do not want to lapse into or adopt, and situations you want to avoid. Keep your individual goals under constant review. As your knowledge and experience increase, the nature of your goals should change accordingly, perhaps to be defined more precisely, perhaps to be adapted, or perhaps to be completely replaced. Do not limit yourself by getting locked into your first goals.

The ability to identify goals for yourself is very much a matter of practice. Many of you who have not had to do this often may be feeling quite threatened by this talk of personal objectives. You may not have any special goals that you are aware of, and be perfectly content to accept the school's objectives without expansion or elaboration. That is quite acceptable for now, but you should certainly develop specific plans to meet your own interests and needs as you proceed through the programme.

This programme will, to a large extent, be for each of you what you make it. You should not be concerned with just getting through but in getting the most out of the opportunities available to let you develop in ways best suited to your temperament, skills and needs. In addition, you should do what you can to make the experience the best it can be for your classmates. To do this, you will have to get involved with the programme and with your peers. They need you.

II. Students' reactions

Reactions of a student from a conventional undergraduate programme
Before I was asked to contribute to this paper, I had done quite a bit of thinking about the changes which I have had to make in my methods of learning since coming to medical school, after completing an honours programme in biology at this university. There are four different kinds of adaptation which I can identify. They are the changes necessary in moving from a research-oriented approach to a more practical and applied one, the changes necessary in the style of studying, the need to develop the ability to approach, on my own, subjects about which I know nothing, and the need to develop greater integrative skills. I will describe my experience in relation to each of these in the following paragraphs.

In my undergraduate programme, emphasis had been placed on the ability to analyse and criticize original research, to understand the importance of experimental design and to weigh conclusions drawn from results. I was therefore used to approaching a problem by going to the most recently published original research, and although I quickly realized that this led me in medical studies to too much detail and too narrow a view, I found that I did not completely overcome this tendency until the end of Phase II (*the second ten weeks of the programme*). By that time, I had learned where to look for good review articles or summaries. By going to these first, I saved time which would otherwise have been spent on tracking down original papers, and avoided the tendency to go into too much detail. I also found that I had become comfortable in accepting that I could not get a detailed knowledge of all I was studying. Although my undergraduate education did make this adaptation necessary, at the same time it helped me to make it. My knowledge of biology enabled me quickly to conceptualize possible mechanisms, and gave me the confidence to make good guesses as a starting point for exploration.

In the lecture system which I had been used to as an undergraduate, I had been accustomed to reading relevant material quickly before each lecture, and having the identifying and sorting out of what was essential done by the lecturer. Now I spend much more time on reading about a topic. I re-read several times and underline, before I can be sure that I have isolated all the important concepts. I felt reasonably confident about this by the middle of Phase II. Each student works independently to some extent, but our tutorial groups are crucial to us for checking that our concepts are accurate. As an example, in my present group we posed the question of what two laboratory tests are the most important in the initial diagnosis of diabetes. All the group members researched the same area and acquired the same information, but individually had different perceptions of what considerations were relevant in answering the question. A very lively hour of information exchange, challenge and rethinking was necessary, before all the group members had agreed on the answer and on the qualifying statements attached to it. This kind of exchange is most fruitful when the question of what information is essential is raised, when the information and the concepts generated are confirmed and when individuals' contributions are integrated and augmented. I have found that in only one of my tutorial groups did these benefits not result. They are dependent on the attitudes of the group members and their willingness to share their knowledge and question their own and other people's concepts.

From my undergraduate education, I was also used to being introduced to new subjects by lecturers. I did not have to worry about defining the dimensions of the subject or identifying a starting point. Now I have to be prepared to start alone on any appropriate new subject. The approach which I have used and which took me until the end of Phase II to get comfortable with, is to ask simple questions, one at a time, at the start. The questions gradually get more complex as the framework of a concept is built up and then filled in. This takes time and a lot of patience, when the urge is to find out everything at once. It suits my style to get some knowledge of the anatomy of the relevant area or organ as a starting point. This provides me with visual references for further information. More recently, I have been finding that the embryological development of relevant tissue or organs is often my best starting point.

The final adaptation which I made was the easiest. I had to accept responsibility for integrating knowledge, which formerly I could rely on lecturers to do. Indeed, I can remember specific examples of this happening in lectures and many pieces immediately falling into place. For me, it was enough to know at the start of the medical programme that this was necessary. I was able, with deliberate effort, to make connections to expand my understanding, and to relate new knowledge to my pre-existing knowledge. I try to do this with the information I have gathered in individual study before tutorials, and the work of the tutorial reinforces this.

Now, at the end of Phase III (40 weeks made up of four units of organ system study), I am able to see what changes I have made. I find the increased degree of my personal involvement in my studies to be fun and I enjoy the chance to be a detective. The need to defend one's information and one's concepts makes them more of personal possessions.

Reactions of a student with previous unconventional, self-directed educational experience
I was an independent ('freewheeler') student long before arriving at McMaster Medical School. My high school — Nohant School — comprised a band of 40 teenage outlaws. These renegades from convention abandoned their respective schools and established a small, private sanctuary of learning, which they ran, without benefit of budget, building or paid faculty, for five school years. Nohant 'hired' a faculty of 25 volunteer teachers from the community at large, established headquarters in a public library, and held classes most evenings in private homes. Each of the 40 students carried one-fortieth of the responsibility for the smooth function and good government of the operation, and 100 per cent of the responsibility for the implementation and success of their own personal learning programme. No student was obliged to show up at all, ever. No student — this, by decree — had to do anything he or she didn't want to. The dictum we came to prefer, as we matured philosophically, was that all students at Nohant were free to do anything they *did* want to do. Mostly as a result of the unfettered enthusiasm of our staff and students, and the excitement generated by the adventure, much was accomplished, both in terms of the growth and development of the participants as human beings, and in terms of cold, hard, provincially recognized academic accomplishment.

My undergraduate programme, Integrated Studies at the University of Waterloo, Ontario, amounted again to a licence to do as I pleased. The programme was twice the size of Nohant, but was still completely student run, through weekly school meetings and committees, whose jurisdiction extended to the hiring and firing of faculty, dispensing a considerable budget, student programmes, and other issues bearing on the operation and growth of the programme. The only compulsory requirement was that each student submit a summary, by the end of the year, of the year's academic activities. Otherwise, students were free to 'go where they would, do as they wished': they could study the violin in Vienna, literature in London, biology, philosophy, journalism or mathematics. One of my own years in Integrated Studies was spent in Montreal, with Dr Hans Selye, founder of the theory of stress in human disease, and the year following I became a co-worker in an amateurish but successful attempt to develop an injectable treatment for malignant tumours in rats.

One of the first things that struck me on arrival at McMaster was that adjusting to independent learning could still be difficult for students from conventional programmes. Seeing it again reminded me very much of my days at Nohant, and the growing pains we all went through. New students invariably suffered a period we called the doldrums. Realizing that one was in a school which allowed unqualified freedom to do as you pleased made the idea of doing absolutely nothing absolutely irresistible for a time. Many a carefree afternoon was spent languishing in the sweet clutches of freedom. Over endless cups of coffee, and uproarious conversation, we toasted the end to repression, to being told what to do. Then, for each person in turn, came 'the morning after' of the victory celebration. This was the day on which the individual awakened to the realization that doing nothing was not freedom; that in fact we were being controlled by our need to prove our autonomy . . . defining ourselves by the hold our enemy no longer had on us. That is, we still saw ourselves as what we weren't, but not by what we were. This was the moment of truth; when we had to accept as *proven* that no one could tell us what to do. We then buried once and for all our vanquished enemy, disposed of the half empty coffee cups, revved up the generator and got down to work. The successful 'freewheelers' came to understand that being truly free meant doing things because one was free to. With the externally imposed structure, reward and punishment systems gone, we resolved to build our own internal structures, and become genuinely self-directed. A.S. Neill recognized the 'pre-free' or doldrum stage in students at Summerhill School in England. He estimated that it took from three months to ten years for his students to become successful self-starters.

During my first several months at McMaster the often-voiced complaint from some students was that there wasn't enough work to do. They felt that, having been geared up in anticipation, medical school was providing nothing to sink one's teeth into. It was, in short, too easy, which made some students very uneasy. What these newcomers to independent learning didn't know was that while they were going through their 'pre-free' period, waiting to be *told* what to do, other, more autonomous students (from whatever background) were having the most arduous, busy time of their lives, having fired their *own* starter's pistol. This was partly a function of some students having no background in biology or physiology, and being panic motivated. But more so a reflection of the two different attitudes; the one, fostered by conventional education, of awaiting orders from the top in order to begin learning; the other, engendered by successful independent programmes, or acquired naturally, of self-motivation.

So, according to A.S. Neill's schedule, somewhere between three months and ten years post-entry begins the process of self-actualization. Another stage often intervenes, sometimes at Nohant and often at McMaster. This is the penance stage. It occurs when a remorseful student decides that he has just frittered away several weeks/months of precious time in unproductive leisure. By this time he has accumulated a veritable mountain of unresolved, merciless guilt. As a form of penance, the guilt-ridden student makes a solemn and serious vow to work himself to the bone, burn the midnight oil, put his nose to the proverbial grindstone. The problem arises when this otherwise valuable energy resource is harnessed to some almost fruitless task. McMaster students, for example, may sign Lehninger's *Textbook of Biochemistry* out of the library, and attempt to 'work through it', chapter by chapter. This allows one to trade suffering for guilt. It seldom, however, results in much productive learning. Proponents of problem-based learning claim, and I agree with them, that in order to be of real value, knowledge should ideally be gained in solving a specific problem; then, in order to be retained, this knowledge should be exercised in solving other problems. The trouble with chapter reading as a learning style is that it involves trying to gobble up reams of information passively, without actively using this information. Instead of having questions, and searching out the answers which are thereby incorporated into one's thoughts, it means working through pages and pages of 'answers', never having asked the questions to begin with. Certainly there may be something to gain in chapter reading, but as the 'penance' worker often finds, as he throws down Lehninger in despair, there is no limit to the information one can find to 'gobble' and one can very easily choke on it. A certain amount of chapter study is useful in acquiring background, say in a new area. Few people go through our system without it (not even freewheelers). But this is distinct from the penance activity of throwing oneself headlong at some impossible task in the name of working hard, rather than working well.

Barbara asked me to offer comment on the adjustment of students in the programme, and myself, to McMaster medicine. The biggest problem I've faced at McMaster is the loneliness of the long distance runner. For many of us, it has been a dawn-until-midnight routine from day one — six days a week, 11 months a year. Not every minute is brain-breaking, but it's all medicine, without let-up. I've all but run out of friends, abandoned hope of ever falling in love, and am now a little uncomfortable in the company of 'outsiders'. It has become hard to let loose, relax, and be frivolous and warm with people, having become so accustomed to 'life in the monastery'. As Rod says, when one finally takes a night off to see an outsider, one unconsciously begins taking a health history and physical, which is the relationship we have become most comfortable with. This skill has a limited value in social settings.

I don't know if anything could change all this; with all the long hours and seclusion I still don't feel I've accomplished anything *near* the learning I should have so far. But some days the loneliness and struggle make me nauseous. At other schools, students face exam pressures and the endless boredom of lectures, none of which I could ever tolerate, nor do I see these as constructive. But McMaster can be its own brand of hell on earth, and when you stand alone it's just you and the flames. Loneliness and anxiety are rampant in the programme. I guess really they are in life also.

Lauren was saying the other day that two years in the programme changes a person; that by the end you almost don't recognize yourself. She claims to feel uneasy at the morning mirror, not knowing whose teeth she's apparently brushing. The greatest personal changes for me were induced by working in tutorial groups. Tutorials are the learning focus of McMaster medicine. In them, five students and a tutor 'problem-solve' each other to near delirium. With several days' preparation, the group works through explaining a given health history to the best of their acquired knowledge.

One doesn't win favour in tutorials by saying nothing. Nor will a group tolerate a member who dominates the proceedings. Somewhere between the two extremes lies the elusive happy medium. Groups are much like life, in which, as Martin Buber says, 'Secretly, and bashfully, every person waits for a yes'. I have wanted, like a bear wants honey, my groups to recognize my thinking as right and correct, and praise my memory. Performing well in tutorial is all that has mattered for me at McMaster. From this I derive all my sense of self-worth and personal value. I don't sleep well the night before, and do so the night after only if all goes well in tutorial. In a programme which allows little or no time for love or friendship on an extra-curricular basis, the tutorial group becomes co-workers, friends, lovers, family — the individual's only mirror of himself for two long years. The group's bi-weekly meetings come to represent much more than mere academic forums. Whether the group likes you as a person on a particular day determines to a large extent whether you like yourself in any given week. For example, the other night I had dinner with my friend (- - - - - - - -). An otherwise jolly and warmhearted person, on this particular evening he was the picture of melancholy. Something was bothering him, and it hurt so much he couldn't even discuss it. Twice over dinner his eyes grew red, and I sensed him holding back tears. Later that evening, some checking around turned up the problem. Someone in (- - - - - - - -)'s group, whom he had looked on as a friend, had commented in the day's 'evaluation session' that he had made them feel uncomfortable since the group began. He was devastated. And N.B., my friend is no fragile youngster — he's a graduate in engineering, been all but married once or twice, and even lifts weights. In 'real life' the comment wouldn't have flattened my weight-lifting friend, but in the vulnerable, 'need love' condition of a McMaster medical student, it was nearly lethal.

Another thing Lauren commented on the other day was that tutorials challenge one to be maximally assertive and minimally aggressive. I agree strongly (but nicely). My foremost goal in tutorials has been to learn to speak with such self-assurance and cogency of thought that no one would dream of contradicting me before thinking twice, yet at the same time to perform in such a way as not to make any other group member feel intimidated, put-down, or inferior. This is the real art of tutorial success: to be respected, and at the same time liked by one's peers. The assertive/aggressive balance is a delicate one in the best of groups where the sensitive issue of what one knows and has learned is always in the air. The need to develop confidence in myself has made me more assertive than ever before in my life. The need to be liked prohibits building up my own sense of worth at the expense of someone else's feelings. In a group without trust, this is an impossible challenge.

One of my groups consisted of five almost incompatible students, with a thoroughly disreputable tutor. The tutor intimidated everyone, and played our feelings mercilessly one against the other. Why should he, one might wonder: but why are people ever unkind? A stronger group might have weathered him, but ours broke ranks. It established a mood of every man for himself from the beginning, and what both fascinated and annoyed me was that the quality of the tutor had such an impact on how the students related to one another. This tutor has had a similar effect on all his groups. Winning his approval meant joining in a game of mental fencing in which, by fair or foul, one was meant to jab at one's opponents, and if possible render them sensitive and off balance by hurting their feelings. A group which might otherwise have stood a chance was lost in constant one-up-manship and scrapping. Twice the group met in private to consider why they weren't getting along. Both times we recognized that somehow the tutor had undermined our sense of trust in each other. This helped immeasurably, although it was too little, too late.

I consider this trust issue an important one in all my groups. It means a lot, for example, for someone to say in the first meeting of a group, something to the effect that they feel a group is a place where one should never be afraid to be wrong, because we're all here to help each other in any way we can to maximize the learning experience. This sets an important tone — to have the thought expressed is crucial. It is not enough to assume that everyone knows this. It is similar in my mind to dealing with patients, who, like students, are in a very vulnerable position. On the evening of an operation, it's important for a patient to be told that events are planned for the day after the operation. The patient knows he will probably wake up after the operation is over, but it is often important to hear from someone else what one already knows. Groups which don't establish an atmosphere of trust, and don't respect each individual's need to be right once in a while, don't work, in my experience.

What I have forgotten to say, but naively assumed the reader knows, is that despite my complaints, the learning and growth I have undergone at McMaster have provided among the most satisfying moments of my life to date. I am feverishly loyal to the programme, and consider it one of the most profoundly successful educational experiments ever.

III. Graduates' opinions

The question of whether the public can be assured of the competence of graduates of programmes in which student autonomy in learning exists, is usually posed in relation to professional education. The immediacy of the question is tempered in Canadian medical education because the licence to practise medicine is awarded by a body independent of the universities and is based on performance in a written examination and successful completion of at least one year of internship. It is still, of course, of vital interest to those involved in medical education at McMaster to know how well the programme has met its objectives and the needs of its graduates in practice.

McMaster graduates, who have experience of no formal written examinations while in the programme, have performed close to the national average in the licensing examination. Their success in being accepted by the internship and residency programmes of their choice is also similar to that of graduates of the other Canadian medical schools (Woodward and Neufeld, 1978). Studies of their performance in postgraduate training in comparison to graduates of other medical schools are in progress. Some information is already available on our graduates' assessment of the programme in the light of their current activities, and of their own preparedness for internship in comparison to that of graduates of other schools.

Surveys of two classes (1972 and 1975) have been completed with a response rate of 92 per cent (Woodward *et al*, 1979). Approximately half of the members of these classes have completed their postgraduate training and are in practice. In response to questions about their preparedness for internship in relation to their peers from other schools, they reported themselves, as would be hoped and expected, as better prepared in areas emphasized by the McMaster programme such as independent learning, problem-solving and self-evaluation. They found themselves to be generally equally prepared in patient management skills (ambulatory patient care, in-patient care, follow-up care, care of social and emotional problems, emergency care, preventative care, diagnostic skills, and therapeutic management). Somewhat surprisingly, perhaps, they found themselves also equally prepared in knowledge (basic science, behaviour science, clinical science and public health). Thus, although our medical students frequently express fears that they will be less prepared than graduates from other schools, the members of these surveyed classes found, in general, that they were at least as well prepared to begin an internship programme.

In another series of questions, these graduates were asked to assess, in the light of their current activities, the emphasis given in their undergraduate medical education to a variety of areas including those mentioned in the preceding paragraph. In general, no area was found to have been overemphasized. The majority of respondents found that 17 out of the 20 areas had received appropriate emphasis, and that 3 areas (practice management skills, therapeutic management and drug effects) needed greater emphasis. In responding to these questions, the graduates were not asked to make comparisons with other programmes.

The graduates identified self-directed learning, along with early patient contact, small group tutorials, independent study, flexibility and problem-based learning, as a strength of the programme. Lack of definition of core material and the anxiety level created were reported to be its deficiencies. It is interesting that it appears that these strengths and deficiencies are related, in that lack of precise definition of core material and consequent anxiety may be a necessary price to pay for self-directed learning.

We do not know how graduates from other medical schools would have answered these questions, but the results do show that the members of these classes do not, in general, perceive themselves to have been disadvantaged in any way by the emphases of our programme, and that they recognize considerable advantages in having been able to direct their own learning.

9. Preparing for Contract Learning

Mary Buzzell and Olga Roman, *School of Nursing, McMaster University*

> A learning contract is a document drawn up by a student and his instructor or advisor, which specifies what the student will learn, how this will be accomplished, within what period of time, and what the criteria of evaluation will be. (Donald, 1976, p 1)

In this chapter, we propose to examine the use of the learning contract in the fourth and final year of the bachelor of science nursing programme at McMaster University. We will address ourselves to the implications this process has for changes in the roles of teachers and learners. The chapter includes a description of a workshop designed to help teachers and students become accustomed to the changes in orientation and practice entailed by the use of learning contracts; one student's personal account of her reaction to the use of learning contracts over a period of time; and finally a case study illustrating the importance of the consultation which occurs in the development of a contract and the learning which can take place at this stage.

We believe that a major educational goal is to help students gain skills in learning. Contracting for learning contributes to this goal by making learning personal for each student through involving him or her in decision-making regarding the formulation of learning goals, learning methods and evaluation. It also heightens motivation by placing responsibility for learning on the student.

The following description from the course calendar provides an indication of the overall aims of the fourth year course:

> Increasing emphasis is placed on interpersonal skills, independent learning and leadership qualities. Learning takes place in an environment conducive to openness and sharing amongst faculty and students. Emphasis on small group tutorials and self-directed learning promotes the development of self-evaluation skills and problem-solving abilities. This necessitates students taking responsibility for identifying their learning needs and, therefore, utilizing resources and experiences appropriately. Development of interpersonal skills is based on a sensitivity towards people, awareness of personal potential, and willingness to grow and share with others. (Nursing at McMaster: The BScN Programme School Calendar, p 3)

McMaster University School of Nursing
An adviser self-diagnostic tool for student-centred learning in Year IV
(for new advisers)
RELEVANT COMPETENCIES

Adviser: ....

	SELF-RATING			
	Don't know	Weak	Fair	Strong
I. SELF CONCEPT				
A. *Climate* Do I have the ability to:				
1. create a climate of trust and mutuality between teacher and student, as joint inquirers.				
2. understand the differences in assumptions about learning and the skills required for learning under teacher-directed learning and self-directed learning and the ability to explain these to others.				
B. *Diagnosis of Needs* Do I have the ability to:				
1. involve student in self-diagnosis of learning needs, personal and professional, and in the development of a learning contract.				
C. *Evaluation of Learning* Do I have the ability to:				
1. help students develop criteria for evaluating their learning experiences.				
2. help learner to measure his/her own competencies.				
3. Initiate opportunity for feedback from students regarding his/her faculty performance.				

	SELF-RATING			
	Don't know	Weak	Fair	Strong
II. EXPERIENCES				
Do I have the ability to:				
1. draw on past experiences of learner and relate to new learnings.				
III. READINESS				
Do I have the ability to:				
1. utilize students' interests as learning priorities.				
IV. STUDENT-CENTRED LEARNING CONCERNS				
Do I have the ability to:				
1. facilitate learning by focusing on the students rather than subject matter.				
2. diagnose and consult with peers regarding student-centred learning problems.				

Figure 1

Adapted from Knowles, M S (1970)

Introducing the use of learning contracts

The use of learning contracts has profound implications for the role of academic staff. The relationships between staff and students becomes critical as the role of teachers shifts from that of being content experts to that of being learning facilitators. This implies that teachers become learners alongside their students, and that through their interdependence mutual discovery and decision-making are developed.

Carrying out the contracting process necessitates planned staff development. Many academic staff members come to us knowing only the traditional teaching role, believing that all information lies with the teacher, and that rewards are received for the efficient preparation and presentation of content. Expressions of anxiety, fear and inadequacy in making the transition to the role of learning facilitator, are common. These feelings bring forth such expressions as: 'I'll need help'; 'It's hard to switch to a new way'; 'I feel my role as a teacher will disappear'; 'It's uncomfortable to think of myself as a learner'.

Acknowledging these concerns, we developed a one-day workshop to help teachers and students with the contracting process. Contributory objectives were to:

1. increase understanding of the characteristics of the adult learner and the implications for teaching and learning
2. understand the steps of the learning contract
3. apply course standards to individual learning contracts: development of a learning contract
4. develop an appreciation of the teacher as a learning facilitator.

In preparation for the workshop, each participant was given two articles on adult education which highlighted the following areas: self-concept, experience, readiness to learn, and orientation of maturing adult learners. Teachers were asked, as well, to complete an individual assessment tool which provided us with baseline data for workshop planning (see Figure 1).

The atmosphere set for the day was crucial, as this was to become the model for future work with students, and we believe that students, given the right circumstances, will grow and behave responsibly. Exercises were built in to promote the sharing of ideas and concerns, and to assist participants in dealing with them.

Our workshop outline was as follows:

9.00 - 10.30 am *The Adult as a Learner:* implications for teaching and learning.

Methods: Presentation of material associated with pre-reading on the characteristics of adult learners.
Participants' questions and concerns arising out of pre-reading and related to Year IV learners.

10.30 - 10.45 am Stretch break

10.45 - 12.00 noon	*The Learning Contract:* the how, where, when and why in Year IV.
Methods:	Begin the development of a learning contract and share with peers for clarity and relevance to objectives set: faculty/student dyads. Illustration of two completed Year IV learning contracts with different learning objectives.
12.00 - 1.00 pm	Lunch with Year IV learners
1.00 - 3.45 pm	*Learning Together*
Methods:	Discussion of roles, responsibilities and learning objectives. Faculty as facilitators — implications for faculty and students. Dyads: getting to know each other as people and as learners.
3.45 - 4.00 pm	*Wrap-up:* reactions to the day.

Feelings and concerns flowed easily during the day in our community of learners. Both sets of learners had entered a critical beginning with realistic visions of how they wanted to work together.

Some of the most meaningful comments arising out of the discussions were:

- ☐ 'How will I know if I am a good learning facilitator?'
- ☐ 'What if I can't help the learner meet her learning needs?'
- ☐ 'If I wait for readiness to learn, how can I ensure course completion?'
- ☐ 'What other ideas can you give me for building a learner's past experiences?'
- ☐ 'How can I improve my ability to give constructive feedback?'
- ☐ 'How do you involve students in contributing to their evaluation so that standards are maintained?'

These questions reflected the struggle involved in coming to grips with the contract learning process. Our purpose was to lend support and to provide experience in the development of the learning contract.

Acknowledging the fact that the learning contract is the major learning tool in Year IV, practice in its use was built in. Principles of contracting were reviewed and participants worked on developing a learning contract. This process was individual initially, followed by work in faculty/student pairs, while workshop leaders acted as resources. Through this experience the students learned to help one another — a helping model to be continued in their future work. The room became alive with self-help activity as contracts were shared, exchanged, and refined. At this point, two completed learning contracts were presented on overhead projectors for discussion, to illustrate how the melding of individual and Year IV goals could be achieved (see, for example, Figure 2).

SAMPLE LEARNING CONTRACT

Student . . . . : Maureen D.   Clinical Setting . . . . . : Doctor's Office
Course . . . . : N4J7/4K7   Date . . . . : 19 Sept – 8 Dec 1977

OBJECTIVES	STRATEGIES AND RESOURCES	EVIDENCE	CRITERIA AND MEANS FOR EVALUATION
Develop knowledge about the normal anatomy, physiology of the female reproductive system in the pregnant woman and to apply this knowledge to the development of skill in the physical assessment of the pregnant woman Eg – palpate fetal position, – auscultate fetal heart, – measure fundal height. *Modification of Objectives* To develop knowledge of psychosocial and normal physiology of the pregnant woman. To increase skill in physical examinations, interviewing and teaching of the pregnant woman.	1. *Books* – Literature A & P Interviewing books 2. *People* Office nurse Office physician Adviser 3. *Videotapes* Reproductive system Interviewing Pre-natal teaching	1. Written summary of anatomy and physiology in chart form with a verbal explanation of content. 2. Direct observation of physical assessment skills by clinical staff. 3. Tapes of interviews.	1. Evaluation of charts by my adviser as to: i) Degree of clarity and comprehensiveness of charts. ii) Degree of understanding of subject matter as illustrated by my oral explanation of content of charts. 2. Evaluation by myself and a clinical staff member of physical assessment and interviewing skills according to following criteria: i) Degree of accuracy in taking physical measurements and assessment of fetal position. ii) Degree of confidence shown in approaching physical assessment. 3. Taped interviews and direct observation to be evaluated according to the following criteria: i) What degree of confidence is demonstrated? ii) Do I demonstrate ability in assisting the patient to find ways of dealing with her health problem? iii) Do I give appropriate information to the patient about her health problem? (including resources available.)

Legend for Evaluation of All Criteria

to a great extent	above average	average	some-what	not at all

Figure 2

The strategy and resource column of the learning contract was the subject of some dispute. Traditionally, teachers assumed responsibility for designing learning strategies; now they were expected to assist students in the development of their approaches and outcomes for learning. Teachers now needed to give thought to the fact that learners on their own 'hop and skip' around to meet their learning needs.

The word 'evaluation' has a very strong emotional component. Because of this we gave each person an opportunity to experience positive and negative evaluation. Each had responsibility for receiving and giving feedback about the learning contracts developed. Some past experiences about evaluation were shared:

□ 'My experience with evaluation meant another person giving me bad news.'
□ 'Evaluation seldom helped me, more often destroyed me.'
□ 'I rarely knew what I was being evaluated on.'
□ 'My evaluations were all so one-way and so final.'
□ 'I've never had input into my own evaluation in my life.'

These comments reflect the low value placed on learner growth and development and highlight the fact that imposing evaluation often leads to resistance. Evaluation, in terms of the contracting process, means redefining learning gaps, emphasizing assets rather than deficits. This led to more practical questions about the final column of the learning contract — criteria and means for validating evidence. 'What am I, as a facilitator, really going to evaluate?' 'How can I evaluate the student's learning objectives?' 'Should I be evaluating the student's learning objectives if they are hers?' 'Has the student the ability to evaluate her own performance?' These questions reflected additional concerns about learning achievement.

Through the development of the learning contract, some of these questions were answered. Participants learned that mutually set goals must be evaluated by both teacher and learner throughout the experience.

The responsibility for assigning a final grade weighed heavily on our participants. Fears were expressed about lowering professional standards, fairness to students, and the handling of discrepancies between students and faculty. A change in self-concept from that of *teacher* to that of *learning facilitator* requires an emphasis on what is happening to the student rather than on what the teacher is doing. Knowles describes the significance of this change, 'I divest myself of the protective shield of myself as an authority figure and expose myself as me — an authentic human being' (Knowles, 1975, p 33). These thoughts were the basis for the 'Learning Together' experience with teacher and student dyads. Time together was spent exploring roles and relationships and mutual expectations.

Within the dyads there was discussion about one another's learning styles and learning needs. The sharing of expectations of one another for their regular meetings was begun. As this was to be only the initiation of a continuing helping relationship, learners and teachers were left with important questions to consider on the ingredients needed for a helping relationship:

- ☐ 'How can we develop a trusting relationship over the year?'
- ☐ 'What can we establish to promote clear, open communication?'
- ☐ 'How can we acknowledge each other's interests and feelings respectfully?'
- ☐ 'Are my actions promoting growth in a non-threatening manner?'

A student's view of contract learning

The student's view of contract learning which follows illustrates both the intensity of the initial struggle to come to terms with the demands of contract learning and the eventual reward in terms of increased awareness of the processes of learning.

Our 'bible' was Knowles' *Self-Directed Learning* (1975), with its concept of learning through self-direction. Our major learning tool and constant companion was the 'contract' which we each had to write. In the beginning it was very painful. Our teachers were learning about self-direction and contracting at the same time. Anxiety levels ran high, causing many fears and rude remarks about contracts. At one point, writing the contract became our major assignment for the year! That is, rather than a means to an end, it became an end in itself. Many, many hours of student and faculty time were wasted that year because we lost sight of the contract as a learning tool and tried, instead, to produce the 'perfect' contract.

As time went on, the process took on new meaning and became easier. We were learning how to learn, not just until we finished our degrees, but forever. 'The problem is that education is not yet perceived as a lifelong process, so that we are still taught in our youth what we ought to know, rather than know how to keep finding out' (Knowles, 1970, p 23). We were learning how to keep finding out, by gaining sufficient insight to know our strengths and weaknesses, setting objectives for correcting the weaknesses, building on the strengths, being aware of the available resources and strategies, and evaluating whether or not we had met the objectives.

Year IV was a joy! Faculty and students, alike, had reached a level of comfort, even affection, with the contract. We had learned to write it with ease and use it with confidence. It had become the indispensable tool it was meant to be, which made our learning uniquely our own. We would be hard put now to sit passively through hours of lectures, for we are 'active' learners. Telling us what we should learn would not go down well, for we are in tune with ourselves and are aware of our learning needs. We set our own pace, for each of us is different, with different life experiences and styles, responsibilities and needs. We are 'mature' learners in the true sense of the word, and we will not stop learning or growing

when we are handed our degrees. This is only the beginning of the rest of
our lives, and we intend to take advantage of the opportunities life offers.
We know how to go about that because we have learned how to learn
through being self-directed.

Becky Jill Hollingsworth

Case study

One example of how a learning contract might be established is shown by
the case of Maureen, a nursing student in the fourth year of the
baccalaureate programme. She completed 13 years of elementary and
secondary schooling, and worked as a secretary prior to entering nursing
as a mature student. She is in her early twenties.

The case study finds Maureen with her adviser in the first week of the
autumn term. Before this first meeting Maureen had reviewed the course
requirements and visited the setting for her clinical placement, a physician's
office. In preparation, she had made an assessment of her learning needs.
This requires the learner to consider both the activities of the clinical area
and the course requirements and reconcile these with her own needs.
Maureen came to the meeting to discuss this and the development of her
learning contract with her adviser. As part of this meeting, her adviser is
responsible for initiating a climate of free communication and support
and providing for freedom of expression. Both student and adviser are
expected to see each other as learners valuing each other's knowledge and
experience; both assume responsibility for the maintenance of this climate.
Maureen's needs determine the nature, content, and scheduling of the
meetings; her adviser acts as a resource person and learning facilitator,
reviewing the relevance of her objectives for the course requirements and
providing an opportunity for later modification or change.

The focus for the initial meetings with her adviser related to her first
objective: to develop knowledge about the normal anatomy and physiology
of the female reproductive system in the pregnant woman, and to apply
this knowledge to the development of skills in the physical assessment of
the pregnant woman.

Maureen's concern related to the achievement of skills in the physical
examination of the pre-natal mother. Her plan was to involve the
experienced clinic nurse in evaluating her knowledge and performance.
But, when she discussed this proposal with the nurse, a conflict arose: the
nurse wanted to focus on the technical details of the examination rather
than the total needs of the patient which Maureen assumed would include
the emotional as well as the physical aspects of patient care. Maureen
wanted to explore alternative ways of meeting her objective with her
adviser. The way they chose to do this was through role playing. Her
adviser assumed the role of the clinic nurse and Maureen was given the
opportunity to express her frustration and try out possible alternatives
for resolving the conflict. The aim of this was to help Maureen understand
her own learning needs and her own feelings before she returned to the

clinical situation and to enhance Maureen's total learning from the incident. Through this process Maureen was helped to identify strengths and weaknesses in herself, in the nurse, and in the situation. She was able then to realize that her objective could not be met with this particular nurse. With continued analysis of this clinical situation, Maureen readjusted her learning focus. Now that she had defined her own strengths more clearly she was able to accept broader learning challenges and reassess her objectives, and was able to seek out an interdisciplinary learning situation with a physician-nurse team in the same office which would be able to meet her objectives more effectively. This required an explicit extension of her objectives beyond physical examination to include both physical and psychosocial aspects, and health teaching.

Consultation with Maureen progressed to the ways in which she could demonstrate the achievement of her learning objectives. She presented evaluation scales which could be used to assess her performance by herself and clinical staff in the physician's office. These related to physical examination, charting, and counselling skills (see Figure 2).

A variety of ways for achieving the knowledge component of her first objective were explored. Maureen rejected the idea of writing another formal paper, of presenting a case study, or of giving a formal seminar; she preferred to do a project that would be creative and stimulating. Her adviser engaged her in a brainstorming session to help her expand the range of projects from which she could select. The result was the development of a number of charts that integrated anatomy and physiology of the reproductive system. (The charts were so simply and creatively developed that they were found valuable for teaching patients, and the staff in the clinic requested that they be left for continued use.)

In addition to this aspect of assessment, an overall course grade is required, and students have the opportunity to negotiate for the grade they are aiming for. Initial discussions regarding grading revealed that Maureen wanted to work towards a 'B' grade. Prior to completion of the term, Maureen was asked to review all her learning, continuous assessments, and course requirements. She was encouraged to examine the modifications made to her learning contract which reflected not only increased knowledge and skills, but creativity and initiative. It was agreed, mutually, that Maureen had achieved an 'A' grade.

This chapter finds us facing the continuing challenge of developing better ways to facilitate learning. Our hope is that you will be inspired to find new ways to stimulate growth in your learners, for we are reminded that 'it is a fact that rarely has there been much attention given to *learning* though there has been an enormous amount of concern about teaching' (Kidd, 1968, p 15).

10. Student Planned Learning

John Stephenson, *Head, School of Independent Study,*
North East London Polytechnic

Background

Since 1974 the School for Independent Study at the North East London
Polytechnic has been helping students to plan and carry out their own
programmes of study up to Diploma and Honours degree level. In all,
over 600 students have been enrolled and many of these have successfully
completed their work. This development arose as a response to a genuine
concern about some basic problems of the nature and purpose of
education generally, and of higher education in particular, and is seen by
its organizers as a possible solution to some of those problems. This
chapter sets out those problems, describes what we do and how we do it,
indicates some of the difficulties we have encountered, and reviews some
of our progress so far.

The educational problems to which the School's work may be a
potential solution are many, and were discussed at great length by the
development team over a period of two years prior to the first enrolment.
A brief summary is given here. First, the changing nature of society has
meant that social practices, moral codes, and personal relationships are
becoming less standardized, with more onus on the individual to establish
his or her own code of practice. A second problem is the changing nature
of employment. Gone are the days when a vocational training could set
someone up for life: such is the rate of technological and economic change
that few people can rely upon doing the same kind of job in the same kind
of way, even five years hence. The critical ingredient nowadays is
adaptability, and the ability to learn.

The third problem is bound up with the traditional view that the
teacher and the subject are both autonomous and self-justifying. Syllabuses
and teaching methods are often determined by the needs of the subject
and the interests of the teacher. Courses are devised for large numbers of
students who are assumed to be identical for educational purposes, with
little effort made to accept each student as a person with something
distinctive to offer with his or her own peculiar starting point and desired
end. Only lip service is paid to a genuine client/consultant view of the
educational service.

The fourth problem is the restricted range of entry to higher education.

In spite of a generation of expansion, still only a small minority is catered for, with the premium on middle-class backgrounds and the ages of 18 to 21. The Polytechnic is situated in an area of London where the tradition of education beyond compulsory school leaving age is the least developed in the country, so an expansion of educational opportunity demanded a radically new approach based on a wide variety of student backgrounds and experiences.

A fifth problem relates to our view of the nature of knowledge and how it advances. All knowledge is provisional, waiting to be challenged, refuted, extended or developed; it advances by constant attempts at refutation which when successful produce further knowledge. Yet most educational practice assumes knowledge to be established. Students are encouraged to acquire, store, classify and use it. If they are involved in any practical activity, it is often aimed at verifying existing knowledge; they are not often encouraged to challenge it. But it is surely more important not only to have the ability to acquire knowledge but to have the ability to formulate problems and to challenge or test formulations as a means of achieving a more sophisticated reformulation. In brief, we rejected the notion that the starting point of education should be the identification and understanding of a body of knowledge, or that the purpose of the course was to take the student on a conducted tour. Such an approach would be unlikely to lead to the development of the kind of independence and autonomy referred to earlier.

A sixth problem was our observation that much existing education required students to be passive, whereas people are quite capable of learning by 'having a go' and learning by mistakes. How could education claim to be helping people to become competent and independent if they were not allowed to experience independence in the learning environment?

The result of our consideration of all these problems was our commitment to method rather than content, and in particular to independent study. Education should enable students to become competent and independent, able to cope with the unfamiliar without dependence upon traditional solutions or on other people. Students should develop these characteristics by practising them on the course itself. Accordingly, the School has no predetermined syllabuses but instead aims to provide opportunities for students to:

1. formulate the problem of their own education and to negotiate their own appropriate programme of study;
2. expose their proposals to rigorous external scrutiny prior to obtaining approval for their programme of study;
3. gain access to appropriate tutorial expertise and resources;
4. demonstrate their achievements;
5. gain public recognition for their work.

Since the School exists within an established institution of higher education, these opportunities are offered within two course structures, the Diploma of Higher Education and the Honours Degree, both validated by the Council for National Academic Awards (CNAA). The Diploma of Higher Education course runs for two years full-time and is equivalent in standard to the first two years of an honours degree. The Honours Degree is a period of one year's further study leading to the award of BA or BSc by Independent Study (Honours)

The Diploma programme

Most of the School's experience has been with students on the Diploma course, so the description which follows relates exclusively to this programme and is presented in terms of the five aims listed above. The Diploma is a terminal qualification in its own right but fits into a general course network in which students can move, if they wish, into other academic vocational courses either immediately or after an interval. It enables students to delay their vocational choice as long as possible. Over 60 Diploma courses have been established since 1974, but so far the North East London Polytechnic Diploma of Higher Education is unique in that it aims to develop general competence, encourages the development of transferable skills, and requires students to demonstrate their competence in both individual and collaborative situations. The programme therefore has two concurrent elements, one in which the student works in his or her own specialism, and another called Central Studies which uses projects and skill workshops to develop general competence in group situations.

1. Student planning

This is the most important educational activity in the programme. Not only does it ensure a student's high commitment to his course, and its great relevance to his or her needs, but it also provides a most valuable educational experience in its own right. An essential element of general competence is the ability to formulate problems and to devise solutions which are then tested. The problem to be formulated is the problem of the student's own education. Planning takes place during the first term and concludes with the completion by the student of a learning contract, or statement as we call it. The statement consists of a signed agreement between the student, the School, and the specialist area, and is amplified in detail by six appendices (see Figure 1).

The statement has three stages. First, Appendices A, B, and C represent the formulation of the student's educational problem as perceived by himself; secondly, D and E represent the proposed detailed educational solution to the problem; and finally, Appendix F represents the basis on which the completion of the solution is to be tested. What follows is a brief description of how they are produced.

STAGE ONE: THE FORMULATION OF THE EDUCATIONAL PROBLEM (A, B, C)

This takes place in the first three or four weeks of the programme. During this period the student is with a group of 15 peers with a personal tutor. Each

---

INDEPENDENT STUDY STATEMENT

Proposed statement by . . . . (student's name)
of a programme of study leading to the award of the Diploma of Higher
Education in the context of his/her present position and intentions.

Appendix A *Experience*
I present here a critical appraisal of my educational and other
experiences.

Appendix B *Present position*
I am able to identify the following areas of knowledge, skills
and experiences which I indicate as strengths/weaknesses and
regard as potentially relevant to the development of my
programme of study.

Appendix C *Intentions*
I am able to identify the following intentions, personal,
academic and vocational on gaining the Diploma.

Appendix D *Knowledge, skills and experience needed*
Consistent with my stated intentions I am currently able to
identify that by the end of my programme of study I will
need to have acquired the following areas of knowledge,
skills and experience.

Appendix E *Proposed programme of study*
In order to acquire the above areas of knowledge, skills and
experience I have formulated the following plans for
individual work and central studies.

Appendix F *Assessment*
In order to demonstrate that I have achieved my targets
I propose the following form of assessment.

Signature of student. . . . .

Signature of personal tutor . . . .

Signature of individual work tutor. . . . .

Approved: Yes/No.   Date of approval/rejection. . . . .

Signature of Clerk to the Validating Board . . . .

Figure 1

appendix is written in sequence and preparation for each lasts about a week.
For Appendix A the task is to encourage the student to feel sufficiently secure
to be able to open up about himself. Use is made of team building exercises to
boost support from peers and develop a cooperative climate for learning.
Students are encouraged to write down their personal histories, focusing
on what seems to them to be important, and to discuss them with their
colleagues and tutors. As often as not, this process of mutual exchange of
experiences and reactions leads to a more thoughtful and penetrating
personal history by the end of the week. Students are able to compare
their own lot with that of others and very quickly find themselves talking
at great length about themselves and in return asking searching questions
of their fellows. The group of 15 frequently divide into sets of four to six
for this activity so that a variety of experiences and reactions is

encountered. The School provides specific inputs such as seminars on the aims of education in general and, in particular, on the value of planning educational experiences and the importance of starting with the student rather than the subject. Wherever possible the activities are made enjoyable and everyone is made conscious of the need to support others. There is no rigid timetable of activities, except on the few occasions when an input is required for the whole year group (eg an introduction to the staff of the Polytechnic's counselling services) which means that groups operate rather like an infant class where the class teacher has the freedom to switch activities to suit the moods and changing needs of the group.

Appendix B is a more analytical version of A: now the student is encouraged to set out his strengths and weaknesses. This is particularly difficult and students find themselves constantly adding to their personal inventories. The pattern of activities is as before with the addition of self evaluation exercises. Tests of specific skills, such as literacy and numeracy, are available but for other less obvious skills group exercises leading to mutual evaluation are used. Access to the Polytechnic's counselling tutors and other specialists is arranged as required. Inevitably there is constant reference back to Appendix A which continues to develop during this phase. Appendices A and B together represent the student's initial self-diagnosis and are the point of reference for everything else. They ensure that decisions about programmes begin precisely at the point where the student actually assumes himself to be, supported by the critical feedback of a variety of his peers and of his tutor.

For Appendix C, access to careers advisers and ideally to specialists in the chosen field is very important. Students are encouraged not only to indicate likely destinations but also to explore the implications of getting there. For instance, a student wishing to become a teacher would need to know the requirements for gaining recognition, the different ways in which it can be achieved, some indication of his preferred route, and to show some understanding of the place his DipHE would have in it. Again, discussions in small peer groups are very useful in helping students to make explicit what it is they want to do. For many of them it is the first time they have been required to think seriously about the future. It is quite legitimate for students to remain doubtful about their intentions provided they are clear about the area of doubt and that it is expressed in such a way as to form a useful basis for educational planning. An example would be 'I wish to work with adolescents but I wish to keep open the options of probation work, teaching, or youth and community work. The implications of keeping these options open are that my Diploma programme should contain . . .'.

Appendix C is a clear statement of intent and represents the completion of the student's initial problem formulation. Together with A and B, he has identified where he is, and where he wants to be. His educational problem is to get from the one to the other.

STAGE TWO: SETTING OUT THE PROPOSED SOLUTION
The student identifies for himself a general field within which he
explores a solution. Activities are arranged to enable him eventually to
state precisely the learning objectives to be achieved (Appendix D), and
the preferred way of achieving them (Appendix E). For instance, a
potential teacher of deaf children would be introduced to those
Polytechnic staff who share the same interest and who have appropriate
experience and expertise. Preliminary background work is begun, schools
for the deaf are visited, practising teachers in the field are interviewed, and
arising from all those discussions, observations, self-assessments of specific
abilities, and negotiations, the student is able to complete D and E with
some confidence. The student's own specialist tutor is crucial in this
activity, acting as adviser, critic, assessor and source of information and
contacts. The contract between them not only spells out the content of
the programme, but also indicates the learning methods, frequency of
tutorial contacts, types and amount of assignments to be completed, and
location and duration of field placements. Together, D and E represent
a syllabus with content, objectives, and learning methods. In the context
of the statement, the syllabus is peculiar to the student, and is devised as
a solution to his own formulated problem.

STAGE THREE: TESTING OF THE SOLUTION
Here the student is required to indicate precisely how he intends to
demonstrate the achievements of his programme. In this he must keep to
the objectives he set for himself in Appendix D. The questions asked by
the assessment board are 'Has this student achieved what is set out in
Appendix D in the manner indicated in Appendix F?', and secondly,
'Has he done so at a level comparable to that which would be expected
of an undergraduate completing the second year of his Honours Degree
course?'. If the answer is 'yes' then a Diploma is awarded; if 'no' then it
is not. Students are encouraged to understand that the more precisely and
unambiguously they state D and F, the more control they themselves have
over their programme. The objectives in D, if carefully defined, represent
the basis of their assessment and the criteria to be applied when judging
them. Normally students are not capable of completing this section in its
entirety until later in their course when their greater experience of the
work enables them to carry out some 'fine tuning'. Nevertheless they are
expected to include in Appendix F some indication of the kind of
product they are aiming for (eg 'a 15,000-word report on some aspects
of the difficulties of preparing educational activities for the deaf, suitable
for the use of teachers training in education for the deaf: this piece of
work will demonstrate my understanding of the knowledge areas and
competence in the skills referred to in D.')

2. Validation of proposals
The School recognizes that before embarking on a course designed by
himself, the student needs to know that what he proposes to do is a valid

programme of study in its own right, and if completed would be worthy of the award of a Diploma. The Polytechnic needs to know that the student's proposed programme can be resourced. Last, and by no means least, the public have a right to feel that the fact that programmes are designed by the students themselves does not mean that they are in some way deficient. Accordingly, a system of validation has been devised. Validation is extremely important to the student: unless his proposal is validated, he does not have a programme of study and there is nothing to assess. Preparation for validation is, therefore, taken very seriously and has the urgency normally associated on other courses with assessment. Most students are able to set out a tentative statement sufficient for them to commence work after only three weeks, and the fully specified statement is submitted for validation after 12 to 14 weeks.

The process of validation has three stages. First, the student's personal and proposed specialist tutors indicate the extent to which they can support the statement. Secondly, the School, by means of an internal validation board, endorses the tutor's view, or otherwise. Thirdly, the School's judgement is exposed to an external validating board. Only when all three have been satisfied is validation complete. The criteria for judgement used internally are published in advance, and are:

1. Do Appendices A and B provide sufficient evidence of critical self-appraisal?
2. Is a sense of direction indicated in Appendix C? Is there an awareness of the implications (vocational and academic) of stated intentions?
3. In Appendix D is there:
   A clear statement of learning objectives which relate to both individual and group work?
   A consistency between these objectives and the goals indicated in Appendix C?
   Sufficient emphasis on content (skills/knowledge) especially in terms of individual work?
   A clear reference to transferable skills in terms of group and individual work?
   Evidence that objectives are sufficiently refined as to be manageable within the context of the programme?
   Sufficient regard for coherence and presentation?
4. In Appendix E is there:
   An overall awareness of the reality of implementing objectives outlined in Appendix D?
   An outline of the substantive elements of individual work?
   A clear statement of commitment to a specified output of work within the individual work context?
   Sufficient indication of the phasing of work in terms of time and emphasis?

Some indication of the nature and frequency of contacts with special interest tutors?

5. In Appendix F is there:

A reference to the skills and knowledge (outlined in D) to be demonstrated via individual work?

An indication of the individual work final product showing sufficient relationship to the above?

When the School's judgement is clear, a sample of the statements is sent to a panel of people outside the Polytechnic who meet together to decide whether the School's judgement is appropriate. As a board they interrogate the School on its judgement, and interview all students whose statements are in some way in doubt, plus a selection of the rest. Once validated, the statement represents a commitment by the Polytechnic to resource the programme and under arrangements agreed with the CNAA becomes the basis for assessment for the award of DipHE.

Members of the board are individuals who, by their status or achievement, represent success in the outside world. It is a deliberate policy that they are not conventional external examiners. At present they consist of an ex-senior civil servant, a retired inspector of education, a business consultant, an architect, a former senior local government official, and a business executive. Preparation for validation is a formidable task for the student and is of considerable educational value. A good deal of effort has to be put into making as explicit as possible the precise nature of the student's educational problem and the proposed solution and into communicating the proposal as clearly as possible. The effect of this is that students are made to be explicit to themselves and to be as clear in their own minds as they can be about what they want to do, why they want to do it, and how they propose to do it. Their commitment to completion of the programme is higher as a consequence. Students begin to learn quickly how to communicate more effectively both orally and in writing, how to analyse complex situations, how to give and receive critical advice, how to support others in group situations, how to set out a problem, and above all how to negotiate their way around a vast bureaucratic institution.

3. Access to resources

With staff planned courses, materials and expertise are assembled before the students arrive. With independent study this is clearly not possible. During the past five years we have developed the following ways of coping with this. With students' specialist studies, the problem is largely one of referral to appropriate areas of the Polytechnic. It is important to establish that the School for Independent Study is located within a large conventional institution with something like 700 full-time academic staff working in eight faculties. Conventional academic and vocational courses are run, and appropriate libraries and specialist facilities are provided. When a student has completed his earlier statement appendices and is able to identify the general area of his specialism, he is referred to the appropriate faculty. Each faculty has a link person who takes responsibility for giving some preliminary advice, and arranges contact with an appropriate specialist tutor. Often tutors have specialisms other than those which they spend most time teaching and such contacts offer useful opportunities for the tutor as well. If both student and tutor are happy to work together, the tutor will help the student with the planning of Appendices D, E and F. When the programme is validated, the tutor will take responsibility for helping the student proceed. On this one-to-one ratio, clearly the tutor cannot see the student for more than one hour or so each week. Much of this tutorial time is spent advising the student on what to read, the lectures to be attended, the placements to be arranged and on reviewing the student's progress so far.

In this way the student is able to use the full range of workshop, laboratory, and lecture provision for other courses. The whole Polytechnic is like a library, to be browsed and used. The important point is that students must always negotiate each access, usually with the help of the specialist tutor. In this way the student is able to use materials and expertise from a variety of different courses and sources as appropriate to his or her own needs. Many students successfully complete programmes of study which are not based on the use of existing courses; but it is crucial that the student should have access to specialist resources and specialist advice. If this is provided in the form of a research activity or a workplace then it is just as useful as an existing course. Three examples illustrate the wide possibilities. One student, interested in politics, was placed with a Member of Parliament for whom he worked as a research assistant; he had an office in Westminster and had regular discussions with his supervisor in the Polytechnic. Another was interested in underwater technology, so worked for British Petroleum in the North Sea and exchanged tutorial material with the Polytechnic by post. A third, interested in the learning difficulties experienced by teenagers when studying mathematics, worked with mathematics teachers in a variety of types of urban school. Existing lectures are only used when it is convenient to do so.

Within the School, different kinds of specialist resource provision are made, covering three main areas. First, there is what we call 'back up' studies which help students brush up on basic skills which they feel have been neglected. These include study skills, reading and writing, numeracy, etc. Secondly, to help students work on projects in collaboration with other students, there are skills workshops covering things like questionnaire design, group interaction skills, report writing, interviewing, information retrieval and processing, problem formulation, etc. Thirdly, there are opportunities for students working in similar specialist areas to work together exploring common intellectual problems, to enable them to place their specialism in a wider context. Students mainly find these resources by their own initiative, but often only after discussion with their personal or project tutor. Provision of resources is of three kinds. There is the 'instant checklist' or handout which can be removed from a resource centre and used as appropriate. Then there is consultancy where individual students or groups of students arrange tutorials with School staff who specialize in helping with particular skills. Thirdly, there are mini-courses, usually running a cycle of six to ten weeks, which students can join as and when appropriate. The staff of the School need to be prepared to vary their work in response to demands and to mount new mini-courses and prepare handouts at short notice.

4. Demonstration of achievement

The School provides opportunities for students to demonstrate their general competence both as individuals and in collaboration with others. For group work, students are randomly put into groups of five and given about eight weeks to demonstrate their ability to collaborate in the formulation of a problem relating to the local community and to use the project to demonstrate mastery of the transferable skills they had identified in Appendix D. Throughout this project, students are supervised by a tutor who is responsible for assessing their performance. Examples of such projects from the 1979 assessment include 'An examination into the problem of lack of caring accommodation for the aged in the Borough of Newham', 'What's wrong with going to the dentist?', 'Investigation into the availability of certain forms of alternative medicine', and 'Safety and security in fairgrounds in relation to their social benefits'. Students submit individual reports on their own participation in the group project, and these are the bases for their assessment.

For their specialist work there is much more variety of practice. The common factor is that students are required to submit 'a product' prepared during the last few weeks of the course which should be capable of demonstrating the achievement of the specialist objectives referred to in Appendix D. Many submit written reports or dissertations, but we have had photographic exhibitions, working models, experimental environments, films, and a prototype motorcycle. From the 1979 list, the following selection gives some indication of the variety: 'Personal growth and awareness skills of use in police work', 'Report on the patterns of tenancy in the Borough of Waltham Forest', 'Publicity campaign for a toy library in Kensal'. 'The Laughter of Woman' (a novel), 'Creative, commercial and still life studio photography', and 'An underwater life support system'. These individual products are assessed first by the student's specialist tutor, and then by a second specialist who has had no previous interest in the student.

5. External recognition

Just as it was necessary to secure public recognition for students' proposals, so it is for their achievements. At the purely practical level, students need a marketable bit of parchment, but they also need the confidence of knowing that the work which they planned and completed is regarded by the academic establishment to be comparable to that of other students on conventional courses. The Polytechnic needs to be satisfied that student-planned work does not lead to a lowering of its educational standards. The School therefore decided to secure for its students the conventional awards of DipHE and BA/BSc.

For Diploma students, details of assessment plans, as validated, are submitted for approval to a meeting of an assessment board constituted in exactly the same way as for any conventional course, including a wide range of external examiners amongst its membership. For individual work, students are required to specify in more detail than was possible in Appendix F precisely what they intend to present and to indicate which of the objectives from Appendix D it will demonstrate. When completed, the work is seen by two internal assessors and a selection is scrutinized by the external examiners with discrepancies ironed out by means of vivas. The greatest difficulty is the identification of level, particularly with there being no opportunity for ranking performance with an arbitrarily defined cut-off point. Each case has to be judged on its merits. Further, there is often no direct comparison between a student's field of study and a conventional field. A glance at the list of topics above indicates that. The solution we use is to require clearly defined statements of objectives to be agreed in advance by the student, his tutor and the assessment board; to choose as a second assessor someone who has had experience of working and assessing standards on honours degree courses in similar fields; and to have a range of externally appointed examiners covering between them most fields of study. The critical question asked is, 'Is the student working at a level at which you would expect a second-year undergraduate to be working?'. By some mystical process, widely used and respected throughout the academic world, such experienced examiners know by the 'feel of their bones' whether the work is up to standard. This 'bonesmanship', as we call it, is at least supported by evidence related to clearly specified objectives, which cannot be said of all of the assessment practice in the academic world.

One interesting by-product of this exercise is that tutors who have been assessing students for years are having to articulate to others outside their specialism the criteria they use when judging whether work is of first class honours or pass degree standard, and the subtleties of demarcation between upper and lower seconds. We hope some day to publish our accumulated experiences in this.

For group work, the randomly established groups are required, after about two weeks, to submit to the assessors, including the externals, full plans for their project in which they are required to justify the value of the project itself, but mainly to indicate the ways in which their individual objectives will be met. When the work is completed the same use of internal and external assessors is made as for individual work. The final stage is when the external examiners feel able to report to the Council for National Academic Awards that in their view each student listed has completed work at the appropriate level, following full discussion of the evidence by a properly constituted assessment board.

Our experience with students

We have now had four intakes of students who have completed the DipHE.
Annual intakes are shown in Table 1.

	1974	(%)	1975	(%)	1976	(%)	1977	(%)
A level	29	40	17	17	18	20	8	9
Mature	34	46	72	71	58	65	71	77
Non-standard	10	14	12	12	13	15	13	14
Total	73	100	101	100	89	100	92	100

Table 1 *DipHE student intake by qualification*

Clearly the largest category of intake is the mature age entry which
according to the CNAA is anyone over the age of 21. The non-standard
entry refers to students under 21 without formal entry qualifications.
This pattern of entry reflects our commitment to meet the needs of the
local community where take-up rates of higher education are the lowest
in the UK, and to the attraction of the opportunity to pursue studies
which build on expertise and interest other than that gained from formal
education.

When comparing success rates of students in these three categories we
find that whilst caution should be exercised because of the small numbers
concerned, entry category appears to make very little difference to final
performance (see Table 2).

	1974	1975	1976	1977
A level	83	60	73	33*
Mature	83	80	72	73
Non-standard	83	57	70	75
All students	83	76	72	72

* Only three assessed — small A level intake with large percentage
  transferring during course to other courses.

Table 2 *DipHE student success as percentage of those assessed*

Of greater concern to us has been the high rate of withdrawals, shown in
Table 3. There have been several reasons for this. One has been that at the
end of the planning period, several students have found that their best
interests lie in pursuing regular courses, often elsewhere in the Polytechnic.
Secondly, the greatest numbers of withdrawals are mature students with
personal difficulties ranging from pregnancy and spouse job changes to
financial difficulties. Thirdly, some mature students simply find themselves
unsuited to working by independent study. These are students who are

unable to embrace the principle of planning ahead, or whose view of personal freedom does not include any notion of accountability to the public. For the intake of 1978 these lessons were incorporated into the School's admissions procedures and at the completion of their first year their number has reduced from 98 to only 92.

	1974	1975	1976	1977
A level	21	71	39	50
Mature	32	38	38	28
Non-standard	40	42	23	45
All students	29	44	36	32

Table 3 *DipHE student withdrawals as percentage of entry*

In terms of longer-term student benefit, it is too early to report. We have a substantial study under way which is not yet complete, but preliminary indications suggest that most students claim to have derived considerable personal benefit on which they have been able to capitalize in their jobs or lives generally. However, a large number have experienced problems when applying for jobs in competition with holders of qualifications gained more conventionally. This is partly because of the unfamiliarity of the course to employers and the generally depressed state of the graduate market. However, this is beginning to show signs of easing.

Some difficulties

One of the major difficulties has been referred to already, namely assessing level. In particular there is the problem of identifying level of performance in affective skill areas. We have not resolved this by any means except to assess the complexity and degree of unfamiliarity of the context in which the skills are demonstrated. A much greater problem is to persuade the traditional academic establishment that work produced by independent study is comparable to work done by students on conventional courses. One example is of a student who presented for his degree assessment a major thesis on a new design for ships' propellers complete with manufacturing and commercial assessments of its feasibility. He had secured from the director of one of the foremost research and development units in this field in the UK a full appraisal of the work which commented on the fact that the work represented a breakthrough which would be of use to the research team. The specialist engineering examiner was reluctant to approve the award of an honours degree, whilst admitting that the work was more like a PhD thesis, on the grounds that we had no means of knowing that the student 'actually knew all about fluids', and was not just capable of solving a specific problem within the general field of fluids. Had the student pursued a normal lecture/laboratory course in fluids and successfully completed a three-hour unseen written examination paper, there would have been no problem for the examiner; but there would have been no design breakthrough.

Another difficulty concerns the tutors, who find themselves having to discover for themselves a totally new role. This problem immediately emerges whenever someone asks 'What do you teach?'. The reply always involves a long exposition of the greater importance of learning as opposed to teaching, and the use of some inadequate jargon like 'I'm a learning facilitator'. Personally, I cope by saying 'I don't teach, I give students the opportunity to learn'. The independent study tutor is not a source of knowledge, nor is he the holder of answers to the question: what should be learned? Yet these are the traditional roles of teachers and the normal expectations of students. Without these agents of control, the tutor can feel impotent and exposed, constantly being confronted with his own inability to solve the learning problems of his students. In its place the tutor needs to develop a commitment to helping the student to solve these problems for himself. This requires the tutor to be capable of: building up the confidence of the student; offering sharp criticism of student performance and proposals; and providing access to specialist advice and information. The most difficult judgement to be made is when to intervene to support a student who is in difficulties. Learning to confront and cope with difficulties is one of the most valuable experiences which students can have, yet instinctively tutors feel compelled to prevent it happening.

Another difficulty concerns the place of the School within the Polytechnic, and is likely to be experienced if independent study is attempted in other conventional institutions. On the one hand the conventional faculty structure is a great advantage in that tutors and specialist resources are readily available. On the other it perpetuates a discipline-based ethos to education. As a result our staff and students must constantly conduct dialogue with everyone else about the ways in which our work is totally different. Whilst challenging at first, this activity rapidly becomes wearing and eventually frustrating. It takes up a great deal of energy which could be put to other purposes. It has been responsible for some student withdrawals, or eventual transfer to conventional courses. Over the five-year period this process has had the good effect of educating individual tutors who have had the often pleasant experience of working independently (an effective staff development programme) but it has also emphasized to faculty managements the extent to which we, in effect, challenge the very basis of their existence. Faculties are subject-based; independent study is student-based. The implications of this reach into all aspects of college administration, not least of which is the allocation of resources. We give money (capitation) to students; they give it to staff. The bureaucratic pressure on us to conform is considerable and has taken the form of incorporating us within the Faculty of Humanities. Another aspect of this is the question of academic control. Host faculties serving our students do not have control over what they study, nor of their admission to the Polytechnic. They are never regarded as 'their' students and as a consequence are always given low priority. This becomes particularly difficult when resources are scarce and faculties are planning their schedules for coming academic years. The worst threat we offer is to their own academic status, especially if mere students can devise a totally different curriculum from the one which the faculty asserts to its other students is the only way to study this subject, and can get an honours degree as a consequence. Independent study, I think, must accept the inevitability of this problem and learn to live with it without conceding its principles. The best hope is that over the years the accumulated experience of hundreds of successful relationships between individual students and tutors will gradually erode these traditional barriers.

The author acknowledges that this report is based on the accumulated experience of the staff and students of the School for Independent Study at the North East London Polytechnic. Further accounts of the School for Independent Study can be found in Burgess (1977), Percy and Ramsden (1980), Robbins (1977) and Stephenson (1980).

11. A Decade of Student Autonomy in a Design School

Barrie Shelton, *Department of Environmental Design,*
Tasmanian College of Advanced Education, Hobart

Introduction

The School of Environmental Design is part of the Tasmanian College of Advanced Education (the equivalent of an English polytechnic) and offers a three-year undergraduate course in environmental design leading to a BA degree. It also offers three-year graduate courses which lead to professional qualifications in architecture, building, landscape and urban planning.

In the awards that the School offers, it is similar to several American Schools of Environmental Design and not unlike many Schools of Architecture and Planning throughout North America, the United Kingdom and Australia which offer three-year undergraduate courses followed by professional courses at graduate level.

However, in other ways the School is far from the norm. For instance, prospective students decide on whether or not they will enter (if there are more applicants than places, the fortunate ones are picked from a hat) and, once entered, it is the students who design their own learning programmes and subsequently pass or fail themselves. That is, of course, at all points in the courses except those at which final awards are given: here, students submit projects prepared over set periods (minimum duration four months) and receive panel assessments, pass or fail, for the work.

This system had its first full year of operation in 1971 and so I am writing this in its tenth year. It is my ninth year with the School. In this case study I shall reflect upon those years of experience. It will not be a rigorous course evaluation in the sense that it is the result of a careful research programme. Rather, it will be the impressions of an enthusiastic participant, albeit an enthusiasm tempered by what I hope is a healthy suspicion of what I am naturally inclined to support.

In this context I shall attempt to convey how the School came into being, why I came to join it, what it is the School has been trying to achieve, how it has gone about achieving its aims, and what trends, triumphs and tribulations I have witnessed there. Finally, I would like to offer those conclusions which I feel confident in drawing from the experience.

Background

The Director and his ideas

In 1970, Barry Hugh McNeill was appointed as the Director of School. At 32, his first decade of adulthood had coincided with the idealistic 1960s although his own education had been a conventional one. On leaving school he pursued tertiary studies at an intensity which left little time for questioning the education received. (At one stage, Barry was working substantially full-time in an architectural practice, studying for his BA degree as well as completing a course in town planning.)

During this period, Barry recalls a few surprises which influenced his later opinion. He was surprised at his level of achievement for what seemed little effort. Also, having been led to believe that the *raison d'être* of universities was the pursuit of truth, he was disenchanted with what he actually saw. Dedication amongst staff was unusual. In the case of political science and psychology, he expected those subjects to leave their mark on the political values and self-awareness of the students undertaking them but this was not apparent. In short, he began to doubt the integrity of tertiary institutions and the effectiveness of their programmes, if he was not yet critical of their methods.

At the same time, the value of practical experience was fully appreciated, for Barry felt strongly that he learned much more from architectural practice than from formal studies.

However, it was not until an overseas study tour in 1968-69 that these embryonic doubts were reinforced, extended and clarified. In particular, elements of various American tertiary programmes suggested an alternative and more effective approach. At Antioch College, field (ie practical) experience was assessed and accredited as a part of the students' educational programme. In the same vein, assessment by project work had replaced that by examination in certain schools. At the Rhode Island School of Design, he witnessed an art foundation programme (ie a common 'starter' programme for all design students) which was problem- rather than technique-oriented. And in MIT's foundation programme there was no grading, merely 'pass' and 'fail'.

In North America (as compared to the UK and British Commonwealth) there was greater separation between professional bodies and academic institutions and this emphasized the possibilities for developing more than the values, skills and knowledge of the existing profession. Other characteristics of American education which seemed to have merit were: (i) undergraduate programmes tended to emphasize general education rather than professional training, the latter following at a graduate level, which allowed for a more informed and committed judgement about career; and (ii) the absence of set syllabi for courses but instead, the opportunity for choice from a wide range of options.

Further, as a result of teaching on return from the USA, he observed an enormous discrepancy between the knowledge and skills which students were taught in formal classes (and supposedly demonstrated by way of examination) and what they later demonstrated when a project demanded its application.

It was during this period in particular that Barry recalls making the connections between those aspects of the American educational scene which had held most appeal, his own experiences in teaching and learning, and his former university readings in psychology, especially those of Carl Rogers and the humanistic school with their emphasis upon people as individuals — a rewarding synthesis.

It is not difficult to see how these connections were the forerunner to views on education expressed in a paper to a 1969 architectural education conference:

> Formal preparation for a professional career has tended to emphasize . . . specified techniques, a defined area of factual information, and a description of the nature of acceptable solutions.
>
> To enable the architect to contribute to an everchanging society . . . the individual (must) develop an understanding of his community and his relationship to it. The techniques, facts and solutions of today are likely to be superseded . . . even if basic problems do not change.
>
> Whilst . . . (schools) . . . have accepted the concept of education as personal development, tertiary education, even in the so-called 'liberal arts', is still essentially a humdrum procedure of the exchange of third-hand information in a detached arid environment . . .
>
> Architectural education now has to cease paying lip-service to the principles of progressive education and see the 'first-stage' of higher education as a vital opportunity for the individual to enhance his self-awareness and develop meaningful ways of relating to his fellows and his community.
>
> The waste of these intense and idealistic youthful years on trivia not only frustrates the spirit but also does a disservice to the community, which has paid for tertiary education but upon which the young architect is inflicted to begin his *real* education.
>
> The acquisition of techniques, facts and the knowledge of currently acceptable solutions must be recognized for what it is — a continuing and never-ending process throughout one's life.
>
> There is no one path. Individual differences must be recognized and their potential exploited . . . (with) . . . the development of special areas of interest based on motivation and the self-awareness of special abilities.
>
> I argue for the rejection of the concept of 'training' and view the acquisition of skills as a complementary but secondary aspect of professional education, best attained when motivated by the individual's need to understand or solve problems which have intense personal significance.
>
> Architectural education, if intended to 'produce' creative, flexible, alert practitioners, ought therefore best to be viewed as general education. (McNeill, 1971, pp 26-7)

Although directed towards architecture, the comments are sufficiently general to apply to all the design professions, indeed to most professions.

These views in turn set the scene for the School of Environmental Design course proposals:

> The basic aim . . . is to provide each student with the resources, opportunity and advice to enable him to pursue his own interests and those matters which he considers are most important.
>
> Each student has the opportunity to initiate his own programme and the only direction will be that . . . he must cover a certain range of problems

and problem-solving situations, eg scale, time, group, reality, limitations.

There will be no formal attendance requirements except that each student will be obliged to discuss his work programme with an adviser every three weeks.

Formal lectures will be replaced as the main teaching instruction by a weekly meeting programme which will mainly be constructed on a seminar basis but which will also provide for informal discussions, interviews, question and answer sessions, field project presentations and, if there are special visitors whose material is not available in another form, lectures.

There will be no formal examinations. Students will nominate their methods of assessment, eg research essays, field studies, pilot projects.

The basis of accreditation must be the student's assessment of himself since this has the greatest educational value.

An assembly of staff and students (and outside professionals) should meet at least once a term to review operations and suggest new directions in policy.

Since the student is able to initiate his own programme and method of assessment, the course of study will become more demanding for both students and staff. However, with the encouragement of greater student motivation it is expected that a more valuable and effective experience will result. (Final year assessment would be by a panel consisting of a member of staff and two people from outside the School [one of whom would be nominated by the student].) (McNeil, 1970)

My own ideas

My own background contrasts sharply with that of Barry McNeill. I had a protracted tertiary education through leaving one course at one institution and starting another course elsewhere. In the intervening period (over two years), I sought only occasional work but was far from inactive. I lived something of an itinerant life visiting friends at many universities, read profusely, and tackled projects of my own accord. I tried to meet people whom I thought could contribute to the development of my ideas: I sat in on seminars where I thought these could do likewise. Some of these ideas had much to do with the problems of learning which I myself had received and long questioned: I searched for alternatives.

What I did over this period was, in fact, to work at things in which I had a personal interest, at my own pace and in a manner and sequence which seemed appropriate. It was very much a period of 'autonomous learning' and I found it most rewarding, which reinforced my doubts about formal teaching.

I returned to university only when much surer of what I wanted to do and after I had developed for myself some reasonably cohesive notion of how education might be more effective. I withdrew from one course as an angry young man. I commenced another with a clearer vision about educational alternatives which, perhaps surprisingly, enabled me to show more tolerance of a system which I considered to have serious shortcomings.

I also observed the ease with which my student circle sailed through their courses. To this extent, I think some of the advantages which I enjoyed out of college could also be enjoyed within. One of the privileges I think a university education traditionally offered was the opportunity for the students to think about their own development and key issues facing the world in a sympathetic environment, in that it was relatively unpressured with regard to time; it allowed, if not condoned, excesses in behaviour; and removed young people from the usually constraining parental influences. I suspect this freedom was recognized, consciously or otherwise, in the older universities and to have been an important factor in contributing to a 'diplomatic sensibility' in many of their graduates.

But in the great expansion of tertiary education in the 1960s, I saw newer institutions trying to assert themselves with tighter scheduling and more formal teaching; they gave greater emphasis to the social sciences. Often, the aims of these courses were directed explicitly at personal development and changing values. 'Education is a subversive activity' became a cliché. But like Barry, rarely did I see significant shifts in awareness and values, or even a maturing of attitude. The attempts, as often as not, backfired with ritual learning and a sense of achievement that was more apparent than real, ie not internalized. In other words, however well-intentioned, there was often less opportunity to address important issues in a manner which was personally meaningful.

Schools of Architecture featured particularly as part of this trend. There were more and more packages of knowledge to be consumed with less and less opportunity to see how they related to each other and to architecture. Like planning, architecture is an integrating activity: it brings together information from widely disparate sources to a particular task at hand. It is hard, therefore, to define a body of knowledge for these professions. The important abilities to develop in design students are those of creative inquiry and synthesis — how to ask the right questions, how to seek out relevant information, how to put it together thereafter.

Yet the Schools, in the admirable pursuit of a well-rounded and widely knowledgeable architect, devised tighter programmes which tried to cover everything with a smattering of many subjects. These subjects guaranteed more attendances, more swotting, more worry and frustration, but not necessarily more learning.

I did not deny that the new subjects were potentially of value to the architect and that specialist information had to be available to students. It did not seem, however, that the solution lay in bringing in specialists to lecture to repeated timetables but rather in making the sources more easily accessible to be used according to need.

Subsequent teaching and practice consolidated my ideas before I joined the School of Environmental Design for the 1972 academic year.

The institutional framework
Innovation in any sphere is not only a matter of individual or group belief and pursuit, for innovations have to contend with institutional inertia and resistance to change. Indeed, many would argue that the ideas are relatively easy; their acceptance and implementation are more difficult.

In the case of Environmental Design, coinciding with the appointment of the Director of the School, the education of architects and town planners in Tasmania was transferred (and upgraded) from technical college to advanced college (or polytechnic) status. Further, the Royal Australian Institute of Architects who had developed a liberal education policy (and on whom professional recognition of the architectural course depended) were critical of the then existing course and pressed for change. Thus, with pressure from the professional institution and the School sitting in a sort of institutional no-man's-land (neither the technical nor advanced college exercised a strong influence) the climate lent itself to innovation. As a consequence, a group of tertiary courses came into being which, to my knowledge, were unrivalled in Australia in the degree to which they allowed students to direct their own learning.

The School

The general programme

The School's formal *raison d'être* (ie why it receives funds) is to produce graduates for the environmental design professions. At present there are courses in architecture, urban planning, landscape planning and building operations which follow on from a more general undergraduate course in Environmental Design.

The nature of all courses is such that there is no curriculum in the sense of a programme which is prearranged and repeated each year. There is a range of tasks for which graduates are expected to have a working knowledge. But how and where and in what sequence students acquire their knowledge and skills is wide open and a matter for discussion and negotiation between the student and the School. It may be through our own School activities and resources (projects, seminars, workshops, visiting speakers, books, videos etc); it may be through practical experience in the work place; through courses offered outside the School; it may be through travel or whatever resources can be identified or invented. Discussion between a student and a member of staff is constant but particularly important at the beginning of a semester, when a student sets out a personal programme for that period and at the end of semester, when progress in that programme is assessed. The decision to progress into the next level of the course or remain in the present level (ie 'pass' or 'fail') is the student's.

However, the student has eventually to present a project which will be assessed by a panel of three people whose special interest or expertise lies in the area of the study. In the undergraduate course, such a project (the 'Major Project') is prepared over a whole semester and presented at the completion of the third year (for the Bachelor's award). In the case of the graduate programme, the project (the 'Professional Project') is of one year's duration and presented at the end of the sixth year.

The School's programme is summarized in Figure 1. In the following sections I shall take each element of the courses and describe them as well as comment upon the key changes and issues which have occurred

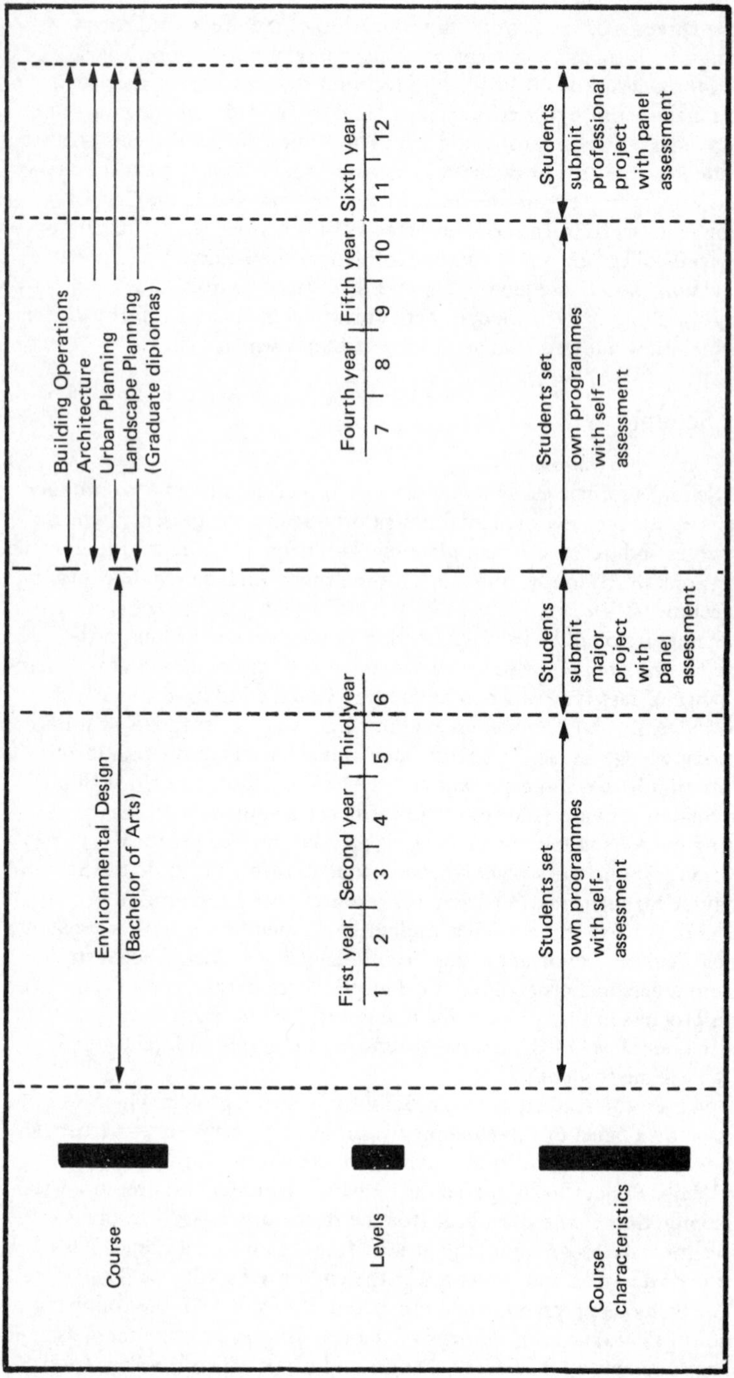

Course
Levels
Course characteristics
Environmental Design
(Bachelor of Arts)
Building Operations
Architecture
Urban Planning
Landscape Planning
(Graduate diplomas)
First year
Second year
Third year
Fourth year
Fifth year
Sixth year
1
2
3
4
5
6
7
8
9
10
11
12
Students set own programmes with self-assessment
Students submit major project with panel assessment
Students set own programmes with self–assessment
Students submit professional project with panel assessment

Figure 1

within them. I shall take the elements in the sequence that the student meets them as he passes through the course, namely entry, programme setting, learning and assessment. In addition, I shall focus on the various resources which support the courses, namely the staff and facilities, as well as on the machinery which keeps the system running (and changing), namely the government and administration of the School.

Entry

Entry standards are 'matriculation or equivalent': in practice, the latter is virtually taken as a minimum age limit. The reason for this is that academic performance at school serves as no reliable guide to performance in the course: to use it would therefore exclude many people with the potential to succeed.

The procedure for entry is that all applicants are interviewed. The function of the interview is not to select but rather to inform the potential student as much as possible about the School and its courses: also, to learn about the students, their interests and potential. This should allow for an informed judgement about whether to enter and at what level. The School attracts many mature students and for these, 'credits' are given for previous experience *both* in college and in the workplace. The important question facing incoming students is therefore: how much preparation and how long is it going to take before a project can be undertaken in the third year which is likely to meet the assessment criteria for a degree?

A tough decision perhaps, but my experience is that students are mostly realistic in assessing their abilities. Having perused work of former and existing students and talked to their peers and staff, newcomers tend, if anything, to underestimate themselves. Inevitably a few do otherwise, usually through blind enthusiasm (which is a useful weakness in at least getting started) although more likely through blind ambition.

If there is a wide disagreement between an adviser and a student about the latter's ability, a short project prior to entry can often serve to demonstrate strengths and weaknesses.

Initially advisers were asked to offer an opinion to incoming students as to their potential for success in the course: students were to have a 'reasonable chance' or be likely to experience 'some difficulty'. But this practice was dropped believing that students would behave according to the 'labels' imposed. There were, anyway, some opinions which were afterwards proved wrong by a student's performance in the course, to make them of dubious worth. Opinion or no opinion, it has been the student who decides whether or not to enter.

Programme setting

There are two levels of programme setting: one at the School level which involves devising a programme of activities for the School which students can then choose to attend or not; the other at the individual level with students devising their own personal programmes of study. I shall deal with the latter first.

Every semester, each student is asked to set himself a study programme. In doing this, students are asked to identify what they need to learn and why and to arrive at a set of learning aims for the semester. They are also asked how they are going to achieve those aims and, in turn, what evidence they are going to present to show that they have learned what they intended. Thus, in setting out such a programme, a student enters effectively into a 'learning contract' although it is not formalized in the same way as those described in Chapter 9.

For most, setting a programme is not an easy task. It demands a fair level of conceptualization and forward planning. The tendency is to produce a 'shopping list' of proposed activities (for instance, to attend seminars x and y and undertake project b) without rationale for doing them and without any indication of how they might be assessed.

To tell students that they have produced a 'shopping list' doesn't normally hold much meaning. It calls for a probe, sometimes obtusely, into the ideas and aims behind the list. One may discover that a student has fallen on hard times and needs quick cash and has hence chosen a project that might realize a little money. One may discover an intricate web of background thinking that makes one realize how much one underestimated one's 'client'. The former may elicit a little sympathy where previously there was none. The latter is a delight.

One often discovers that a student's proposed programme is based on a false set of assumptions. Among newer students the image of the design professions is commonly narrow and technical: for instance in architecture the resulting programme may cover little more than drafting and a house design. This would prompt a discussion about the range and complexity of architecture which may or may not be fruitful at that stage. One may have to wait until the completion of at least the first design project to prove the relevance of that early advice through the weaknesses in what the student does. Programme setting, like design, is a problem-solving exercise, and as such cannot be taught but only developed through experience, encouragement and criticism.

Programme setting at the School level involves organizing and offering a set of learning activities which can broadly be categorized into three types: projects, support studies and work study. In *projects,* students address themselves to solving particular problems such as a building or landscape design, a pollution problem, etc. *Support studies* include the more traditional activities such as seminars and lectures, and these attempt to give knowledge and skills for application in projects. *Work study* allows for practical experience in the workplace recognizing that there are some things better learned in the 'real world' than in a protected 'school' environment. In addition, there are some other activities such as study tours which make up an inevitable 'other' category.

The nature of the activities within each of these categories has, however, not been constant, nor has the balance between them.

I shall take projects first. Initially, I recall projects being generated mainly by the students themselves: either they had some personal significance (eg designing furniture for oneself) or were of a hypothetical nature (eg new buildings for future needs). Many of these, although very involved in terms of their process, failed to conclude with a product. More recently, we have witnessed a swing towards 'live projects' which in the School's language means projects with a real client: in these, members of the public approach the School seeking assistance with design and planning problems. With this shift in the type of projects undertaken, emphasis in working through problems was given more to the end-product and less to the process. In these live projects, students learned a great deal about the importance of timetabling, cost constraints, honouring contracts and management; but such projects have their weaknesses in a teaching context for they are not conducive to diversions (thoroughly exploring related knowledge, pondering over alternative approaches, etc) which are very necessary in an educational situation but not generally possible 'on the job'.

Currently, more projects do seem to be being generated (in the sense of problems being identified) from within the School but which also have a 'live' quality in that they do relate to and involve community groups. In such projects there is usually some leeway for review, and yet they have real application which is important for the integration of theory and practice. It is, however, difficult to know how much this current turn is a reflection of the slump in the economy (ie outside work is not being generated) or a result of people within the School trying to reverse what they perceived to be an unhealthy trend. I suspect both.

In support studies, there have also been changes. In the School's formative years, there were regular seminars in several broad but predetermined knowledge areas. There followed a period in which groups met on the basis of level and then decided what they wished to pursue. The popularity of these waned, and for a while the support studies programme was very bare. In turn there was a tendency to design the support studies programme in response to student requests for activities. And to facilitate this there developed a formal process whereby student requests were transformed into a collective programme.

Students played a key role in this organization, first on a voluntary basis and later as paid assistants. Staff played an increasing role and eventually took over. And while these changes took place, so-called 'core subjects' appeared in the programme which are regulary repeated. Staff offerings now feature more prominently in the programme and I think staff figure more prominently in the activities.

> In some ways students have been encouraged to be less active through the generation of a large range of support study groups from which to choose or drift between. This has also encouraged staff to set programmes for these groups, as it gives them something to focus on. Hence, we have staff over-responding to sometimes tentative or non-existent requests. (Fourth year student working on the organization of the Support Studies programme, 1977)

Changes have occurred also in the balance between project work and support studies, the latter having been on the ascendancy for several semesters. At the same time, programme setting tended towards a mere listing of support study units. However, there is some indication that the growth of support studies has now curbed: that students are concluding that they have been over-valued.

Given the two trends: (i) that more projects seem to be being initiated from within the School and (ii) that the level of the support studies programme is at least reaching a plateau, if not actually tailing, then the trend towards what is in fact a more conventional programme may have been arrested.

This I believe to be a healthy change. The choosing of projects and study units from an externally arranged smorgasbord of learning situations is some way from the degree of autonomy in learning which the School had previously achieved. My own experience of students who choose passively is that the resulting study units seem to serve as conscience salvers for they equate 'doing' or even 'attending' with 'learning'. In this way, passive choice substitutes for critical self-evaluation: conscience-salving substitutes for problem-solving.

The third component of the course is work study. There is a limit to which an educational institution can effectively develop a student's professional skills and abilities from its own resources. While the School is in a better position to do many things such as understanding the key social issues affecting the practice of a profession, introducing students to new and emerging task areas and to theory, etc, the office is more likely to develop more quickly many practical skills (eg in architecture, drafting skills, specification writing), a working understanding of current practice, job administration, etc. Work study is intended to be more than a mere practical experience but a speeding up of learning in the workplace through the School monitoring progress there. This means helping students set aims for their own development and reviewing progress thereafter (as for School-based learning).

In this context, the School is building up a network of work study positions, which we refer to as 'internships' into which students can be placed. This network is the equivalent of a teaching hospital but decentralized.

Although the quality of work study positions is somewhat variable, disseminating the concept and developing the positions are areas in which the School has made steady and consistent progress. Perhaps surprisingly, we have not found great difficulty in placing students, even in the current difficult economic circumstances. The main problems to be faced in work study are, I believe, the attitudes of the participating parties. Many offices see the occupiers of work study positions as technicians rather than as trainee professionals. Students themselves tend to separate 'work' in the office from 'study' in the School. And with staff, work study visits tend to get relegated below other more convenient (ie on campus) and more attractive teaching activities (which centre upon their own interests).

The commonest 'other' studies are the use of audiovisual learning packages and, in particular, travel programmes. The latter may include short periods of study in other colleges or universities to broaden the student's general experience and/or pursue some study in which that institution specializes.

Learning and assessment

The various levels in the courses have very different emphases: in most the emphasis is upon 'learning'; in the others, it is on the 'demonstration' of one's abilities, this occurring at the end of each course.

In 'learning levels', assessment is self-assessment but in 'demonstration levels', it is external with a panel assessment of a project.

In a 'learning level', having first formulated a programme and subsequently pursued it a student will assess his progress at the end of the period and decide whether or not to 'pass' into the next level. This is done in consultation with an adviser but is ultimately the student's decision.

Broadly, one tends to be confronted with four situations in assessment. There are students who have done a great deal of work and also learned much from it. Others may have been very busy but learned relatively little. On the other hand, there are students who appear to have done very little but made considerable progress. There are those who have done little and progressed accordingly. And there are all shades between.

Not surprisingly, there is a high correlation between those students who have a clear learning programme at the start of a semester and who subsequently both do and learn a lot. These are the self-starters who know where they are heading and it is usually very rewarding to work with them. It is the more conceptually-minded students who try to see things in their complexity and who are more inclined to address themselves to the world's wider problems and new fields (energy questions, economic depression, social problems, etc). These students will often set their sights beyond what is realistically possible and it is difficult, as an adviser, to know how much to intervene and thwart their enthusiasm. Ironically, it can be some of the more motivated and conceptual students who therefore take an extra semester, having failed in their first externally assessed piece of work through overreaching themselves. To these students an additional semester is rarely seen as a handicap and is usually viewed rather philosophically as a further opportunity to satisfy their appetites for experience and learning.

Other students may appear to be self-starters in that they are able to sustain their application and maintain a high work output, but in fact show surprisingly little development for their efforts. It is often difficult to convince them that this is so, for to them 'doing' and 'learning' are synonymous. These students tend to be among those who produce shopping lists of proposed activities at programme-setting time without real explanation of why they are undertaking these activities. They may pick up some technical skills in the process but remain rather static in terms of their general educational and personal development.

171

> I felt much more secure in Queensland. There were a lot of things about which
> I did not have to think. I had a goal — that was to pass a year. Down here I have
> to think more about why I am doing things. (Third year student)

Here, the 'doing' seems rather like an act of conscience-salving within the framework of the Protestant work ethic. Ideally, the approach required to learning in our School is more akin to a problem-solving exercise, the problem being one's own learning which requires critical self-assessment. And while ultimately, to become a competent professional, one can only learn through practice, one has to know why one is doing what one is doing. It is this latter question which is avoided when 'conscience-salving' replaces 'problem-solving'.

It is, nevertheless, difficult for an adviser to know how much criticism is appropriate in such cases. 'Doing' gives some students their reason for being: to attack this too quickly may be very destructive. It is my experience that if only some basic skills can be acquired through a somewhat thoughtless programme of 'doing', this can give students a certain level of confidence within themselves which becomes the springboard for more self-questioning and probably more profound progress.

On one occasion, I remember a colleague showing me what he thought to be a model study programme from a student. I recall looking over it and not feeling the same appreciation. It seemed somewhat false and shallow — as though the student was producing what he thought was wanted without a thought-out underlying purpose. That student worked very hard for a couple of semesters. Staff and students alike admired his application, and in the process he undoubtedly acquired some basic skills. Thereafter, he appeared to falter: he seemed less confident, more aimless and produced less. (I suggest it was an expressed appreciation of his attitude from other members of the School that kept him moving for as long as he did with a sort of compulsive activity which prolonged the change.)

I believe he had been in the conscience-salving category and not been questioning what he was doing in any depth. There followed a period in which there was far less doing and production, more introspection and self-evaluation and, eventually, a great deal more progress in terms of general knowledge and personal development. There was a coming to terms with himself and an ability to put together what would previously have been disparate bits of information into general patterns: there had developed a frame of reference which made subsequent studies more meaningful and enjoyable, and learning more rapid.

In a sense, the student made a 'false start' which led to a period of introspection and, in turn, to 'take off'. In the more conventional course, the tendency is, I believe, to produce more false starters who realize rarely that that is what they have done.

Periods of introspection are not usually the most productive (in terms of tangible results) for anyone, not only students, but they so often result in marked progress, especially in personal development. It is common for students who are asking themselves basic questions about their future to experience difficulties in programme-setting. They will submit a programme (ritualistically perhaps, for it is mandatory) but then veer from it because the pursuits outlined in it are overshadowed by nagging questions — relating to the scope, practices, social context, etc of their intended profession and their place in relation to it.

While writing this paper, I met a student who joined the School a few months ago: he is a very competent technician who is dedicated to architecture and wishes both to expand his knowledge and better his qualifications. On entering, he quickly set himself a programme and got on with it. Having attended various activities assiduously, he came to my office and proceeded to talk about his new-found confusion: how architecture is taking on a new complexity; how his concept of the profession is changing; how he no longer appreciates buildings that he once did. While telling me this, his expression contained smiles and frowns together — excitement and bewilderment. His initial programme was obviously falling apart and, as yet, he had not much to replace it with. I predict that he will have a hard time with himself at his next assessment: but I also have no doubts that a measure of clarity will emerge quite soon which will allow him to pursue his studies more efficiently, with more confidence and even greater fervour.

Lastly, there are those students who both do little and learn little. The reasons for this vary. Some are conscious of what they are doing and make it plain that they have no wish for it to be otherwise. They are aware that this will not lead them to a successful completion of their course. Sometimes they are explicit; sometimes they pretend it to be otherwise. They are not difficult to identify and some straight talking may or may not persuade them to leave. There are, of course, a few such students in most courses: in ours, their numbers may be marginally higher because self-assessment does allow them to hang on for longer and hence there is a cumulative effect. However, contrary to what many of our critics would like to believe, these students are few and not a problem.

Some students know that they are doing and learning little and, try as they might, cannot do otherwise. These are also few in number and probably the saddest group. They are generally the most difficult to assist. If one can at least channel them into pursuits outside the course more appropriate to their potential, then that is a considerable achievement and their stay has not been without benefit.

There is a final group of students who do relatively little but believe themselves to be making more progress than they really are. Here, there is often ambition for professional status coupled with a rather flippant attitude towards their professional area. Their typical programmes are lists of activities directed towards basic skill acquisition rather than general knowledge and thinking abilities. This correlates with a simplistic notion of the professional as a technician — a notion which they do not wish to relinquish for it makes life safer and easier. During self-assessment, they will argue for a pass, receive advice to the contrary but probably persist in recording a pass for the semester. Their work will have been criticized by an adviser: they will say that they were aware of these weaknesses, excuse them and say that this will change with their project for external assessment. To be fair, occasionally it does change, in which case the student knew himself far better than the adviser knew him. But generally it does not, and the same criticisms are spelled out by the three panel assessors. Thus, with self-assessment, for these students poor decisions become cumulative, with consequent failure — a rude awakening and another try.

In programme setting and assessment, advisers must clearly be astute to the various situations described above. In some ways their role is more akin to that of a counsellor who also has a knowledge of and involvement in the professions for which the students are preparing themselves. In projects and support studies, the role changes with an adviser more likely to be passing on skills and knowledge. Assessment is a crucial activity. One can advise a student of his proposed programme's inadequacies at programme-setting time but it is at assessment time when the student finds, in the absence of an adequate programme, self-assessment to be difficult and so discovers the wisdom of the earlier advice. Similarly, it is when a project is submitted for critical comment that an adviser can, through asking the right questions, demonstrate the inadequacy of aspects of certain information that has been overlooked; whereas, try as one might to tell someone of its relevance during the event, it may not register. (In the conventional course it may register only for the purpose of producing what the lecturer wants — for obvious reasons — but is not internalized.)

Final-year panel assessment is a very different ball game from self-assessment. Panel assessment is not uncommon in colleges and universities, especially at a postgraduate level, although the rationale behind the selection and composition of our panels is probably unusual. The School believes that there should be representatives of the professions and wider community which it is serving. A panel enables there to be a depth of evaluation which would not normally be possible from within the School, since its range of expertise and staff time are limited. A panel also ensures fairness through a variety of opinion. This latter point is underlined by the method for appointing panels: a panel consists of the student's adviser, an outside (but approved by the School) nominee of the student and a nominee of the School.

Assessment is based on the student's project, but is essentially an assessment of the student himself: thus he not only submits his project but also has a lengthy interview upon the project. At third year (BA) level, the project is of one semester's duration; at sixth year (Graduate Diploma) level, it takes a full year. In the third year the panel is looking for 'professional potential' with the emphasis in assessment upon the student's general approach to the project with rather less attention to detail or specific professional knowledge. In the sixth year it is looking for professional competence with emphasis therefore upon both.

One criticism of our assessment system is that a single project is not capable of covering a broad enough range of skills and knowledge. Such criticism fails to recognize that no assessment system can test all relevant activities and that most abilities are anyway transferable in their application between tasks. Also, projects of a year's duration (especially in the context of our assessment criteria) are inevitably broad-ranging. Further, since questions on any aspect of professional activity that can be linked to the project may be asked at the interview, I suspect such a criticism is as much a reflection of the critics, who themselves have difficulty in generating wide-ranging questions from the project (ie thinking laterally).

Although I would have to admit to some variation in standards between panels, I see no greater and, if anything, less variation in standards between panels than between individual staff within the School. Since the latter occurs on any faculty, it could be argued that panels are an evening force. Certainly, within panels, my opinion is that a unanimous opinion occurs more often than not.

Generally, a panel ensures a thorough, fair and balanced assessment and one which is not out of touch with the world beyond the School. In my opinion, panel assessments have been successful, and excepting what might be considered to be minor modifications (eg an option to present additional work from other levels of the course as part of the assessment), I have not heard significant criticism.

Staff

It must be obvious by now that teaching in the School is somewhat different from the conventional teaching role. There is no curriculum, only some general objectives (eg a range of professional task areas for which one should be able to demonstrate a working knowledge and competence at the end of one's studies) and some general procedures (eg for programme setting and assessment). How staff actually work within this framework is in their own hands, collectively and individually; in practice, mainly the latter.

Teaching consists, in part, of imparting professional expertise and general knowledge. It also involves assisting students to set programmes, to monitor and assess themselves. It is thus partly a counselling role for which there is no standard approach for all students or even the same student all of the time. This counselling role is emphasized by some of the personal situations, outlined in the last sections, of which advisers need to be aware.

Yet our staff come from professional backgrounds with little or no special preparation for some of the roles which they have to perform. How do they fare?

The feeling of being drained of energy is a repeated theme of conversation. While I know this to be common in the teaching and helping professions, I believe it is particularly strong within the School. Given an 'unstructured' learning framework, it is very easy for staff to do one of two things: either to indulge in one's own thing to the detriment of the students or, alternatively, to respond too much to students to the point where one's own identity is subjugated to the detriment of oneself. The latter means being 'drained' from forever giving of oneself without revitalization. The former can precipitate a permanent sense of guilt with a similar effect: it gives rise to negative feelings and defensive behaviour against the School (the oppressor) as well as undermining the sense of achievement from doing one's own thing. The two feelings are not mutually exclusive and can even be mutually reinforcing: for the more one's guilt is triggered, the more tarnished is one's attitude towards the School and the lower one's patience in giving to the students.

The reality seems to be that the structure (or lack thereof) which exists in the School demands people who have a very high degree of self-awareness and emotional self-sufficiency.

Other terms often heard over coffee and around corners are of the 'no direction' variety — 'chaos', 'anarchy', '*laissez-faire*', etc. An absence of structure is seen to be synonymous with no direction. The absence of structure is, however, only relative. There *are* goals, and procedures which allow individuals to structure their own lives in pursuit of those goals; it is simply that the structure is more abstract. The School therefore requires staff who can conceptualize, and again, who have a strong sense of personal direction. Without these qualities, it must appear as a confusing place and this image will to some extent be transmitted to the students.

Yet another criticism is that students are 'lazy' and 'don't do anything' although different members of staff have very different images of the students, some perceiving them as being generally hard-working and others seeing quite the opposite. It is, however, not unknown for staff to emphasize the 'farcical', non-compulsory framework and the opportunities that exist to legally satisfy the regulations with little effort, rather than to stress the necessity for practice and criticism as a means of progressing. This can only encourage student laxity, which is then raised as evidence of weakness in the course and the students! Ironically, it is a case of demolishing what structure does exist without replacing it with anything more positive, when it is more structure that the critics have asked for.

What these critics want is more authority over the students: to *make* them do things. I would argue that if there are more controls on students then there should be similar controls on staff. If, for instance, students have to submit semester programmes (which they do), so should staff. If students have to submit a substantial project every semester (for which there is some support), staff should be required to write a substantial critique of each project. And if there is evaluation of students, should there not also be a mechanism for constructively evaluating staff performance? But such suggestions are not easily accepted.

> I can't see how the obligations implicit in a Handbook . . . can be met unless we make certain learning mandatory.

> A problem arises for some staff because they feel that they cannot discharge
> their responsibilities because of the way the School operates. For example:
> fully optional programmes; lack of power to require output from students
> (aggravated by other staff discrediting such efforts); lack of power to enforce
> certain standards during self-assessment. (Member of staff, 1978)

Another aspect of the School which deserves mention is the attempt to
equalize tasks between staff with everyone doing a more or less equal
share of everything. This has failed on several accounts. Since students
choose their advisers, some staff are more in demand as advisers than
others. Some staff are, anyway, reluctant to advise but prefer conducting
projects and/or support studies. Some staff are reluctant to take on
administrative tasks. And very important, the externally imposed college
organization whereby some staff have higher salaries than others has
proved a real obstacle to sharing.

The above observations, even if only partly right, stress the importance
of certain personal qualities in 'teaching' in an unstructured learning
environment. In a professionally-oriented school, there arises an
immediate conflict, for one has also to consider professional experience
and expertise. While selection panels have taken personal characteristics
into account, they have usually given more emphasis to professional
criteria.

Although I have indicated some disgruntlement, discord and difficulties,
not all staff have been critical: in fact, the majority have not. Currently
we have nine academics on staff. While no one denies that improvements
cannot be made, I perceive that feelings for and against our mode of
operation are about equal.

While there is value in having a range of opinion in any school, there
is also a threshold beyond which the conflict becomes destructive: the
conflict becomes the main preoccupation and thereby undermines the
main purpose of the institution, namely teaching and learning. I believe
that we have sailed dangerously close to the wind.

Administration and facilities
If students determine their own programmes, if the School programme
arises out of the pattern of individual pursuits, and if resources are
organized to meet learning needs which can only be identified at short
notice, then it is obvious that the problems of organization,
communication and administration are immense.

Generally, the less structure a course has the more sophisticated its
communication channels must be. The hub of the School's
communication network is a set of pigeonholes and a programme board:
the amount of paper that passes through these is colossal and, as a School
concerned with the environment, of some concern. There is also a huge
programme board which allows people to pin up details of meetings,
seminars, or any other events of relevance as they are organized. Further,
each week these details are taken from the board and put on to a
telephone tape such that people can ring in for the programme. I might

add that with the build-up of support studies to dominate the programme, because these tend to be organized to a weekly timetable, use of the telephone and even the board itself has waned.

Staff carry out more administration and organization in a course such as ours than in a more traditional one: this load is something that most staff feel overwhelmed by sometimes. But a more frequent and not unrelated complaint is the slowness at which decisions get made. Every attempt is made to get important matters affecting the School discussed by as many students, staff and interested professionals as possible — which makes decision-making inevitably slow. A School meeting, known as the General Assembly (the 'GA') and open to all staff, students, and invited professionals, was a feature of the School from the outset. It met several times each year with reasonably well-attended meetings (20 plus with up to 50 for the occasional crisis issue). But as the School grew, GA attendances did not follow suit, and eventually fell. The GA was never recognized as an official body by the College and as such, could only be advisory to the Director: nevertheless, the Director said that should a significant difference arise between it and himself on a matter of policy, he would resign. During these early years the Assembly set up many *ad hoc* working groups to deal with particular matters (eg reviews of procedures for project assessment, reviews of the orientation programme, etc) and, in general, there was no shortage of volunteers from staff and students.

A couple of years back, there was a recognition that GAs were poorly attended and increasingly ineffective. At the same time, the College was reviewing its academic government: each School was asked to set up a Board of Studies consisting of at least one-fifth students.

In its wisdom, the School transformed the Assembly into a Board of Studies but also set up a Board of Studies Standing Committee (18 members) upon which staff, students and professionals have equal representation. Each member of the Standing Committee is seen to represent certain interests (eg architecture, planning, students, professionals, etc) and thus be under some obligation to attend. The Standing Committee deals only with non-policy matters and has to put policy matters to the whole Board through referenda (ie the entire School and more). Although it is still early days for the Board, indications are that the numbers who will vote in referenda are no more than those who attended General Assemblies in the School's formative years — in fact, proportionally less.

Further, many matters concerning the operations of the School and which were once dealt with by *ad hoc* working groups of volunteers (eg planning the semester's support study programme) are now dealt with in organized administrative groups which on paper include staff and students but in practice are mainly staff.

Parallelling the development of these administrative groups, there seem to be many more petty regulations which are there for administrative convenience rather than educational purpose (deadlines for projects, programmes, submissions, etc). Such arrangements were once the preserve of each adviser and student which is consistent with the notion of managing one's own learning programme. The more standardized deadlines and procedures become, the more this encourages advisers and students alike to think mechanically rather than educationally about their learning programmes. In fact, with the growth of support studies, the course appears to be perceived by many as a mix of structured support studies and a calendar of deadlines. Further, as more aspects of the operation become standardized, so more circulars emanate from administration, replacing friendly notes from individual advisers. The sense of autonomy slips while that of bureaucracy increases, with consequent alienation.

To take deadlines as an example, my own observations are that things do not happen much differently with or without them. (If anything, the reverse may even be the case.) With or without deadlines, most things occur in reasonable time out of an understanding of their context and a sense of responsibility: deadlines will not enhance these qualities which are surely a purpose of education. If they do not occur, this will be for a variety of reasons which a multitude of checks and regulations are unlikely to change.

On facilities, I shall merely describe some changes which have occurred in the School's accommodation on the assumption that the built environment is a mirror of the organization which built it.

For several years, the School was housed in temporary (although new) accommodation: this was essentially one large space (56′ by 52′) plus a workshop. Within this, the School designed and built its own quarters out of a meccano-like steel frame and chipboard. What emerged was a labyrinth of narrow corridors, tiny cubicles (for students and as staff offices), some slightly larger teaching spaces, a larger 'tools of trade' library, and an even larger social gathering space. None of these spaces had much privacy in that there were no doors and most walls finished some distance below the ceiling (at least, after the Fire Officers had made their inspection!). The natural colour of the chipboard quickly gave way to paint, slogans, notices, pearls of wisdom, peepholes, etc. Some student cubicles were both complex (one was three storeys with an overall height of nine feet) and highly personalized through decoration (somewhat reminiscent of gypsy caravans and canal barges). Parts of the School were periodically demolished and rebuilt according to new needs. Some of the tinier student spaces became too claustrophobic after the initial novelty wore off and were amalgamated into larger shared spaces. I heard the place referred to as 'the warren' and a 'slum' by other sections of the college; there was even a request by someone that curtains be hung at the corridor windows to screen us from the eyes of their visitors. We were also known as the School of the beanbag philosophers, since the most conspicuous activity was that of sitting around talking on brightly coloured beanbags.

> The walls are painted, covered in comments, graffiti and diagrams. The whole
> appearance is of complete informality. The staff do not hide away in offices,
> do not separate themselves from students by the use of titles such as 'Sir' or
> 'Mr' and do not use formal lectures with a 'me talk, you listen' basis. Everyone
> is on first name terms. Staff advise rather than instruct. (A visiting university
> student, 1972)

A little less than two years ago, we were given new accommodation. While
there was some attempt to involve a wider group, the design work was
done primarily by two members of staff and building went to outside
contractors. Now staff have spacious private offices. Two or three social
spaces serve as extensions of a central corridor, to break up a layout that
would otherwise be a corridor with offices and teaching spaces either side.
The new structure is too permanent to be changed with any regularity.
People sit on chairs rather than beanbags. And while there are many
notice boards intended for various categories of information, the
opportunities for cans of spray paint are nil!

The story of the School's pigeonholes or mail boxes highlights the
same theme. It was the students who first saw the need for every student
to have a pigeonhole, and over the years there have been four versions.
The first two were student-designed and built from scrounged materials.
Mark III pigeonholes were student-designed and staff-built. Our present
set were staff-designed and contract-built (and, I have heard it said, work
worst).

Some concluding observations

It should be evident from the foregoing that a good many changes have
taken place in the School since its inception. In this paper I have focused
upon a few which I feel to be among the most significant: the ascendancy
of support studies with staff increasingly prominent in their organization;
some tendency for programme setting to turn into a passive choosing
from a smorgasbord of 'classes'; the growth of internships for practical
experience; a growing dissatisfaction among some staff, and a reluctance
to advise; falling participation in School meetings and administration; a
proliferation of petty regulations; and the changing face of the School's
premises with less opportunity for students to leave their mark.

Long-standing students reminisce about the 'good old days' — a little
over half a decade ago. They talk of the parties, the camps, the characters
and the student publications; of begging, borrowing and improvising for
accommodation and equipment; of staff being more accessible; they recall
a spirit about the place which they say is now missing. To what extent
these memories are justified is hard to say.

Students then were generally younger (and more impressionable?).
They were fewer in number (and therefore more likely to know each
other). The School was new and fighting for survival and was more
conspicuously different from other educational places. I do not know if
there are fewer camps and parties although they are not as apparent as

they were. Staff are less accessible if only because they now have offices (!) spread over two floors where once there was one. Smart accommodation and a steady flow of supplies replaces the begging and improvisation. School news-sheets (and similar student endeavours) have been taken over by administration much in the manner that governments take over functions from voluntary agencies.

If the reader detects an air of disappointment in myself then he is probably correct. While some changes have undoubtedly brought about improvement, others have had the opposite effect. The balance sheet is, in my opinion, slightly in the red.

A factor influencing some of these changes which has, thus far, passed without discussion, is the School's size. Staff numbers have increased threefold over the period. The inherent uncertainties in an open learning situation increase exponentially with each additional member of staff, for each newcomer makes the system increasingly difficult to read which can, itself, be a source of stress. When I arrived there were four academic staff and a secretary shared with other departments in a typing pool: now there are ten academic staff and four technical and administrative staff. Student numbers have had the same effect: these started at about 60 and have since more than doubled. It is, however, the composition of the student body which has probably brought about greater changes within the School. Initially, the School established a nation-wide reputation (sometimes glowing, sometimes infamous) and students came from far and wide to join the programme. There were many transfers from other colleges and universities. Beards, blue jeans and sleeping bags descended upon Hobart from every Australian state and even from overseas. We had transfers from all but two of Australia's 14 equivalent Schools. In Tasmania itself, there was initially some suspicion of the programme; I am sure there were prospective Tasmanian students who wished to have studied at home, but who opted for the security of a more conventional course. Thus even on home territory there was a 'natural selection' of students willing to accept a challenge from the unconventional. Some had no intention of making a career in the design professions, but came for the undergraduate course and moved elsewhere afterwards. In short, students were enrolling for what they believed to be a unique educational opportunity. Student numbers 'soared' to a record 140.

Further, the interstate students had few local contacts and the School tended to become the focal point of their lives, assuming a significance beyond that of a place of learning. The students, willing to accept a challenge, tended to be idealistic, highly motivated and concerned with social issues. They were eager to effect change within the School and therefore willing to get involved in its organization. They were thirsty for knowledge rather than intent upon acquiring a professional ticket (an attitude facilitated by a social and economic climate which was itself idealistic and in which jobs were plentiful).

Since then the School has become more established and accepted. Students graduated and found jobs. There were some criticisms that students were deficient in skills (which incidentally is a universal criticism of architectural graduates by the profession); there were also many positive comments, especially on the thoughtfulness and analytical abilities of graduates. Changes occurred in other schools which brought them closer to our mode of operation: one school of architecture (where two Hobart graduates had joined the staff) instituted a similar course and had the added attraction of being in a big city.

As a consequence, the student body changed. Students coming from interstate dwindled. Tasmanians joined the course who may have shunned it previously. Students were joining the School because of the professional areas in which courses were offered rather than the educational approach. In addition there was an increase in the number of adult learners: women escaping housewifery; people who had left one form of employment and sought retraining; people with a great deal of office experience and technical skills but without qualifications — in other words, more mature people who were more certain of their direction, or at least who had more constraints upon their lives.

The tide turned. With important exceptions, newcomers are not so concerned with the educational approach; many have simply less time: they are therefore less inclined to affect consciously the direction in which the School develops. Their interests appear to be more immediate. The tightening economy must have affected student mobility which may partly account for the drop in interstate enrolments. Funds in education have shrunk and the students are very much aware of this, especially in a School which tries to involve students in budget decisions. Buildings and planning programmes in public and private offices have contracted with even fewer funds directed towards research activity. Unemployment has grown and the job market become more uncertain. Society-at-large emphasizes the worth of technician and trade skills rather than a learned society. These changes permeate the School. For a few, they are perceived as a new challenge. For many, they erode morale and confidence. For most, they seem to lower horizons and sap idealism.

In a more traditional department, the effects of these changes are probably delayed. But in our School the day-to-day operational links are many, through the work study programme, outsiders on assessment panels, 'live' projects and a high proportion of part-time staff with outside involvements. Thus, the School is not well cushioned against such influences, and it is both a strength and a weakness that its open structure allows the changing values and attitudes of the wider world to permeate quickly. What is crucial in these difficult times is that it is only the activities which change within the open structure. But clearly, if it is the structure which changes, the trends will be much more difficult to reverse later.

The general social and economic climate of which the School is a part has to be accepted. On size, student numbers have levelled off at about 120, which is, I believe, still too large to allow all students to at least know of each other and to encourage attendance at School meetings. But to reduce numbers is to reduce opportunity and is therefore unthinkable. It is not inconceivable that we could run two parallel streams within the School each with its own distinctive flavour, thus satisfying the size criterion and perhaps alleviating some of the discord, but this would be fraught with difficulties institutionally.

An area which has to be addressed is staff morale and discord. As clearly inferred there exists a range of opinions reflecting very different philosophical viewpoints. There has been an airing of those philosophies over many years with differences at least clarifying themselves. It is neither desirable nor realistic to obfuscate those differences: they represent a range of viewpoints to be found in the wider society and it is educationally desirable that these be visible within the School. Very crudely, some staff wish the School to continue to exist with minor improvements, while others seek greater authority over students 'to make them perform' (and presumably, therefore, learn). At the same time, all staff are appreciated by some students, which is indicative of a similarly wide range of opinions within the student body.

The framework which asks staff to contribute equally in all tasks is, to some, irksome. The lack of ultimate authority which the staff have over student assessment is particularly contentious. Is there a framework, therefore, which allows all staff and students to function in a manner which suits their individual values, interests and abilities?

There is currently a proposal from the Director which envisages some degree of specialization within the staff. Briefly, the proposal runs something like this. Some staff should act as advisers in programme setting and assessment with only limited other teaching duties. Other staff would be responsible for specific teaching duties (projects, seminars, etc). Staff could determine the terms by which the students would undertake their teaching units (attendance, work, assessment). Thus it would be possible for activities other than final year projects to emphasize performance (in the form of product) rather than progress (learning). The emergent programme would be genuinely pluralistic in that a student could progress through the course either on the basis of self- or external assessment (assuming that some staff impose the latter), or some mix.

This model recognizes that different students learn best similar things from different sources, by different methods, at different rates and in different sequences. The brief personal histories of Barry McNeill and myself are testament to this: both of us hold similar educational viewpoints but derive these from very different circumstances and experiences. In this context, even the idea of general education preceding professional training which is implicit in our two-tier course structure is not entirely valid. The new model also recognizes that students learn most from those things for which they see a purpose and which they enjoy doing.

The new programme would allow tight instructional courses to be offered within a wider framework of choice. However, insistence upon tight instructional courses alone would restrict the ways in which learning could take place.

If an aim of education (as it is of the School) is to achieve a balance between the conflicting aims of personal development, general education and training, there will be a focus upon values, knowledge, and skills respectively: different teaching and learning activities lend themselves to development in these different areas. Advising (and project work, especially in groups) assists development in all areas but advising aids particularly personal development: on the other hand, support studies (lectures, tutorials, practical classes) can expose students to new knowledge and assist in the acquisition of specific skills.

Further, if one views values, knowledge and skills as a gradation, then to give undue emphasis to either end of the spectrum results in an imbalance in learning: one is likely to have graduates who either lack skills or, alternatively, are narrow technicians.

Initially, it is possible that we overreacted. At one stage there were few support studies. In this context the growth of these programmes was a positive development. However, their growth to the neglect of advising and projects was dangerous (this is implicitly a criticism of traditional courses). Support studies have to be chosen within a context: development of that context is what takes place between student and adviser. Support studies should be seen, as their name implies, as *supportive* to something else.

In short, I see all teaching methods as having merit providing they take place within an unstructured general framework which permits students to learn in alternative ways. It is for these reasons that I see the proposals for some staff specialization as more than a workable compromise between two groups who have difficulty finding common ground but as a positive improvement.

In retrospect I believe we have made certain errors. The most basic is that we underestimated the importance of personal qualities which are necessary to work in an unstructured teaching situation, especially as an adviser-counsellor. We placed too great a weight upon professional experience and expertise as a criterion in staff selection. Secondly, we allowed the support studies programme to become more than 'supportive' to the detriment of other and more fundamental aspects of the programme (advising and projects). And in tandem with this, we produced too many petty regulations for the sake of administrative rather than educational efficiency. However, these changes can be reversed (and this paper may even form part of that process).

A possible error is that there was a complete break with the familiar in setting up the School. It may have been a better strategy to dangle a series of 'progressive carrots' in the midst of tradition and in doing so, harness the collective energies of staff and students in pursuit of those directions. This could have resulted in continuous change towards a desired goal without the excessive trauma which occurred for some and without that sense of retrogression now felt by others, for both undermine morale.

Finally, while writing this paper, a few comments from a former college principal kept milling around in my mind. The gist of these runs something like this: first that education is ultimately an act of faith and it is difficult to prove one approach as greatly superior to another: secondly, that no matter how carefully planned an alternative approach may be, the staff will sooner or later bring it back into line. I hope he is wrong.

Part III Reflections

12. Putting it into Practice: Promoting Independent Learning in a Traditional Institution

Malcolm Cornwall, *Department of Applied Physics, Brighton Polytechnic*

Introduction

The arguments and case studies presented so far in this book provide a persuasive — one would like to think convincing — argument for the introduction of more opportunities for independence in learning within the general framework of tertiary education. Let us assume that you, a typical reader, are persuaded or perhaps even convinced by them, and have now decided that you would like to go ahead and introduce much more independent learning into your own courses. There remains the problem of putting the idea into practice in *your* particular course, with your kind of students and within the constraints of your particular department and institution, all of which are, of course, not quite like those of anyone else.

Are there therefore any general lessons to be learned from the case studies and from the general experience of others which can help you in your particular circumstances? I think there are.

The case studies illustrate several widely different ways in which one may convert innovative enthusiasm for the general ideas into practical and successful concrete realities. But through all the case studies, there runs the common strand of a carefully thought out organizational structure or framework within which students can develop and exercise independence in their learning. The need for such structuring is, I believe, the major lesson that can be learned from the diverse experience of earlier innovators. And it is the main topic of this chapter.

There are, too, among the case studies, several hints of the inevitability of institutional resistance to change and the problems of educational innovation. When we are faced with proposals for new approaches, or simply with new ideas, which challenge some of our most cherished beliefs about the 'right' way that teaching and learning should take place, not surprisingly we will be inclined to argue against them and resist their implementation. For the proponents of independence in learning these reactions can create very severe problems. Some of these problems and possible ways in which they can be tackled are dealt with later in this chapter.

All innovators in the field of independent learning will, however, find that their initial problems are not so much practical ones, but are those related to the misunderstandings, anxieties and straightforward prejudices of their colleagues. In the final section of this chapter, therefore, I consider some of the more familiar arguments against independent learning, attempt to analyse them and outline some of the counter-arguments that might be deployed.

But before we can properly discuss the organizational and innovative issues and problems, it seems to me that we must first define in 'operational' terms what we mean by 'independence' in learning. As a preliminary to my later discussion, I will first consider one approach — a tentative and rather simplified one — to the problem of definition. My suggestion is that a measure of the degree of independence in learning that a course provides can be indicated by the amount of *choice* that a student is allowed within the curriculum.

Degrees of independence in learning

In higher education our methods of teaching are notoriously ill-defined and loosely described (Atherton, 1972). Even the lecture, the ubiquitous workhorse of the academic world, describes a wide variety of activities and is by no means a unanimously agreed set of procedures. It is therefore not surprising that the much richer concept of 'independent learning' can materialize in such a variety of organizational formats, as illustrated in the case studies. All the contributors would be very likely to subscribe to the general definition of 'independent learning' proposed by John Heron in Chapter 3 and endorsed and discussed in the chapter by John Powell. But what in *practical* terms have each of these (and many other) approaches to independence in learning in common? One such characteristic, perhaps the most crucial, is that they all provide the learner with *some degree of personally significant choice* in one or more aspects of the course of studies. After all, 'independence', in common parlance, implies that the individual has a large degree of choice, considerable autonomy, in decision-making affecting his or her aims and activities, and the values he or she puts on them.

Some of the factors in the curriculum, in terms of which we might 'measure' the degree of choice with which a course of study provides a student, are suggested in Figure 1.

In this diagram I have also attempted to indicate an approximate ordering or 'hierarchy' of these factors. My criterion for the suggested order of the 'steps' is the extent to which the provision of choice in each of these aspects of the curriculum is likely to require reorganization of a conventional 'teacher prescribed, teacher-presented, teacher-paced and teacher-assessed' course. For example, allowing students choice of their specific objectives is likely to have more impact on the conventional curricular pattern than, say, allowing only the choice of the ways in which learning takes place. But allowing students to choose assessment methods and criteria is likely to create the need for even more profound reorganization of the 'normal' course pattern.

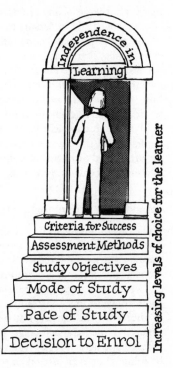

Criteria for Success

Assessment Methods

Study Objectives

Mode of Study

Pace of Study

Decision to Enrol

Increasing levels of choice for the learner

Steps to independence in learning?

A hypothetical heirarchy of choice in learning in terms of aspects of the curriculum.

Figure 1

It is worth emphasizing that the suggested hierarchy is based more on practical organizational and innovative considerations than on any logical interrelationships. The factors I have indicated are simply those that, *in practice*, are aspects of the curriculum within which students can be given more or less freedom of choice.

In practical terms, as the student moves up the 'steps' he is in effect being required successively to ask himself questions such as: 'Shall I join this course?'; 'When and how fast will I study?'; 'In what way will I study?'; 'What books or other resources shall I use?'; 'What specific objective shall I pursue in my studies?'; 'What particular knowledge, skills or attitudes do I wish to acquire?'; 'How do I wish these to be assessed?'; 'What should be the criteria for my success or failure?'.

It will be obvious that defining any course of study in such a one-dimensional way is a gross oversimplification of the true range of variability which can exist between courses which seem to offer the same degree of 'independence' to the learner. Nevertheless, there does seem to be some relationship between the extent to which a course allows choice in the sense I have outlined, and the organizational and innovative problems it raises. The further your course is, or you would like it to be, up the hierarchy, the more radical are the issues that are raised and the

191

bigger are the problems of implementation and organization.

One might add in passing that in the present context, it is the relaxation of the prescriptive and controlling influence of the teacher and of the education system that is our concern. The individual is still subject to the pressures, coercions and inducements of the 'real' world, and to the constraints and limitations of his own abilities and character, no matter how 'free' he is allowed to be within the sometimes rather cosy educational world. We might even interpret our advocacy of 'independence' in learning in higher education as an attempt to remove, or at least reduce, the mediation of the teacher between the learner and the 'real' world of unformulated problems, non-predigested information, personal decision-making and value judgements.

Providing a framework: some prerequisites for success

The case studies illustrate the fact that giving independence to students does not mean abandoning one's responsibilities as a teacher; that giving up the rigidly teacher-centred structure of the traditional course in tertiary education does *not* mean having no structure.

Certainly, a move towards independence in learning and a relaxation of some conventional constraints, must be associated with greater freedom of choice for the learner; but, as seems to be the case for freedom more generally, one may well create greater real autonomy by imposing a well-defined and agreed set of 'rules of the game'. Occasionally, the 'rules' can be minimal or even just taken for granted. Thus there have been some successful examples of courses of independent study in which students have been given nothing but the general indication of what it is they are expected to do, and a final deadline.

The School of Independent Studies at Lancaster University has used a minimal framework along these lines for several years. Likewise in most colleges and universities in the USA students can earn academic credit by 'independent study', in which a small section of a course is given over to the private study of self-selected topics, on which 'term papers' must be submitted for assessment. Approaches like these certainly seem to work for some students, but they do tend to put a premium on the almost unaided efforts of students to learn by themselves.

It is not accidental that options of this kind, whether formally offered or not, are often taken by mature students, who already possess some of the necessary skills for working in this way. For the typical entrant into tertiary education sudden immersion into this sort of independence is more likely to lead to sinking rather than learning to swim. Independence, like freedom, needs a framework to nurture and support it.

The general features of a framework or structure for independent learning are as follows:

1. clearly defined goals
2. availability of the necessary material and human resources

3. an understanding of the roles and responsibilities of both the teacher and the students
4. arrangements by which both parties can be prepared for the new demands to be imposed on them and can acquire some of the appropriate skills in a 'fail-safe' way
5. means by which the success of the course can be checked as it proceeds and if necessary changed without bureaucratic snags.

These, it seems to me, are the minimum requirements of 'structuring' that it is desirable to include in any innovative course. For courses which aim to promote independence in learning they are essential.

But can we go beyond these generalities? Unfortunately, the reader expecting any neat recipe or blueprint for promoting independence in his own course will be disappointed. This is not only because there are obviously a large number of varieties and degrees of 'independence', nor only because there is also an infinite variety of local conditions and constraints. Even if other things were equal, the educational environment and, above all, people, are never quite the same from place to place or time to time. Ultimately the minor and often unexpected details of an educational situation can make or break an innovation. Most important is probably the accidental and largely uncontrollable mix of personalities, interests, motivations and aspirations to be found among the participants in the average course — most important, the teacher him/herself. There is no neat formula for dealing with these variables. However, it is worth saying a little more about two of the aspects of structuring listed above, as they are particularly important. One is the need for *careful preparation* and induction of both students and teachers; the other is the desirability of careful 'quality control' or *evaluation* of the processes and the outcome of the course. I will also discuss briefly some of the possible implications for structuring of the differences between 'regular' and mature students.

Preparing students and teachers
Too often, it seems, students and their teachers are plunged into new ways of teaching and learning on the assumption that they can pick up the new skills needed. Sudden and unprepared imposition of the demands and responsibilities of extensive autonomy in learning can be counter-productive. As John Powell emphasizes in his contribution, both students and teachers need to learn to cope with the new kinds of role they will be expected to play. This process cannot be rushed and time for adjustment is very important. It is not simply a matter of acquiring new technical skills: long-standing assumptions about the function and behaviour of an academic teacher may need to be changed.

Telling students or teachers in talks or in introductory notes about the new pressures and roles is not enough. Gradual and controlled introduction of the actual experience of working within the new framework should be built in as part of the innovation itself. The need for gradualism in this respect has been emphasized in a different context by Kelly (1955) as quoted by Gibbs (1977). Kelly describes the process of acceptance of new ideas as one of cautious negotiation. He emphasizes the great importance of the existing way in which people construct their personal worlds. This personal construct cannot be lightly abandoned on the say-so of another or because of the sudden appearance of new kinds of demands. Change must come about in a gradual and piecemeal way.

Throughout the process of weaning students into greater autonomy and responsibility, a major role of the teacher and of the course structure must be to provide guidance and support. The learner must be assured that a 'safety net' exists and that he is not entirely dependent on his own (probably initially rather meagre) resources. One of the problems for the teacher, like the parent, is to judge correctly when and to what extent to let go of the hand of those for whom he has a responsibility. There is no way, unfortunately, in which this can be done without taking *some* risks. It is particularly in this respect that a gradual approach is necessary.

There are examples among the case studies of ways in which students may be prepared for independence in the educational context. There are also descriptions elsewhere of other ways in which students and teachers can learn some of the skills involved using various forms of workshops, games, simulations and group sessions (eg Northedge, 1975; Gibbs, 1977; Cornwall *et al*, 1977). Certainly there should be no serious organizational (or innovative) problems in most institutions about introducing small components of independence into otherwise conventional courses. For example, students in small groups can be asked to prepare over several weeks short reports on a subject of their own choice (within the subject area of the course) and to present a talk on it to a full session of their fellow students; or students can be asked to study a part of a course independently, using the teacher as a consultant. These minor innovations are undoubtedly trivial when compared with the more full-blooded approaches to independent learning described in the case studies. Nevertheless, they can provide a very useful first taste of independence for many students and their teachers. Even a small component of such activities within an otherwise closely prescribed and directed curriculum seems to loom very large in the perceptions of most students, when they first experience it.

A final innovative tip concerns the need to use what might be called the Jesuit approach; get them early and they are yours for life! In the present context this is not as sinister as it may sound. It means simply that the skills and attitudes appropriate to independent study are likely to be best promoted by allowing students to experience *some* autonomy as early as possible during a course of study. The attitudes and expectations of students about what is expected of them and what are the usual methods of teaching and learning, seem to be firmly established quite soon after they enter the new and unfamiliar world of higher education. If part of that normal pattern of activity includes elements of independent study, the later introduction of 'real' independence is likely to be much easier, and will not be so likely to be regarded as deviant.

Innovative problems

Innovation — the introduction of the new or unfamiliar — is difficult in any field. In tradition-bound higher education it is more difficult than in most. The introduction of independent learning is likely to provoke maximum resistance, since it challenges some of the more basic preconceptions of how learning can and should take place, and of the teachers' role. It is wise for the would-be educational innovator to be fully aware that many of his colleagues are going to be less than enthusiastic about innovation in general and independent study in particular. Because the capacity and taste for change seems generally to decline with age, whereas formal status and authority usually increases with the same variable, the eager innovator can expect to encounter resistance where he is least likely to be able to deploy countermeasures! There are of course the usual arguments against change which have been well documented (a recent and directly relevant discussion is the book by Astin, 1976). These arguments may take the form of the 'not-invented-here' syndrome, or the 'we haven't done it before' response or, perhaps, the many variants on the theme of deference to potentially disapproving higher authority of the 'mother-wouldn't-like-it' type. Among such institutions are one's academic board or senate, the accrediting bodies like the Council for National Academic Awards in the UK, the various professional bodies like the Council for Engineering Institutions or, more diffusely, 'Industry'. Such arguments must be treated seriously, if not always with respect. At the very least they force the innovator to reassess his own arguments, to build in safeguards, to plan and prepare the ground more carefully than he otherwise would. It is not unknown for an over-eager innovator and his followers to allow their enthusiasm to carry them across the logical gaps in their arguments or organizational proposals. The rationale and the organizational plans may look impeccable on paper but the reality will not be anything like as neat.

Those who put some form of independent learning into practice as the basis for a whole course must be prepared for special difficulties. Roughly speaking, the amount of innovative effort necessary will be proportional to the location of the innovation up the 'steps' in Figure 1. How much you can 'get away with' depends to a great extent on how much you want to rewrite the conventional script for the roles of teacher and of student. It is well to remember that the would-be heretic who rejects the established pedagogy too radically, risks severe censure and even the educational equivalent of excommunication. Roskilde University Centre in Denmark is an institution which has based itself largely on 'problem-orientated project-organized' study in which students are required to exercise very considerable autonomy in every aspect of their courses — study itself, assessment, organization, administration and even to some extent in financial matters. For several years after its foundation it suffered a succession of serious clashes with the educational establishment ostensibly concerned with questions of 'standards' and demands for conformity to the general pattern of university assessment in Denmark. It survived. And now it is establishing its pattern of education as a valid alternative which is attracting the attention of the traditional institutions for more positive reasons. Bremen University in the German Federal Republic is also based largely on group project work in which students exercise considerable autonomy. This university, too, has become a focal point of hostile criticism within (and to some extent beyond) German higher education. Unfortunately, the pressure towards conformity (including revised national statutes on the government of universities) does seem there to have caused a substantial degree of retrogression compared with the original ideals of the founders (Cornwall *et al*, 1977). On a smaller and less publicized scale there are undoubtedly many other examples of attempts to expand the independence of students, which have been thwarted by the various forms of resistance to change. Unfortunately, initiatives which suffer in this way are not usually described in print — success stories are both easier and more rewarding to get published.

New approaches in teaching and learning seem rarely to be initiated by institutions at a formal level, even though they will, if successful, eventually be formally endorsed by them. The initiative usually arises from the enthusiastic and energetic efforts of an individual or small group. The pioneering spirit seems to be an essential ingredient in carrying through an innovation, especially if it challenges cherished notions of what is possible, right or proper. But this brings dangers. We can probably all think of exciting new developments in our own departments or institutions which flourished briefly but were too closely associated with one or two individuals to survive their disappearance from the scene, or the flagging of their interest and enthusiasm for their own brainchild. For an innovation to stick it must become properly institutionalized; it must become a new tradition. That means that the successful innovator, having proved the feasibility of the new approach, must attempt to get the institutional regulations, especially the procedures for the allocation of resources and the decision-making mechanism, amended so as to provide formalized support for the new approach. This may sound over-legalistic, but when the going gets tough, for example when there is a financial pruning exercise, the innovation which is tolerated as an act of institutional goodwill or simply tacked on to the departmental organization is the easiest to dispense with.

Some barriers to change

The 'authority', especially at the national level, often tends to be thought of as an inhibitor of change and a reactionary maintainer of tradition. In fact, it may be eager itself to stimulate and nurture educational innovation in over-cautious, if not hidebound institutions. The most dominant and immediate resisters of change are much more likely to be one's colleagues whose motives are many and varied (and certainly not always unreasonable!). Administrators, too, are likely to frown upon deviations from convention which threaten to upset the system.

For example, in science and technology departments used to the idea that student attainment can and always should be quantitatively measurable in quasi-precise examination percentages, it is not surprising that there might be suspicion of courses which place emphasis on difficult-to-measure skills and attitudes. The administration also usually demands neat ranking of students according to exact numerical criteria of performance, with pass-fail decisions sometimes dependent on one or two percentage points. It is as if Lord Rayleigh's dictum, which may be paraphrased: 'If you can't measure it, you don't know much about it', has been taken seriously beyond the realms of classical physics itself.

The system is also likely to be thrown into confusion by attempts to schedule a course of independent study in other than the conventional way, ie with teaching hours divided neatly and periodically into one, two or three hour slots once or twice a week for a particular course. Attempts by a teacher to use larger blocks of time or to plan a teaching schedule flexibly according to the likely demands of students at different stages of a course require considerable negotiation with academic colleagues and administrators who may be unwilling to be so flexible. Administrators in particular are very sensitive to any blurring of the apparently well-defined 'teaching hours' criterion which in many institutions is the primary index used to calculate the all-important student-staff ratio for the department and the institution. (These remarks apply particularly to the sciences and technology, and probably more to the non-university than to the university sector of higher education.) These are just a few of the many organizational problems.

I have given several examples of what might be called structural sources of resistance to change. Anyone advocating or trying to initiate independent learning on a significant scale will usually experience a wealth of objections and criticism related to more fundamental educational issues. In the last section of this chapter I have tried to produce a short compendium of arguments against independence in learning (based on actual conversations and discussion), together with an indication of some of the responses that one might make.

© Sue Curtiss, Malcolm Cornwall. 1977

Seven arguments against independent study

Left to themselves students would work at a low level and standards would drop

A common and natural concern of academics is that standards will fall on the introduction of a new and unfamiliar method of teaching and learning. There is, however, much evidence to suggest that the level and standard of work is more often higher in independent study than we would expect from students on conventional courses at comparable stages. Yes, there are students who perform poorly when learning to study independently. But the weak student is to be found whatever approaches we adopt to teaching and learning, and we do not (or should not) judge the effectiveness of a new approach in terms of the performance of the least successful. On average, standards even in conventional terms are certainly not necessarily lower.

Lurking behind this criticism, too, is the assumption that level and standard are to be judged only in terms of the almost exclusive criterion of most conventional courses, namely in terms of the coverage of the standard content of a predigested and conventionally acceptable syllabus.

The outcome of independent learning must be judged at least as much in terms of the acquisition of skills and abilities as of the acquisition of factual knowledge. Not least among these abilities is that of learning autonomously. Moreover, one might question whether conventional courses can inculcate in students the range of intellectual skills which are usually referred to in the statements of aims and objectives of courses. The emphasis, in practice, on the production of 'right' answers would seem to mitigate against any real intellectual relationships between the student and the material studied. He becomes concerned with satisfying the expectations of particular teachers rather than adopting a critical attitude to his subject matter.

It has to be accepted, however, that if independent learning were adopted more widely, the ability to reproduce given areas of content in conventional examinations might decline. This would be more than compensated for by an improvement in other abilities of much longer term importance, not least the ability to plan and manage one's own learning. And although the assessment of these abilities is not amenable to the quasi-precise methods we employ in general in higher education, there are various ways in which we can monitor and evaluate their development.

Finally, the criticism presupposes that the independent learner would be 'left to himself'. But independent learning is not synonymous with learning in isolation. Students have a tutor or tutors (as with research students) and probably a group with whom work can be planned and discussed. The tutor acts as a resource, a counsellor, and maybe even a devil's advocate, who helps the student towards reaching his own ends in his own ways, rather than as a prescriber of given goals and means, as he is in the conventional approach. His function is to be a sounding board or sympathetic ear, and his reactions can stimulate the student to explore more deeply or investigate alternative strategies.

Students are not capable of working independently
This objection is usually based on the assumption that students lack the basic knowledge and skills from which to begin to work independently. After at least 18 years of life in general and 13 years of formal education, students are seemingly unable to take any initiative for deciding what and how they will learn and the task remains the sole responsibility of the teacher. Nevertheless, approximately three or four years later, raw graduates entering the professions or becoming research students are regarded as being capable of a very high degree of autonomy, especially with respect to being responsible for their own learning. Should we conclude that this is the result of a process of maturation which occurs at approximately 21 years of age during the rather sharp transition between student and graduate status? It does not seem at all obvious why three more years of an education almost identical in its approach to that already experienced in school should succeed in creating people capable of continuing to learn efficiently and independently where the previous 13 years have failed. In reality, it is of course the necessity to learn independently which produces the ability. Clearly, the only way to learn to swim is to get into the water, and it is patently better to do this in the presence of someone who can rescue you when you sink and can encourage you to try again, rather than when you are alone and in danger of drowning. From the moment of taking one's feet off the bottom and clumsily splashing about, expertise will develop through a combination of advice from the instructor and watching other people, but mainly through hard practice. So, too, with learning to learn independently. To expect the student to have the skills to operate successfully in the very early stages is an unrealistic as expecting a child to swim on his first day at the seaside. Some students will need to be encouraged into the water, others restrained from rushing in headlong. All will need help in developing their skills over time. But, just as the child of an overprotective parent is unlikely to learn to swim, so the student of an overprotective teacher will not learn to be an independent learner.

It is more efficient and much quicker to use teacher-directed learning than to allow students to find out for themselves
In terms of a set syllabus it is probably, but not necessarily, the case that the independent learner will not so quickly cover the ground. However, if the formulation of problems, the development of approaches to learning and of research techniques, and several other intellectual skills are considered to be at least as important as the acquisition of a body of knowledge, then it will not be time wasted.

At a more fundamental level, the implied 'efficiency' of conventional approaches is questionable. Even in terms of content-centred aims, the economy of teacher-directed learning seems illusory. The academic teacher approaches his subject matter from a position of in-depth knowledge. His teaching is a summary of complex material which by its condensation has, inevitably, lost many of its original subtleties. The process of oversimplification continues as the teacher's comments are transformed into students' notes. Students thus learn to 'know', for example, that the working classes are linguistically inept, and repeat it endlessly in examination scripts. In science courses, too, the artificially neat and closed character of a conventional syllabus belies the real nature of science and its methodology. Teacher-directed learning can easily cover a lot of ground; I doubt that students are necessarily gaining much familiarity with the scenery *en route*. To some critics the 'finding out for themselves' character of independent learning seems to have been misinterpreted as akin to an advanced form of 'discovery learning'. It is, of course, nothing of the sort. There is no suggestion that present knowledge should be kept hidden from the student. On the contrary, through the necessity of using a wide range of media he will be likely to explore well beyond the scope of what any individual teacher might reasonably be expected to offer. It could be argued that learning restricted only to that knowledge which is prescribed by the teacher is potentially far more limited than resource-based learning, and is therefore less efficient.

In a highly structured subject it is essential that students be given a firm foundation of basic facts on which they can build
This objection can be approached at two levels. First, given that the students with whom we deal have already acquired some of the basic material through their school courses, it would not be unreasonable to expect that they have reached a point where they might become independent learners. But it is often claimed that students have not, in fact, mastered the basics sufficiently well to move on by themselves. If this is indeed the case, we need to ask the question already posed: will further instruction of a similar kind succeed where it has failed before?

It might, on the other hand, be claimed that the relevant basic facts are different from those met in a school syllabus. Students will be ignorant of their existence so that even if they are literate and numerate in the broadest sense they will not be aware that the facts are there to be acquired. They will therefore attempt to solve problems without the benefit of relevant knowledge. But this is, of course, the situation of the research student, especially at the start of his work. In his case we seem prepared to accept that the areas of existing knowledge required to solve a problem will become evident with the analysis of the problem, and that the nature of his project will force him to learn at the appropriate levels. If a text proves too difficult he will be forced back down the knowledge hierarchy until he reaches a point which relates to his existing knowledge and level of understanding. In this way, the hierarchical and lateral connections will become apparent through the research activity itself, and the relevant part of the map of knowledge will be brought vividly to his attention. Why is it that this process should not be thought to be possible for the learner on other levels in higher education?

At a second and more basic level one might question the fundamental assumption concerning the way we learn which is implied in this criticism. This assumption is revealed by the metaphor in terms of which the objection is expressed, viz, that learning a subject is akin to building a house; first we must have the foundations (prescribed basic knowledge) and then we can build on this brick by brick (*quanta* of knowledge), each neatly fitting within the existing structure. Clearly, with such a model of learning, it is nonsense to attempt to build the second floor until the foundations and first floor are complete; that is, to expect students to fit in blocks of advanced knowledge before they have consolidated the lower levels. A reflection of this model of learning can be found in the rigidly hierarchical format of most scientific textbooks, where there is an assumed identity between the formal structure of knowledge and the form in which that knowledge is taught and learned.

An alternative, and more appropriate metaphor for learning if we are to remain in the field of construction, is that of building a steel-framed structure in outer space — an interconnected network of potentially infinite extent, to which it is possible to add pieces in almost any order as long as they interconnect in some way, and form a pattern which makes sense to the builder. In this model there is nothing to prevent us completing the whole structure in outline before filling in the finer detail, or indeed starting at one place rather than another. I do not suggest that this analogy is necessarily consistent with all that is known about the learning process. But there is, of course, some support from the well-known work of Piaget, and of Bruner (eg 1966) for such a model of learning. More recently, the information processing school of cognitive psychology (Norman, 1973; Lindsay and Norman, 1977; Rumelhart, 1977) has developed models of memory and of the cognitive processes more generally, based on much empirical evidence, which are consistent with the sort of network model referred to above.

As with any analogy, implicit or explicit, it is tempting but unwise to elaborate it beyond its intended purpose. Here that purpose is simply to attempt to show that the conventional assumption that there is a uniquely definable predetermined body of knowledge which is necessarily a prerequisite for any independent study, does not seem to be in accord with our experience of learning, nor with our growing knowledge of the learning process.

Students don't know what they ought to study

This objection is closely related to the previous one. It assumes that only when, like the teacher, you have a superior knowledge of the subject, can you see what knowledge it is appropriate to acquire at each stage. This aspect has already been discussed.

There are, however, other implications behind the criticism, involving what is seen as the educationalists' responsibility towards the professions and society at large. It may be argued that employers need to be sure that their employees have covered an agreed area of knowledge which they can then take for granted (though employers themselves rarely seem to adopt such a view — see, for example, Jevons and Turner, 1972). These agreed areas are often negotiated with professional bodies consisting of people who have been through traditional courses themselves and who are mainly concerned with the status of their profession. They are people whose central interests are, quite properly, not only different from those of educationalists, but also, it could be argued, different from those of employers. The curriculum dictated by these bodies is not therefore necessarily related to the real needs of the job. Unfortunately the influence of the professional bodies cannot be ignored, whatever our views are as professional educationalists of the validity of their requirements.

Most students prefer to be taught
This is probably true. Being taught is a more comfortable, less threatening situation than learning independently. It is mainly a matter of finding out what you ought to know and how best to regurgitate this back to the teacher.

It is also true that many teachers enjoy the didactic lecturing situation. Although both students and tutors might have private doubts about the effectiveness of this approach to teaching and about the dangers of over-teaching, this mode is still the dominant one. Its dominance can be ascribed to a process of mutual seduction in which each party, while recognizing the undesirability of the situation, is egged on by the apparent willingness of the other.

It would, of course, be inconsistent with my central argument to disregard the preference of students concerning the methods by which they are taught, but preference implies choice, and choice is only real when, firstly, one is aware and has some experience of the alternatives and, secondly, the opportunity to choose is actually offered. In our present system neither condition seems in general to hold. Students, like the people in the advertisement for a famous brand of stout, can claim 'I don't like it because I've never tried it'. Usually they can go further and add, 'In any case it's not available'.

It would be fair to argue, however, that to substitute one approach to learning — independent study — for another is hardly going to increase choice. But even supposing one were to advocate the replacement of the existing approach by independent learning, rather than its introduction alongside the traditional, one would not limit student choice. Independent learning, as this book aims to show, is an aim and not simply a method. To become an independent learner is to attain an ability to use a wide variety of ways of learning including, if available and appropriate, a course of lectures.

You can't properly assess flexibility, adaptability and other such qualities
This view has already been discussed briefly earlier in this chapter. So often in education the assessment tail wags the curriculum dog. Certainly

assessment is important. And the assessment of the skills and abilities
which independent study claims to foster are often much more difficult
to assess than the acquisition of factual knowledge and the ability of
students to manipulate this knowledge in a fairly simple way. But the
difficulty of assessment should not prevent us from structuring our courses
in such a way as to develop other skills and abilities if we consider them
to be important. Even within most existing courses the apparent objectivity
and precision of our formal examination procedure belies the reality of
how, ultimately, our judgements of students are actually made. No matter
how many sophisticated statistical techniques we import into assessment,
at the heart of the matter is a professional judgement based on a largely
intuitive understanding of what we are trying to achieve. In project
gradings, evaluation is often an ill-defined compromise between the
differing professional judgements of various examiners.

Nevertheless, we can and should strive to improve and develop the
means by which we assess the less objectifiable outcomes of our
educational processes. In the meantime, we ought to recognize that we
do make such assessments in the course of our roles as teachers, in
assessing project work, in examiners' meetings, in writing references.
And, whether we can assess them accurately or not, the skills and abilities
which we all accept as important goals for higher education can clearly
be more effectively promoted by certain educational approaches than
others. I have no doubt that independent learning is one such approach.

The teacher's knowledge and expertise would not be properly used ...
Most teachers would not be able to work in this way
These are two separate but closely related criticisms. The first reflects an
understandable anxiety that to allow and encourage independent learning
is to devalue the present skills and capabilities of teachers. In blunter
terms it implies that if we are not careful we will make ourselves
redundant. It is possible to reassure this critic that far from devaluing
his technical knowledge and skills, the independent learner is likely to
recognize and value highly the expert guidance which the teacher can
provide in helping him with his learning difficulties. The second statement
has been discussed briefly earlier in this chapter and it is based on a
recognition that the acceptance of independent learning requires the
teacher to adopt a new and unfamiliar role. Instead of the expert
interpreter and dispenser of specialist knowledge, the teacher needs to be
more of a guide to resources, a consultant. Instead of an overseer of the
progress of students through a prescribed syllabus, he needs to be a guide
and adviser on their learning problems as they develop an increasing
degree of self-direction. As emphasized earlier, the provision of advice,
guidance and, frequently, direct assistance, is crucial to the development
of autonomy in learning. Unfortunately, teachers in higher education are
not necessarily going to possess the skills or experience appropriate to
this non-didactic role. But if one accepts the need to move in a small way
towards the development of greater independence in learning, then the

onus is on us to acquire some of these skills. Staff retraining and development programmes are obviously part of the answer; 'learning on the job' by introducing or extending the degree of independent learning in existing courses in a limited and controlled way, is another. Above all, the continued use of our own skills as independent learners in order to extend our competence in appropriate ways, seems not only the most apt but also the most effective way of enabling us to help students to become more effective independent learners themselves.

Postscript

These, then, are just some of the arguments and counter-arguments that the enthusiast for independent learning should be aware of. You will no doubt hear many other reasons why it 'can't be done'. You might well have thought of a few others yourself. Only a little imagination is needed to generate many possible difficulties and problems. But if, nevertheless, you believe it is worthwhile to go ahead with your own innovations based on independent learning, it is encouraging to be reminded of Mark Twain's comments: 'I've foreseen many problems in my life. Luckily many of them never turned up!'.

13. Moving Towards Independent Learning

J. P. Powell

Reading through the case studies, one is struck by the frequency with which three issues are identified as being especially significant in moves toward a more independent style of learning. These are the difficulties which face teachers, those which face students, and the role of assessment. Each will be examined in turn, and I shall conclude with a brief discussion of the educational significance of independence in learning.

The teacher

Almost all of the contributors mention the difficulties which arise for teachers who attempt to encourage student growth towards independence. Not only are many of the instructional techniques unfamiliar but in addition the whole approach demands a major change of role and a review of the nature and extent of the teacher's responsibilities. David Potts recalls his experience of '. . . a strange sense of loss of role and authority as a teacher', and Jane Abercrombie quotes a teacher as saying: 'Every so often I get in a real neurotic state because I keep thinking this is just too loose for words.'

Traditionally teachers have worked in an authoritarian mode, so that anyone who attempts to shift the centre of gravity of responsibility for learning towards the student is almost certain to experience doubts and difficulties in adjusting to a new role. Most teachers are only able to tolerate a moderate reduction in the degree of control which they exercise in the classroom before this produces anxiety, sometimes associated with management problems which they are ill-equipped to handle.

The parallel theoretical issue is that of clarifying the responsibilities of teachers who are attempting to work in a more independent mode. David Potts argues that to aim at fostering student independence does not imply that the teacher should give up all responsibility for leadership: 'I believe that by putting on a course I have a responsibility to lead, to use my abilities and experience to offer valuable material and ideas.' He adds: '. . . students cannot know without training *how* to do something . . . skills are most rapidly learnt where most conscientiously taught . . .'.

The traditional responsibility of the teacher is to encourage and promote learning and this precludes the adoption of an 'anything goes' approach which leaves everything in the hands of the learner. Where the fostering of independence is a central aim, the teacher must strive to avoid pre-empting and short-circuiting what the student needs to do in order to learn. Much of our teaching is characterized by a repeated demonstration of subject-matter knowledge and skills in such a manner that the student is left with little to do beyond the performance of routine intellectual and clerical tasks. The student becomes a victim of the teacher's role, a receptacle for highly-processed and over-simplified information which is quickly forgotten once it has served its purpose as examination fodder.

Constant intrusions into the student's learning space, although intended to be helpful, serve only to inhibit growth towards independence. This point has been expressed very well by David Potts who argues that students need a protected private space within which to think for themselves: '. . . students' experiences of traditional tutorial discussions are more of interruption than of self-expression'. It is not a caricature to depict much of our teaching as a series of disabling intrusions into the private struggles of learners. One result of this is that many students give up and leave all the running to the teacher. 'The tutor intended only to kick off the ball but ended up scoring all the goals.'

Teachers who wish to encourage more independence in their students must be prepared to adopt an unfamiliar role and the initial difficulties in doing this have been described by a number of contributors. We have to be willing to make fewer choices, decisions, plans, judgements and assessments in order to create opportunities for students to make more of them. This is not as simple as it sounds because our earlier experience tends to make us over-cautious, uncomfortable and distrustful of the students' capacity to make good use of the opportunities offered to them. A powerful constraint is the conventional professional image of the teacher. After all, are we not paid to instruct and examine? The answer to this must surely be that we are paid to educate students and this implies doing everything possible to extend their intellectual and affective development to the point where they become independent of us, their teachers.

Another constraint is the pressure towards conformity which is exerted in a variety of ways by colleagues and by institutional rules and arrangements. The latter are raised in a very direct manner as soon as we pose the question: If control is vested in students where do staff stand in relation to their contract with the institution? Much can be achieved without provoking opposition from colleagues who may be unsympathetic towards the whole idea of independent learning, but it is helpful to seek out teachers who share one's aims in order to share ideas and discuss problems and issues as they arise.

Given the kinds of difficulties which have been mentioned here it seems clear that any major shift of orientation towards independent learning will require initiatives and support at all institutional levels and

especially within individual departments where there is the freedom and
opportunity to re-direct learning and teaching.

The student

Somewhat similar problems confront students when they are faced with
an environment for learning which requires an unfamiliar degree of
initiative and self-confidence. As John Heron points out, the earlier
experiences of students have rendered almost all of them totally
unprepared to exercise independent thought and action in handling their
own learning needs. Accustomed to being passive consumers of courses
designed, presented and assessed by others they are bewildered and often
resentful when it is suggested that they assume more responsibility for
their own learning. Even those who are prepared to tackle less structured
courses, as Harry Stanton shows, lack confidence in their ability to handle
them successfully and need a great deal of help if they are to overcome
their fears and anxieties.

An important issue here is the role which feelings and attitudes play
in the transition to a more independent learning style. Lack of confidence,
inability to respond constructively to criticism from others, and unrealistic
appraisals of their own abilities and intellectual products often combine to
lock students into endless fealty to their teachers. This can only be
overcome by accepting students as they are, and then progressively
encouraging them to move forward as they gain increasing trust in their
own judgements and abilities. The anxieties of students must be fully
acknowledged and handled with sympathy and tact. Unless this is done
most students will reject teaching methods and course designs based upon
theories of independent learning — several of the case studies illustrate
the risks which are involved. These can be minimized by talking frankly
about what we are trying to do. We do not spend enough time talking
with students about our aims and methods and how these connect with
their own learning needs.

Another very significant element here is the character of student
motivation. Many are concerned with little more than obtaining a passing
grade and are thus hostile towards any teaching procedures which are
seen as making this more difficult to achieve. The blame for this must
fall entirely on the system which encourages an overriding concern with
passing examinations and which has consistently failed to develop an
interest in the kind of learning which is personally meaningful and
satisfying. This probably constitutes the most serious obstacle to the more
widespread introduction of teaching and assessment practices which seek
to foster student autonomy. Students are in need of help as much as
staff if these difficulties are to be overcome, and many of the contributors
have described a variety of ways in which this assistance may be provided.
One of the simplest and most effective of these is discussing with students
the nature and purpose of what we are trying to do.

Assessment

References to assessment feature prominently in the case studies and John Heron has discussed in detail a number of the issues to which it gives rise. The main reason for its being such a focus of concern lies in its connection with accreditation, both of students and of staff. Few students would be willing to study for awards which had little currency beyond the walls of the classroom and few staff would wish to be identified with courses which were viewed as being of little worth by their peers. It is also probable that unconventional teaching methods are more likely to be tolerated if assessment procedures conform to institutional norms. Frequently, however, independent learning programmes involve self- and peer-assessment procedures and these are seen as threatening to academic standards and potentially destructive of the self-image of many teachers. That the significance of these points is appreciated by educational innovators is clearly evident in many of the early chapters. Several of the contributors took quite elaborate steps to ensure that their efforts, and those of their students, would not be vulnerable to the charge that they were undermining institutional assessment standards.

This displayed sound political sense. Opponents of educational change often rely upon alleged threats to academic standards to thwart policies with which they disagree. This is also good politics because most academics are reluctant to be seen supporting anything which can be presented as posing a threat to a central element in their professional value system. Leaving aside political considerations, it must be acknowledged that all teachers have an important and legitimate responsibility to 'maintain standards' in the sense of encouraging their students to strive to improve the quality of their work and to learn to apply exacting standards in judging the value of it. The discharge of this responsibility becomes more, not less, difficult when attempting to assess students' progress towards independence. This is because of the complexity of the skills and values which are embodied in the notion of independent thought and action. Assessing student progress with respect to these is a far more daunting — and important — task than operating the assessment procedures which are associated with most conventional courses. Working out the details of how this can be accomplished without hindering the achievement of what is being assessed remains a major challenge to everyone involved with independent learning.

Educational values

What is the educational significance of developing autonomy in learning and why do the contributors to this book attach such importance to it? John Heron's account of what it involves would probably be endorsed by all of the authors. He defines a 'self-determining learner' as someone:

> . . . who can set his own learning objectives, devise a rational programme to attain them, set criteria of excellence by which to assess the work he produces,

and assess his own work in the light of those criteria — indeed all that we *attribute* to and *hope* for from the ideal academic himself.

The choice of the word 'ideal' draws attention to a most important feature of the characteristics of an independent learner, namely, that they are subject to unending further development and refinement. Unlike such skills as spelling and counting they can never be finally mastered and awarded ten out of ten. They develop almost imperceptibly over a long period of time — which helps to explain why teaching, in the short run, is so psychologically unrewarding.

Another important claim which is implicit in this quotation is that a basic aim of academic teachers is to encourage students to become increasingly like their teachers. This is not to be understood as meaning the mere production of replicas but rather the gradual enlargement of a community which shares in the creation of knowledge, ideas, skills and values. As teachers our work is guided by the aim of sharing our intellectual interests and skills and encouraging students to develop these further so that they eventually transcend contemporary academic achievements.

The promotion of independent learning is thus central to the whole enterprise of higher education because the intellectual powers which it seeks to foster cannot (logically cannot) be exercised except in an independent mode. Critical thinking, judgement, creativeness, initiative, interpretative skills, hypothesis formulation and problem-solving capacities can only be made manifest by someone who is operating independently. The contributors to this book are also implicitly saying that these powers of the mind can only be developed in learning environments which offer the learner freedom to practise these skills.

More generally, and quite apart from the specialized academic skills which higher education is concerned to foster, we value a society in which people are able to think and act independently, to exercise freedom of choice after rational reflection, and can conduct their own lives without having their minds made up by others. Independent learning must therefore be viewed as part of a much broader social movement which respects, paradoxically, the values of both individuality and community. For without our own distinctive individual contributions there will be nothing worthwhile to share — a point emphatically made by Voltaire.

Unfortunately, our institutions of higher learning, despite public proclamations to the contrary, display only a very weak commitment to all of this. Much of our teaching, however well-intentioned, is not designed to promote independence of mind. Some of our best students are so 'turned off' that they decide to discontinue. Others find the system sufficiently congenial to be able to persevere to graduation but are then ill-prepared to operate beyond the familiar confines of textbooks and laboratory manuals. Admittedly, some of us survive but this is due either to accidents of personal resilience and native wit or to the, usually unacknowledged, influence of individual teachers to whom we owe an immense debt.

The innovations described in this book bear witness to what can be achieved, and should serve to encourage all of us to persist in our efforts to help students to have more confidence in themselves and, at the same time, to become more like us!

References

Abercrombie, M L J (1960) *The Anatomy of Judgement*, London: Hutchinson; Harmondsworth: Penguin (1969).

Abercrombie, M L J (1966) Educating for change, *Universities Quarterly*, **21**, 7-16.

Abercrombie, M L J (1974) Improving the education of architects, pp 23-43 in Collier, K G (ed) *Innovation in Higher Education*, Slough: National Foundation for Educational Research.

Abercrombie, M L J (1979) *Aims and Techniques of Group Teaching*, 4th Ed, Guildford, Surrey: Society for Research into Higher Education.

Abercrombie, M L J, Forest, A J and Terry, P M (1970) Diploma project 1968-69, *Architectural Research and Teaching*, **1**, 6-12.

Abercrombie, M L J and Terry, P M (1971) The first session: an introduction to associative group discussion. Appendix in 2nd Ed of Abercrombie, M L J, *Aims and Techniques of Group Teaching*, Guildford, Surrey: Society for Research into Higher Education.

Abercrombie, M L J and Terry, P M (1973) Students' attitudes to professionalism as seen in group discussions, *Universities Quarterly*, **27**, 465-74.

Abercrombie, M L J and Terry, P M (1977) A contribution to the psychology of designing, *Journal of Architectural Education*, **30** (4), 15-18.

Abercrombie, M L J and Terry, P M (1978a) *Talking to Learn: Improving Teaching and Learning in Small Groups*, Guildford, Surrey: Society for Research into Higher Education.

Abercrombie, M L J and Terry, P M (1978b) Reactions to change in the authority-dependency relationship, *British Journal of Guidance and Counselling*, **6**, 82-94.

Adams, J D (1974) *Phases of Personal and Professional Development*, unpublished manuscript, NTL Institute for Applied Behavioural Science.

Ali, M A, Thomas, E J, Hamilton, J D and Brain, M D (1977) Blood and guts: one component of an integrated program in biological sciences as applied to medicine, *Canadian Medical Association Journal*, **116**, 59-61.

Allport, G (1960) *Personality and Social Encounter*, Boston: Beacon Press.

Association for Supervision and Curriculum Development (1962) *Perceiving, Behaving, Becoming*, Washington DC: ASCD.

Astin, J (1976) *Academic Gamesmanship: Student-Orientated Change in Higher Education*, New York: Praeger.

Atherton, C (1972) Lecture, discussion and independent study: instructional methods revisited, *Journal of Experimental Education*, **40** (4), 24-8.

Audemars, D, Borel, M and Jacot, J (1977) *Le Petit Guide du Parrain*, Lausanne: EPFL-CPD, (1974), Octobre.

Barrows, H S and Mitchell, D L M (1975) An innovative course in undergraduate neuroscience: experiment in problem-based learning with 'problem boxes', *British Journal of Medical Education*, **9** (4), 223-30.

Barrows, H S and Tamblyn, R (1977) The portable patient problem pack (P4): a problem based learning unit, *Journal of Medical Education*, **52**, 1002-4.

Billings, J A and Stoeckle, J D (1977) Pelvic examination instruction and the doctor-patient relationship, *Journal of Medical Education*, **52**, 824-39.

Bilorusky, J and Butler, H (1975) Beyond contract curricula to improvisational learning, pp 144-72 in Berte, N R (ed) *Individualizing Education Through Contract Learning*, Alabama: University of Alabama Press.

Black, P J and Boud, D J (1977) Counting the cost, in Bridge, W and Elton, L (eds) *Individual Study in Undergraduate Science*, London: Heinemann Educational, 178-89.

Boud, D J and Bridge, W (1974) Keller Plan: a case study in individualized learning, in *Towards Independence in Learning: Selected Papers*, London: Nuffield Foundation.

Boud, D J and Pascoe, J (1978) *Experiential Learning: Developments in Australian Post-Secondary Education*, Sydney: Australian Consortium on Experiential Education.

Boud, D J and Prosser, M T (1980) Sharing responsibility: staff-student cooperation in learning, *British Journal of Educational Technology*, **11** (1), 24-35.

Boydell, T (1976) *Experiential Learning*, Manchester Monographs No 5, Manchester: University of Manchester Department of Adult and Higher Education.

Brown, W F *et al.* (1971) Effectiveness of student-to-student counselling on the academic adjustment of potential college dropouts, *Journal of Educational Psychology*, **62**, 285-9.

Brun, J (1976) *La Parrainage à l'EPFL en 1973-74 et en 1975-75: Résultats d'une Première Enquête auprès des Parrains et des Filleuls*, Lausanne: EPFL-CPD.

Brundage, D H and MacKeracher, D (1980) *Adult Learning Principles and their Application to Program Planning*, Toronto, Ontario: Ministry of Education.

Bruner, J S (1966) *Towards a Theory of Instruction*, Cambridge, Mass: Harvard University Press.

Burgess, T (1977) *Education After School*, Harmondsworth: Penguin.

Chaire de Pédagogie et Didactique (1976a) *Le Parrainage à l'EPFL: Enquête auprès des Parrains et des Filleuls faite au Semestre d'Eté 1976*, Lausanne: EPFL-CPD, Septembre.

Chaire de Pédagogie et Didactique (1976b) *Enquête auprès des Parrains et des Filleuls sur la Formation Pédagogique des Etudiants, faite au Semestre d'Eté 1976*, Lausanne: EPFL-CPD, Septembre.

Champagne, M (1976) *Le Parrainage à l'EPFL: Expérience de 1975. Rapport Résumé de l'Enquête faite auprès des Parrains et des Filleuls et Recommandations à l'Intention des Nouveaux Parrains et des Counseillers de Classe de Première Année*, Lausanne: EPFL-CPD, Octobre.

Chickering, A W (1969) *Education and Identity*, San Francisco, Cal: Jossey-Bass.

Collier, K G (1969) Syndicate methods: further evidence and comments, *Universities Quarterly*, **21**, 431-6.

Combs, A W (1962) A perceptual view of the adequate personality, in *Perceiving, Behaving, Becoming*, Yearbook of the Association for Supervision and Curriculum Development, Washington DC: ASCD, 50-64.

Combs, A W and Snygg, D (1959) *Individual Behaviour*, 2nd Ed, New York: Harper.

Combs, A W, Avila, D L and Purkey, W W (1971) *Helping Relationships*, Boston, Mass: Allyn and Bacon.

Cornwall, M G, Schmithals, F and Jacques, D (1977) *Proceedings of the International Seminar on Project-Orientation in Higher Education, Bremen*, Brighton Polytechnic and University Teaching Methods Unit, University of London.

Crittenden, B (1978) Autonomy as an aim of education, in Strike, K A and Egan, K (eds) *Ethics and Educational Policy*, London: Routledge and Kegan Paul, 105-26.

Cropley, A J (1977) *Lifelong Education, a Psychological Analysis*. Oxford: Pergamon Press.

Dearden, D F (1972) Autonomy and education, in Dearden, D F, Hirst, P F and Peters, R S (eds) *Education and the Development of Reason*, London: Routledge and Kegan Paul, 448-65.

Dearden, D F (1975) Autonomy as an educational ideal, in Brown, S C (ed) *Philosophers Discuss Education*, London: Macmillan, 3-18.

Dewey, J (1928) Progressive education and the science of education, *Progressive Education*, 5. Reprinted in Dworkin, M S (ed) (1965) *Dewey on Education*, New York: Teachers College Press.

Dittman, J (1976) Individual autonomy: the magnificent obsession, *Educational Leadership*, 33 (6), 463-7.

Donald, J G (1976) Contracting for learning, *Learning and Development*, 7 (5).

Dressel, P L and Thompson, M M (1973) *Independent Study: A New Interpretation of Concepts, Practices and Problems*, San Francisco, Cal: Jossey-Bass.

Faure Report (1972) *Learning to Be*, Report of the International Commission on the Development of Education, Paris: UNESCO.

Ferrier, B M and Hamilton, J D (1977) A preparatory course for medical students who lack a conventional academic background, *Journal of Medical Education*, 52, 390-5.

Ferrier, B M, McAuley, R D and Roberts, R S (1978) Selection of medical students at McMaster University, *Journal of the Royal College of Physicians*, 12 (4), 365.

Gentry, N D (1974) Three models of training and utilization, *Professional Psychology*, 5, 207-14.

Gibb, J R (1964) Climate for trust formation, pp 279-309 in Bradford, L P *et al* (eds) *T-Group Theory and Laboratory Method*, New York: John Wiley.

Gibbs, B (1979) Autonomy and authority in education, *Journal of Philosophy of Education*, 13, 119-32.

Gibbs, G (1977) *Learning to Study: A Guide to Running Group Sessions*, Institute of Educational Technology Tuition and Counselling Research Group, The Open University.

Gibran, K (1926) *The Prophet*, London: Heinemann

Gindes, B C (1973) *New Concepts of Hypnosis*, Hollywood, Cal: Wilshire.

Goldman, R M, Wade, S and Zegar, D (1974) Students without harness: the 'SUM' experiment in self-paced learning, *Journal of Higher Education*, 45, 197-210.

Goldschmid, B and Goldschmid, M L (1976a) Peer teaching in higher education: a review, *Higher Education*, 5, 9-33.

Goldschmid, B and Goldschmid, M L (1976b) Enabling students to learn and participate effectively in higher education, *Journal of Personalized Instruction*, 1 (2), 70-5.

Goldschmid, M L and Burckhardt, C (1976) Expérience de parrainage dans une école polytechnique, *European Journal of Engineering Education*, 1 (2), 108-12.

Goodlad, S, Atkins, J and Harris, J (1978) *Undergraduates as School Science Tutors*, Imperial College of Science and Technology, University of London.

Hamilton, J D (1976) The McMaster curriculum: a critique, *British Medical Journal*, 1, 1191-6.

Hare, R M (1975) Chairman's remarks, in Brown, S C (ed) *Philosophers Discuss Education*, London: Macmillan, 36-42.

Harrison, R (1978) How to design and conduct self-directed learning experiences, *Group and Organization Studies*, 3 (2), 149-67.

Harrison, R and Hopkins, R (1967) The design of cross-cultural training: an alternative to the university model, *Journal of Applied Behavioural Science*, 3 (4), 431-68.

Head, J and Shayer, M (1980) Loevinger's ego development measures — a new research tool? *British Educational Research Journal*, 6 (1), 21-7.

Heiney, W F, Jr (1977) 'Practicing what you preach': a plan for helping freshmen psychology majors get off to a good start, *Teaching of Psychology*, 4 (2), 73-6.

Heron, J (1974) *The Concept of a Peer Learning Community*, University of Surrey, Guildford: Human Potential Research Project.

Heron, J (1979a) *Behaviour Analysis in Education and Training*, University of London: British Postgraduate Medical Federation.

Heron, J (1979b) *Peer Review Audit,* University of London: British Postgraduate Medical Federation.

Hunt, D E and Sullivan, E V (1974) *Between Psychology and Education,* Hinsdale, Ill: Dryden Press.

Huntington, J (1980) Power and social influence in the relationship between staff member and course member, pp 35-8 in Anderson, B, Boud, D and Macleod, G (eds) *Experience-Based Learning How? Why?,* Sydney: Australian Consortium on Experiential Education.

Jackins, H (1965) *The Human Side of Human Beings,* Seattle: Rational Island.

James, D W, Johnson, M L and Venning, P (1965) Testing for learnt skill, in observation and evaluation of evidence, *Lancet,* ii, 379-85.

Jevons, F R and Turner, H D L (eds) *What Kinds of Graduates Do We Need?,* Oxford: Oxford University Press.

Keeton, M T and Associates (1976) *Experiential Learning: Rationale, Characteristics and Assessment,* San Francisco, Cal: Jossey-Bass.

Keeton, M T and Tate, P J (eds) (1978) *Learning by Experience — What, Why, How,* New Directions for Experiential Education No 1, San Francisco, Cal: Jossey-Bass.

Kidd, J R (1968) *How Adults Learn,* New York: Association Press.

Kirschenbaum, H (1979) *On Becoming Carl Rogers,* New York: Delacorte Press.

Knowles, M S (1970) *The Modern Practice of Adult Education,* New York: Association Press.

Knowles, M S (1973) *The Adult Learner: A Neglected Species,* Houston, Tex: Gulf Publishing.

Knowles, M S (1975) *Self-Directed Learning: A Guide for Learners and Teachers,* New York: Association Press.

Kohlberg, L (1972) Humanistic and cognitive-developmental perspectives on psychological education, pp 394-402 in Purpel, R E and Belanger, M (eds) *Curriculum and Cultural Change,* Berkeley, Cal: McCutchan.

Kubler-Ross, E (1970) *On Death and Dying,* New York: Macmillan.

Laing, R D (1972) *Knots,* Harmondsworth: Penguin.

Lewis, H A (1978) A teacher's reflections on autonomy, *Studies in Higher Education,* 3 (2), 149-59.

Lindsay, P H and Norman, D A (1977) *Human Information Processing,* 2nd Ed, London: Academic Press.

Little, G (1970) *The University Experience: An Australian Study,* Melbourne: Melbourne University Press.

Little, G (1975) *Faces on the Campus: A Psycho-Social Study,* Melbourne: Melbourne University Press.

Loevinger, J (1976) *Ego Development: Conception and Theories,* San Francisco, Cal: Jossey-Bass.

Luthe, W (1971) Autogenic therapy: excerpts on applications to cardiovascular disorders and hypercholesteremia, *Biofeedback and Self Control Annual,* 437-46.

McNeill, B (1970) School of architecture and planning — new programme for 1970, *Tasarchitect,* 1 (8) Jan/Feb.

McNeill, B (1971) General education and professional training, *Archetype,* Oct/Nov, 26-7.

Mulford, B (1977) *Structured Experiences for Use in the Classroom,* Canberra: Centre for Continuing Education, Australian National University.

National Union of Students (1969) *Report of Commission on Teaching in Higher Education,* London: National Union of Students.

Neufeld, V R and Barrows, H S (1974) The 'McMaster Philosophy': an approach to medical education, *Journal of Medical Education,* 49 (11), 1040-50.

Norman, D A (1973) Memory, knowledge and the answering of questions, in Solso, R L (ed) *Contemporary Issues in Cognitive Psychology,* New York: Wiley.

Northedge, A (1975) Learning through discussion at the Open University, *Teaching at a Distance,* 2, 10-19.

Pallie, W and Brain, E (1978) 'Modules' in morphology for self study: a system for learning in an undergraduate medical programme, *Journal of Medical Education*, **12**, 107-13.

Paskow, A (1974) Are college students educable? *Journal of Higher Education*, **45**, 184-96.

Percy, K and Ramsden, P (1980) *Independent Study: Two Examples from English Higher Education*, Guildford, Surrey: Society for Research into Higher Education.

Perry, W G (1970) *Forms of Intellectual and Ethical Development in the College Years*, New York: Holt, Rinehart and Winston.

Peters, R S (1966) *Ethics and Education*, London: Allen and Unwin.

Peters, R S (1970) Review article of Rogers, C R (1969) in *Interchange*, **1** (4), 111-14.

Phillips, D C (1975) The anatomy of autonomy, *Educational Philosophy and Theory*, **7** (2), 1-12.

Powell, J P (1980) Helping and hindering learning, *Higher Education*, in press.

Reason, P (1977-9) *New Paradigm Research Group Newsletter*, University of Bath: Centre for the Study of Organisational Change and Development.

Riesman, D (1950) *The Lonely Crowd*, New Haven, Conn: Yale University Press.

Robbins, D M (1977) A degree by independent study, *Higher Education Review*.

Rogers, C R (1961) *On Becoming a Person*, Boston, Mass: Houghton-Mifflin.

Rogers, C R (1969) *Freedom to Learn: A View of what Education Might Become*, Columbus, Ohio: Charles E Merrill.

Romey, B (1977) Radical innovation in a conventional framework: problems and prospects, *Journal of Higher Education*, **48** (6), 680-96.

Rumelhart, D E (1977) *An Introduction to Human Information Processing*, New York: Wiley.

Sarason, S B, Davidson, K S, Lighthall, F F, Waite, R R and Ruebush, B K (1960) *Anxiety in Elementary School Children*, New York: Wiley.

Schutz, W C (1967) *Joy: Expanding Human Awareness*, New York:.Grove Press.

Schwartz, D (1971) *The Magic of Thinking Big*, New York: Cornerstone.

Sibley, J C (1978) Faculty of Health Sciences, McMaster University, Canada — the 1977 perspective, *Medical Education*, **12** (5), 15-18.

Stanton, H E (1975a) Weight loss through hypnosis, *American Journal of Clinical Hypnosis*, **18**, 34-8.

Stanton, H E (1975b) The treatment of insomnia through hypnosis and relaxation, *Australian Journal of Clinical Hypnosis*, **3**, 4-8.

Stanton, H E (1975c) Ego enhancement through positive suggestion, *Australian Journal of Clinical Hypnosis*, **3**, 32-6.

Stanton, H E (1977) Test anxiety and hypnosis: a different approach to an important problem, *Australian Journal of Education*, **21**, 179-86.

Stanton, H E (1978a) *Helping Students Learn: The Improvement of Higher Education*, Washington DC: University Press of America.

Stanton, H E (1978b) Therapy and teaching, *Proceedings of the British Society of Medical & Dental Hypnosis*, **4**, 5-13.

Stanton, H E (1978c) A one-session hypnotic approach to modifying smoking behaviour, *International Journal of Clinical and Experimental Hypnosis*, **25**, 22-9.

Stanton, H E (1979) *The Plus Factor: A Guide to Positive Living*, Sydney: Collins/Fontana.

Stephenson, J (1980) The use of statements in North East London Polytechnic, in Adams, E and Burgess, T (eds) *Outcomes of Education*, London: Macmillan.

Sweeney, G D and Mitchell, D L M (1975) An introduction to the study of medicine: phase I of the McMaster MD Program, *Journal of Medical Education*, **50**, 70-7.

Talbot, R (1978) *Résultats de l'Enquête sur le Parrainage 1977-78*, Lausanne: EPFL-CPD, Septembre.

Torbert, W R (1976) *Creating a Community of Inquiry: Conflict, Collaboration, Transformation*, London: John Wiley.

215

Torbert, W R (1978) Educating toward shared purpose, self-direction and quality work: the theory and practice of liberating structure, *Journal of Higher Education*, **49** (2), 109-35.

Tough, A (1971) *The Adult's Learning Projects*, 2nd Ed 1979, Toronto: Ontario Institute for Studies in Education.

Tuckman, B W (1965) Developmental sequence in small groups, *Psychological Bulletin*, **63**, 384-99.

University Grants Committee (1964) *Report of the Committee on University Teaching Methods* (Hale Committee), London: HMSO.

Wallace, R K and Benson, H (1972) The physiology of meditation, *Scientific American*, **226** (2), 84-90.

Walsh, W (1978) The McMaster Programme of Medical Education, Hamilton, Ontario, Canada: developing problem-solving abilities, in Katz, F M and Fulop, T (eds) *Personnel for Health Care: Case Studies of Educational Programmes*, Public Health Papers 70, Geneva: World Health Organization.

Wasserman, C W, McCarthy, B W and Ferree, E H (1975) Student paraprofessionals as behavior change agents, *Professional Psychology*, **6**, 217-23.

Wedemeyer, C A (1971) *Independent Study: Overview*, in *Encyclopedia of Education 4*, New York: Macmillan, 548-57.

Welsh Consumer Council (1958) *Patient Participation in General Practice* (from WCC, 8 St Andrews Place, Cardiff CF1 3BE, £1.00).

Wight, A W (1970) Participative education and the inevitable revolution, *Journal of Creative Behavior*, **4**, 234-82.

Woodward, C A and Neufeld, V (1978) *Medical Education Since 1960: Marching to a Different Drummer* (Kellogg Foundation, MSU Foundation), Kellogg Center for Continuing Education, East Lansing, Mich.

Woodward, C A, Ferrier, B M and Mueller, C B (1979) in preparation.

Wrenn, R L and Mencke, R (1972) Students who counsel students, *Personnel and Guidance Journal*, **50**, 687-9.

Index

DATE